CAMEROON HISTORY
for
SECONDARY SCHOOLS
and COLLEGES

MW00979151

Volume 2
The Colonial and Post-Colonial Periods

V.G. Fanso

Macmillan Cameroon Ltd
PO Box 1028, Limbe, Republic of Cameroon
A division of Macmillan Publishers Limited
Companies and representatives throughout the world

www.macmillan-africa.com

ISBN 0 333 48756 7

Text © V.G.Fanso 1989
Design and illustration © Macmillan Publishers Limited 1989

First published 1989

Printed and bound in Malaysia

2007 2006 2005 2004 2003
12 11 10 9 8 7 6 5

Photographic Acknowledgements

The author and publishers wish to acknowledge, with
thanks, the following sources.
BBC Hulton Picture Library pp. 15; 63; 72
Mansell Collection p.51
Ministry of Information and Culture, Buea pp. 39; 136;
138; 139; 152; 156; 158; 159; 160; 163; 164; 169
Other photographs supplied by the author.
The publishers have made every effort to trace the copyright
holders, but if they have inadvertently overlooked any, they
will be pleased to make the necessary arrangements at the
first opportunity.

For
Bongyong, Verkika
and Bonghyuy Bari

Contents

v

List of maps and charts

List of photographs

Acknowledgements

Before expressing thanks for the help I received in writing Volume 2 of *Cameroon History for Secondary Schools and Colleges,* mention should made again of the system of spelling adopted in the two volumes. The spellings of names and places as they appear in official texts in Cameroon have been retained. For example, the official spelling of the following is the same in both English and French texts: Kumba (not Koumba in French), Douala (not Duala in English), Kumbo (not Koumbo in French), Yaounde (not Yaunde in English), and Wum (not Woum in French). However, the standard English spellings for group names have been adopted, irrespective of whether the groups are located in the English or French-speaking provinces. Thus Duala, Bulu and Bamum refer to ethnic groups and not to towns which may have the same name.

In writing this volume, I relied very much on many people, some of them deserving special mention. My mentor Mrs Elizabeth M. Chilver continued to read the drafts and to make very helpful comments and suggestions for improvement. I am especially indebted to her. I owe many thanks to Dr Bongfen Chem-Langhëë (Faay woo Langhëë) who read the entire original draft and proffered advice for improving the structure and language of the text. Madam Liza Sandell also checked the language and helped to make it more suitable for the student audience I was addressing. Dr Lovett Z. Elango, Joseph-Marie Essomba and other colleagues in the Department of History frequently offered academic assistance at different stages of the book. Dr Herman B. Maimo, Jerome Eta, John M. Navti, Henry Kibuh, D. Kukah, Godheart Ndze and George Kidzeeyuf (Mfoome) assisted variously in every aspect of the work. Vensu Alfred Chin typed the drafts and the final manuscript with the same care and accuracy. Bongmoyong, my wife, offered the understanding support, advice and cheerfulness which were instrumental in bringing our private project to completion. All these notwithstanding, I remain solely responsible for whatever errors and opinions appear in the book.

VGF

Abbreviations

ALCAM Assemblée Legislative du Cameroun
ARCAM Assemblée Representative Camerounaise
Ascocam Association des Colons du Cameroun
ATCAM Assemblée Territoriale Camerounaise
BDC Bloc Démocratique Camerounaise
CDC Cameroon Development Corporation
CFA Communauté Financière Africaine
CFU Cameroon Federal Union
CGT Confédération Générale du Travail
CNF Cameroons National Federation
CNU Cameroon National Union
CPNC Cameroons People's National Convention
CUC Cameroon United Congress
CWU Cameroon Welfare Union
CYL Cameroons Youth League
DC Démocrates Camerounais
DO District Officer
EEC European Economic Community
Escocam Evolution Sociale Camerounaise
FIDES Le Fonds d'Investissement pour le Developpement Economique et Social des Territoires
FNU Front Nationale Unifié
FPUP Front Populaire l'Unité et la Paix
GANC Groupe d'Action Nationale Camerounaise
Jeucafra Jeunesse Camerounaise Francaise

KNC Kamerun National Congress
KNDP Kamerun National Democratic Party
KPP Kamerun People's Party
KUNC Kamerun United National Congress
KUP Kamerun United Party
MANC Movement d'Action Nationale Camerounaise
MUN Mouvement d'Union Nationale
NCNC National Council of Nigeria and the Cameroons
OCAM Organisation Commune Africaine, Malagache et Mauritienne
OAU Organisation of African Unity
OK One Kamerun
PSC Party Socialiste Camerounais
PTC Parti Travailliste Camerounais
RACAM Rassamblement Camerounaise
RDA Rassamblement Démocratique Africaine
RWAFF Royal West African Frontier Force
SDO Senior Divisional Officer
UC Union Camerounaise
UDEAC Union Douanière et Economique de l'Afrique Centrale
UN United Nations
Unicafra Union Camerounaise Française
UNO United Nations Organisation
UPC Union des Populations du Cameroun
USA Union Sociale Camerounaise
USCC Union des Syndicats Confédérés du Cameroun

Chapter one
Cameroon on the eve of colonisation

Preamble

Before the coming of Europeans as traders, explorers, missionaries and colonisers from the fifteenth to the nineteenth and twentieth centuries, the territory which constitutes modern Cameroon existed. What did not exist before colonisation as we now have them were defined and demarcated national boundaries clearly separating Cameroon from her neighbours. There was also no Cameroon government covering the national territory. But the ethnic communities were there, some with already established traditions and civilisations, and others in the process of developing them. Some communities were already securely settled where they are today while others were still shifting from place to place, escaping from raids or wars mounted against them by their aggressive neighbours, or looking for safer, productive and comfortable locations.

Cameroon was not without order and civilisation. One thing is certain: that whether a particular community was only just beginning to form and to expand, or was on the move or was already settled, each group already had organised social and political institutions, some with strong centralised governmental, judicial and religious authority. Others were organised in decentralised or uncentralised systems.

Our purpose in this chapter is to examine generally the political, social and economic situation in Cameroon just before the commencement of the colonisation of the territory by the Germans. The aim is to dispel the European argument that Cameroon, like any other Black African country, was a dark territory, that its people were benighted and living in a state of anarchy and primitive barbarity before they were introduced to the light of civilisation which colonialism brought.

Political and social organisation

We have already touched on the political and social organisation in the chapters of Volume 1 dealing with peoples of Cameroon. There were basically two types of political organisation operating in Cameroon on the eve of European occupation. One was a centralised or state political organisation in which there was a recognised ruler or paramount ruler at the centre holding power and wielding supreme political authority as part of his status. Most of the political organisations which had this system surrounded their king with councils and courts. The other was an uncentralised or 'stateless' organisation in which no one was holding political power at the centre. Between the two poles were, of course, a number of intermediate situations. Generally, the centralised organisation was found among the ethnic communities located in the centre and the north, while the uncentralised system was found among the forest communities of the south and the coast of Cameroon.

Among the groups with centralised and institutionalised political organisation were the numerous Bamileke chiefdoms and the large state of Bamum in the Western Province, all the Tikar-derived fondoms, and the Chamba-derived Bali sub-units of the North West Province, the former chiefdoms submerged by later conquest in Adamawa, the Fulbe units, the chiefdoms of the Kotoko and many other smaller states located all over central and northern Cameroon. These groups, which were divided into dialectal states or chiefdoms varying in size generally distinguished themselves by reference to a particular sacred ruler, for example *fon*, to whom its members gave allegiance. Their social structure was of a hierarchical nature with considerable power exercised by the king. Each state also possessed a system of ranked officials often with prescribed duties and a judicial system and provided security for its members. Some of the large states which expanded through peaceful absorption and conquest contained sub-chiefdoms which recognised the paramountcy of the central ruler while at the same time retaining their hereditary dynasties. Other large states like the Bamum absorbed completely their conquered chiefdoms into the central dynasty. A few examples of centralised organisation will suffice.

In the extensive region of Adamawa there existed a well-established and excellently-structured Islamic authority. At the head of the imperial administration was the Emir or Lamido who was both a political and a religious leader. His residence was in the capital at Yola. The Lamido was assisted by a council of notables and numerous officials in the capital. Succession to the supreme position of Lamido was by royal descent. The empire was made up of more than forty districts, each headed by a governor known as Ardo or Lamdo. Only the Emir could appoint or confirm and invest leaders with the authority of a district governor. Each governor had to pledge loyalty in person to the Emir in the imperial capital. The governor had a district council of notables and offices assisting him in the administration of the district. The governor controlled a variety of indigenous populations divided into chiefdoms and villages. The village administration was headed by a local traditional chief known as Ardo who was appointed or confirmed as leader by the governor. Below the village were compounds of extended families led by heads of families. At the beginning of the German occupation of Cameroon the Emir of

Adamawa was Sanda, who died in 1890, and was succeeded by his brother Zubeiru.

The judicial system in the Adamawa Empire was precisely structured with courts at clearly-defined levels of importance. Over and above all the courts was the Emir's Court in Yola. Appeals to this court could only be made as a last resort. There was also in the imperial capital the Alkali Court which served both as a court of first instance for the inhabitants of the town and as a Court of Appeal for the districts. Each district had a governor's or Lamdo's Court and a district Alkali Court. Quarter heads, district and village councillors as well as family heads also performed clear judicial functions at their levels. Appeals could be made from a lower to a higher court all the way from the compound to the imperial capital.

In the large traditional state of Nso in the west-central grasslands, the king or *fon* was a sacred ruler, the overlord of all Nsoland. He presided over councils of state and made final decisions in matters of war and peace. The Fon of Nso ratified appointments to all offices in the land and had the right to remove individuals from office. The welfare of the fondom depended on him. He was 'father' to his people, commanded obedience and displayed the solicitude and gave the assistance of a 'father' to his dependants. But the Nso kingship was not a despotism. Although the Fon was paramount and made the final decision in all matters affecting the fondom, he was also responsible for and accountable to his people. If he acted so as to threaten the welfare of the fondom, he could be called to account as a person. Both the regulatory society, ŋweroŋ and the military association, manjoŋ, might fine him if he acted in a way contrary to the ideals of kingship or to the interests of the fondom. The Nso system of government, like most centralised systems, was one of checks and balances.

The Fon of Nso was assisted in the administration of the fondom by councillors or officers of state who were the great lords of the country. The primary duties of these councillors, who were also heads of their lineages, were those connected with state affairs. Their work was to be near the Fon, to advise him and to judge cases. They, together with the palace stewards, the queen-mothers and the commoner lords assisted the Fon in making the laws of the country. At the same time, all the important palace officers were administrators of their lineages and villages scattered all over the fondom.

There were also local but autonomous *fons* in some important villages and districts. These *fons* recognised the paramountcy and the authority of the Fon of Nso only in matters of foreign relations, war and peace. They too advised the Fon on national matters and were final authority over their people in purely local matters. Some of these *fons* who were incorporated into the Nso state after conquest paid regular tribute in material and personnel to the paramount Fon of Nso. All through, from the family and lineage to the village and district, from the lowest to the highest position in the fondom, law and order prevailed. When the Germans reached Nso for the first time in 1902, they found a well-organised state under Sem II who was succeeded in 1908 by Mapiri. Later, in 1906, Sem waged a major resistance war against German colonialism.

The administrative situation in the so-called stateless or lineage-based communities of southern Cameroon where political leadership was neither centralised nor easy to identify was also not chaotic. Although it was difficult to find a definite national political and administrative structure existing among such groups, there existed nonetheless political and administrative relations in which persons at family or clan level exercised power and authority for the maintenance of social order in the community. There were surely, among such large uncentralised groups as the Beti (Beti-Pahouin, Pahouin or Fang), the Bassa-Bakoko, and the so-called coastal Bantu, internal political and administrative relations between the constituent elements which ensured cohesion and order within the group. Otherwise how can we account for the devotion of the members to the group and their common

linguistic, historical and cultural uniformity?

The political and judicial control in some cases was in the hands of officers of clans, associations, secret societies, age-grades and age-sets and village councils, to whom political authority accrued as a consequence of those positions. The relations between these organisations spread informally throughout the ethnic territory, linking every section as it were to a common political or judicial system. In this way extended families, clans and the clusters were brought together and order, cultural and territorial solidarity maintained. In some cases kinship was used as a means of stating required behaviour. A practical example of political organisation in an uncentralised community may suffice.

The small Beti group of Mangisa is located at the loop of the Sanaga where its tributary, River Ndjim, flows into it. While the loop of the Sanaga forms the natural frontier of the group in the north, the remaining frontier is shared with the Eton, another Beti group.

The traditional administration of Mangisa was organised on a clan basis. Each clan was headed by a *nkukuma* or clan head who was usually a descendant of the founder of the clan. He was selected and installed *nkukuma* by the elders of the clan because he was judged to be courageous and intelligent and in a position to command the respect of the majority of clan members. His power and authority over the clan were delegated to him by the living members of the clan; nothing traditional was bequeathed to him by his predecessors. All that his people expected of him was to help them to organise law and order in the clan. His authority was never absolute, and he acted only when there was a consensus of opinion on an issue. Clan members who disagreed with the leadership of their *nkukuma* often broke away to form another autonomous unit of the same clan. It was in this way that the numerous Mangisa clans were formed.

The fact that each clan was self-governing and guarded its autonomy jealously made it difficult for a national or supra-clan administration to be set up in Mangisaland. But whenever each clan or the group as a whole was threatened by a crisis or external enemy, all the clans easily united in a common national action. In such eventuality, the *nkukuma* who was either the most influential, the most courageous, or the most senior in age would summon a meeting of all the clan heads and elders to discuss the issue and agree on what to do. It was in such situations that the spirit of national solidarity among acephalous peoples was demonstrated. Inter-clan conflicts and national security matters were discussed and resolved in the same manner. The clan head also had the duty to organise the production, distribution and exchange of goods and wealth between his and other clans or neighbouring groups. At the time of the German occupation of Mangisaland. in 1894, the most noted *nkukuma* was Elugu Zoba of the Mbenenga clan.

Neighbourly and territorial relations between groups

What we also need to know about the entire Cameroon society on the eve of European occupation is that each group was historically and socially linked directly or indirectly to other communities. The network of relations between the different groups overlapped from district to district throughout the territory. There were ethnic affiliations and continuities between groups generally located in the same neighbourhood or region. No community was isolated historically, culturally, linguistically, economically or socially from its neighbours.

The numerous chiefdoms and other communities spread throughout west-central Cameroon were unified by their claim to derive from the same stock, their possession of similar institutions and traditions. Thus the similarity of political and social institutions and languages between groups claiming Tikar, Ntarekon and Chamba connections. Even the so-called Kirdi groups of northern Cameroon which formed the majority of the peoples of that vast region and are said to have had little in common, were

already united as a people by their experience of displacement and domination by the Fulbe. Along the Cameroon coast and spreading into the southern interior of the country were groups claiming affinities and particular relations with one another. The Beti groups and the Bassa-Bakoko also claimed relationships and continuities across their ethnic frontiers and across present-day international borders with groups in Rio Muni, Gabon, Congo, Central African Republic, Chad and Nigeria. These werè signs that the people of what was soon to become the defined Cameroon territory already had links with one another.

There were definitely developments of historic importance in terms of culture, institutions, ideas and government taking place in the territory on the eve of colonial rule. No one denies that in some areas of Cameroon people were still living naked, in terror of some of their neighbours, practising traditional (though often highly effective) agriculture and dominated by beliefs of witchcraft. Clothes for those who lived naked were not a necessity. In other words, nakedness was largely a matter of choice, not the lack of local clothes to wear. The insecurity that reigned in many places was largely a result of the European demands for slaves which forced groups to raid upon their neighbours' territory for captives. The people had enough to eat and starvation came only as a result of poor harvests or bad seasons. There was a high level of adaptation to, knowledge and control of their environment.

The economy

The largely subsistence economy of Cameroon on the eve of the colonisation of the territory is difficult to assess. While the coastal inhabitants were involved in a direct struggle and competition in the exchange economy with European traders, the peoples of the interior were united in their production of goods and services needed for their survival. There generally occurred at specific seasons the unity of activities. People cleared farm-plots, hoed and grew crops at the beginning of the rainy season, weeded during the rains, harvested at the end of the rains, and traded or hunted or fished at other times. The division of labour was generally strongly gender-based or according to whether the workers were male or female.

In terms of production, Cameroonians earned their living from the land. Agriculture was the dominant activity, and all other economic activities were set around it. It was not necessary for anyone, for example, to give up agriculture in order to be a trader, craft manufacturer or hunter. Agriculture was important because it provided an assured supply of food and the possibility of a surplus.

Animal husbandry was practised on a large scale in areas of the north. Livestock were kept not only for exchange and prestige, but also for their meat, milk, cheese, butter, hides and manure. Sheep were also kept for wool. Cattle, horses, sheep, goats and donkeys were animals that brought economic wealth or prestige while poultry were raised for food. Pigs were bred on a large scale in the forest region. Hunting and fishing were also important economic activities in the forest and coastlands. These activities, together with agriculture, manufacturing and mining, kept Cameroonians economically busy and self-sufficient.

Markets where exchanges of natural resources, crops and manufactures took place were numerous and distributed all over the Cameroon territory. There were local markets, ethnic markets and international markets in every district or region. Each market was held on fixed days at intervals of between three and eight days. The network of local, ethnic and distant trade routes which converged on different market-places linking and partially integrating different villages, ethnic communities, districts and geographical zones gave Cameroon a tenuous economic unity. These 'thick' networks of trade, no doubt, often extended across present international frontiers.

The market-place was an economic as well as a social centre for all who attended it. It was important not only as a place for buying and selling or exchanging goods, but also as a meeting place for relatives, friends and traditional authorities. Many went to the market-place because they were sure they would hear news, dispatch a gift, pay debts, settle a dispute, meet a fiancée or have companions with whom to socialize. The market day was the day when local age-mates, members of the same profession or trade, periodically organised their thrift or mutual aid associations, *njangi* or *tonte*, the members of which subscribed fixed amounts of money, drinks, and other entertainment items, and each received the money collected in strict rotation. Such associations served as savings banks for many who wanted to save enough money to build a house, marry a woman, enter a profession or begin a business.

Population and work force

The population of Cameroon on the eve of colonisation can only be approximately determined. There had never been an official estimate or counting of the population of any group before the imposition of European rule. Our judgement of the population of the entire territory before 1884 can only be based on the earliest figures provided by the colonial administration. Based on the 1911 estimate of the total population of Cameroon at 2.65 million, we can safely say that the population of the territory could hardly have been more than two million on the eve of annexation. This population was thinly distributed throughout the territory, especially in the low-lying south-eastern forests and the swampy districts along the coast where malaria and sleeping-sickness made life intolerable. The entire population was made up of two principal types of peoples, namely, Bantu and Sudanic, both determined linguistically rather than racially. There were also the pygmies scattered in the areas of eastern and southeastern forests. The population was divided into scattered communities, villages, chiefdoms and ethnic groups. The villages, chiefdoms and ethnic groups in many places were often synonymous. The people lived in huts and houses built according to the traditions of each group.

By all accounts a population of about two million for the entire Cameroon territory on the eve of annexation can be considered small. Many possible reasons can be adduced for both the population distribution and for the low population. First, the population in some districts like the east and parts of the north was low, possibly as a consequence of the inadequacy of natural resources. Fertile and healthy areas like the central and western grass-lands, for example, attracted more settlers and allowed for greater increases in population than poor, unhealthy areas. Second, poor soil and lack of biological resources such as water and salt worked against population growth in arid districts. The availability of water in an area was the most important consideration in the choice of a settlement.

Third, the various influences affecting both the rates of fertility and mortality also deter-mined the growth of population in an area. The African tradition of long child-rearing prac-tices, especially in polygynous families, which reduced the rate of possible births, affected the growth of population. Similarly, mortality from diseases such as malaria, smallpox, sleeping sickness, meningitis, plague, diarrhoea and dysentery resulted in low populations. The average expectation of life at birth could hardly be more than thirty-five. Fourth, frequent movement of peoples from one place to another not only kept the size of groups small, but also prevented people from staying long enough in any one environment to develop and exploit it beneficially. Fifth, epidemics and famine which were frequent in some areas also affected population growth. The influenza epidemics, whenever they occurred, before European medicine was introduced, took heavy toll of Cameroon's population. Famine was frequent in the arid areas of the east, the central high-lands and the north. Finally, inter-group clashes and wars, most of them caused by slave-mongers and expansionist states, often resulted in heavy casualties and low population. The disruption of food production and storage caused by the Chamba and Fulbe raids in areas of central and north Cameroon also retarded population growth. In any event, the fact that the population of Cameroon was low does not mean that the territory lacked sufficient people to exploit the land. On the contrary, there was a workforce organised in its own way to make use of the natural resources available.

The organisation of the workforce followed the traditional pattern. The most important economic unit in Cameroonian society was the family or, better still, the household. The household included all persons living in the house who were not necessarily members of the same family. The predominance of polygynous marriages then (that is, the custom of a man having more than one wife at the same time) provided for the expansion of the household and the recruitment of the required extra labour. (The custom of a woman having more than one husband at the same time is poly-andry. Both polygyny and polyandry are forms of polygamy.) Besides, gender-based communal labour was commonly utilised everywhere. It was exploited by the women and men in the west-central grasslands to clear farm-plots, to plant and harvest crops and build houses. It was also used by the peoples of the forestlands and the mangrove swamps to exploit groves of palm trees, cleaning and constructing market sites, and trapping fish.

Religion and society

The traditional Cameroonian society, unin-fluenced by Islam from the north and Christianity from the coast, was a religious and moral society before European colonisation. Indeed, religion and morality were part and parcel of every aspect of life in each ethnic community. Each member of a particular community tried to live an upright and generous life in order to promote situations which might lead to prosperity in the com-munity. Human life was regarded as sacred and each community used its rituals and sacrifices to protect and safeguard it. Rituals or prayers and sacrifices were often made and offered by each family or lineage to plead the innocence of the members and to ask the gods and the ancestors to lead and protect them from evil. If requests were made during prayers and sacrifices they were usually in relation to health, welfare and fertility in the production of children and crops in the community.

In terms of belief, the people of Cameroon generally believed in the existence of a divine or almighty creator of the universe. Each community believed that the divine creator was responsible for every existence, for human life and for all the events that befell mankind. Each community believed that the divine creator was a High God or Spirit, remote from humanity, omnipotent and timeless. No thought was given to how he came into being, and no one dared to doubt his existence or question his supreme authority. Different communities identified him with such revered objects as the sun and the moon, and some believed he resided in the sky, behind the horizon or some unreachable place, although always near enough to look after his creatures.

There was belief in the existence of numerous minor gods and good and evil spirits, and powers such as ghosts and ancestors, occupying the space between the divine creator and man. These other beings were in no way in competition with the divine creator. These lesser spirits and powers might or might not represent human forces. Unlike the divine creator they resided only in local environments. There was belief in life after death, even if such life lasted momentarily. Finally, there was belief in the existence and power of the forces of good and evil in each human community.

As concerned the living community and the departed, ancestor-reverence was a very important part of the traditional religion of each people. It was strongly believed that ancestors were part of the living society and that they continued to maintain an interest in the welfare of their descendants. They were always ready whenever they were called upon during prayer and sacrifice to intercede with the deities on behalf of the living. The living community used sacrifices as paths of communication and sharing between them and their ancestors.

Each community shunned evil. Evil was thought to be expressed in witchcraft. Witches and wizards were persons engaged in the practice of doing others harm. They were the cause of unnatural deaths in the community. Such persons, whenever they were detected in the society, were either punished by death or banishment. They could never be appeased except with the blood and flesh of someone which they consumed magically. Their evil works or intentions could only be undone by the so-called witch-doctors and diviners who were in a position to combat the practice and save their victims. There are, however, plenty of anecdotes about witchcraft which allege false accusations, the use of torture and death by sasswood, even if only occasionally used. Similarly, crime was severely punished. Thieves and murderers were enemies of the society. If they were judged guilty, depending on the severity of the crime, they were punished by death. Injustice was not tolerated and wrong was easily corrected and cordiality restored.

Of course in the coastal villages and districts clustering round Victoria and Douala, Christianity had been introduced by European missionaries in the 1840s. The concept of a single God made up of the Trinity had been introduced, and people were taught that they would be rewarded as good Christians in heaven or punished for their sins in hell after death. In the region of Adamawa and other areas of the north where Islam had been established, long before the nineteenth century, the population was already familiar with the teachings of Mohammed and the concept of Allah, the only God of Islam. It can thus be said that on the eve of European colonisation, Cameroon had already embraced three systems of belief and worship, namely, traditional religions, Islam and Christianity.

Further reading

David Birmingham and Phyllis M. Martin (eds), *History of Central Africa,* Volume 1 (Longman, London and New York, 1983).

John Middleton and David Tait (eds), *Tribes Without Rulers* (Routledge & Kegan Paul, London, 1970).

M.Z. Njeuma, *Fulani Hegemony in Yola (Old Adamawa) 1809 – 1902* (CEPER, Yaounde, 1978).

Harry R. Rudin, *Germans in the Cameroons 1884 – 1914* (Greenwood Press, New York, 1968).

P.N. Nkwi and J-P. Warnier, *Elements for a History of the Western Grassfields* (SOPECAM, Yaounde, 1982).

Questions

1. List and discuss the types of political organisations in Cameroon on the eve of European colonisation.
2. Name and discuss any five factors that contributed to low population in Cameroon before the German annexation of 1884.
3. How was the judicial system in the Muslim Empire of Adamawa organised?
4. Discuss the importance of the traditional market in Cameroon society before the German colonisation.

Chapter two

The German annexation of Cameroon

The Cameroon coast was already well-known to and frequented by Europeans long before the period of the scramble and the partition of Africa. In fact, by the time of the scramble and the annexation during the last quarter of the nineteenth century, nationals of the three major colonising powers which competed against each other for the occupation of the territory were already numerous and active on the Cameroon coast. The powers concerned were Britain, Germany and France. Germany, of course, won the competition and annexed Cameroon in July 1884.

The indigenous inhabitants of the Cameroon coast

The Cameroon seacoast, which eventually became part of the German territory, extends from the Rio del Rey in the west to the Campo river in the South. Along this coastline are the peoples with whom European traders, mission-

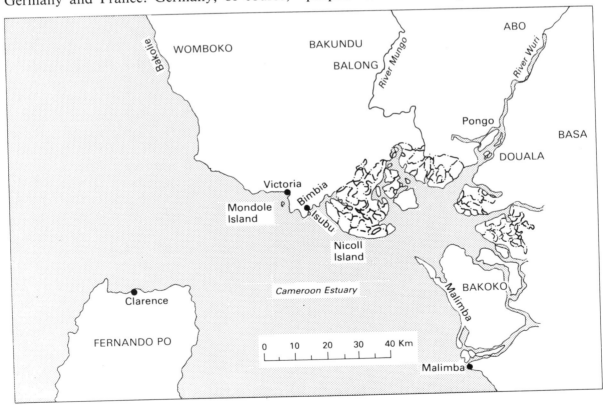

Figure 1 *The Cameroon coast in the nineteenth century*

aries and officials established close contacts in the nineteenth century. Some of the villages, principally Douala, Bimbia and Batanga, became important ports and centres of trade. Their indigenous inhabitants became the most active middlemen in the coastal trade, dominating the import and export markets.

The Cameroon coast is inhabited by some homogeneous and some closely related peoples. Some of these peoples, like the Bakweri, the Duala, the Isuwu or Bimbians, the Malimba, the Mungo and the Wovea, trace their history of origin to the same ancestor. Of these, the Duala group was the most widely known to Europeans in the eighteenth and nineteenth centuries, and Douala township and estuary were the points of convergence for leading white and black businessmen. It is worth knowing a little more about this group before the German annexation in 1884.

At the beginning of the nineteenth century, the lineages of the indigenous society of Duala were still united under one leader, King Bell. By 1815, however, King Bell had lost the hegemony of the group when Akwa, the head of the large lineage in the kingdom, defected and set himself up as king. Other lineages soon followed suit, declaring themselves auto-nomous chiefdoms. By the beginning of the 1840s, there were already two kingdoms and three chiefdoms in Dualaland. It would appear that at this time the importance of a chief or king anywhere on the Cameroon coast was determined not by local tradition but by his wealth, his role in trade, and the support he obtained from white traders and British officials.

As mentioned earlier, the greatest pursuit of the Duala and other coastal inhabitants in the nineteenth century was the middleman monopoly of the Euro-Cameroon trade. Their chief service was bulking, transporting goods to and from the interior, and extending credit. They seized every opportunity to profit from both the import and export trade of the area. They resisted every attempt by both European traders and inland producers of raw materials to break their monopoly of coastal trade and deal directly with one another. Their trade with Europeans was regulated from 1856 by a Court of Equity set up by the British in the township of Douala.

The coastal inhabitants were also the first people of Cameroon to be introduced to Christianity and Western education. Beginning in 1844, when a mission station and school were opened at Bimbia, to the time of the German annexation in 1884, thousands of children and adults as far inland as Bakundu were converted to the Christian faith and taught to read and write. Victoria and Douala townships became truly Christian and educational centres where Cameroonians from neighbouring hamlets and groups converged to learn and believe in Christ. Baptist missionaries who were convinced that literacy was essential for conversion placed much emphasis on education. For them, education would enable the Africans to obtain God's truth and to read and understand His word. For the coastal inhabitants, however, Western education was indispensable in their various relations with the whites. Those who could read and write could conduct their trade with white traders more efficiently, and keep records of their debts, debtors and creditors. Education was necessary for business.

The coastal inhabitants of Cameroon, the Duala in particular, represented, without knowing and without a mandate, the other peoples of Cameroon in some of their major engagements with European officials in the nineteenth century. Beginning with Kings Bell and Akwa in June 1840, the coastal chiefs signed numerous treaties with the British, abolishing the overseas slave trade, establishing friendship and legitimate commerce, and even offering their territories and sovereignty to them. King Bell of Douala and his close collaborators signed the treaty of German annexation of Cameroon in 1884.

The British presence

By the end of the eighteenth century British traders had slowly built up their commerce in the Bight of Biafra and became the leading influential European nationals on the Cameroon coast. British preponderance was to increase enormously in the nineteenth century as a result of the dominant role played by the Royal Navy in the suppression of the overseas slave trade from the area, as well as the arrival and settlement of the English Baptist missionaries.

In 1845 Alfred Saker founded the Baptist Mission in Douala and began a European settlement as an outstation for English missionaries, traders and officials resident at Fernando Po. A second and more permanent English settlement, again begun by Saker, was established at the foot of the Cameroon Mountain in 1858 and named Victoria. Earlier, in 1856, a Court of Equity was set up in Douala by the British Consul for the Bight of Biafra and the Island of Fernando Po to regulate trading relations between the British and the Cameroonians. A similar court, known as the Court of Justice, was set up in Victoria to enforce law and order and impose fines. These two courts were presided over by the British Consul. Through the Courts, British influence in Douala and Victoria was predominant, and Britain became embroiled in the internal politics of the Cameroon coast. Indeed, beginning in the 1860s, the authority of the British Consul was felt necessary to establish the position and importance of any local ruler in the area.

Besides Christianity and education undertaken by the missionaries, the most important activity of the British on the Cameroon coast during the decades leading to the annexation was trade. Legitimate trade between the British and the coastal inhabitants became increasingly friendly and voluminous from the 1840s following the signing of a series of treaties between British officials and Cameroon chiefs abolishing the slave trade and establishing friendship and legitimate commerce. These treaties made the British the most favoured European traders in the coastal townships. Following the setting up of the Court of Equity in Douala in January 1856, British traders and supercargoes (that is, people who sell cargo on

merchant ships) began to flood the region. In 1864 it was estimated that between 150 and 200 British traders could be found in Douala alone at any time. This number usually more than doubled during the export season from February to June.

The overwhelming British domination of Cameroon trade began to subside when the number of traders from other European countries, notably Germany, began to increase substantially in the area. All through, British trade was in the hands of five firms permanently established in the Bight of Biafra. The two dominant British trading companies on the Cameroon coast in the 1870s were John Holt and Company which is still operating in Cameroon today, and the Ambas Bay Trading Company which was absorbed by other companies in 1920. These two companies held their positions solidly in the trading, commercial and political rivalry with other European traders, notably the Germans.

Concerning Christianity and education, responsibility was in the hands of missionaries and teachers of the English Baptist Missionary Society. The missionaries and teachers, who tended to live for long periods in their stations, had a more adequate knowledge of the Cameroon coast than traders and other businessmen who came and went according to the fluctuating prices in trade. When the Baptist Missionary Society was forced to withdraw from Cameroon in 1886 following the German colonial successes, it left behind a Christian community that counted its full converts and novices in thousands.

The arrival of the Germans

German traders probably began to visit the Cameroon coast in noticeable numbers from 1849 when the Carl Woermann Firm of Hamburg began operating on the West African coast. But it was not until 1868 that the C. Woermann Firm was established permanently as a trading firm on the Cameroon coast, with factories or warehouses in the townships of

Douala and Victoria. From 1868 onward, the real German business presence began to be noticed and felt. By that time, as already indicated, there were as many as five British firms operating on the Cameroon coast and virtually controlling the import and export trade of the area. The second German trading firm on the Cameroon coast was set up in 1875 by Johann Thormahlen and J. Jantzen and named Jantzen & Thormahlen.

The setting-up of German firms led to the permanent presence of German traders and businessmen in increasingly larger numbers on the Cameroon coast. Gradually, but in less than a decade, these Germans began to obtain an ever-increasing portion of the Cameroon trade and to challenge the British dominance of it. By the beginning of the 1880s German trade, though still in the hands of only two firms, was known to be expanding faster than that of British. But, in spite of this progressive German challenge to British leadership in the Cameroon trade, British and German nationals visiting or doing business on the Cameroon coast cooperated very well and together controlled the trade of the region from Douala westward to Calabar and beyond. Cooperation and friendly relations with the British allowed the Germans to turn their attention to improving and increasing their trading ventures on the Cameroon coast. Such cooperation also inclined the British to be less suspicious of German colonial ambitions in the region.

The French advance from the south

The third colonial power that was to compete for the annexation of Cameroon in 1884 was France. French interest in the Cameroon coast was particularly noted in the 1840s and given special recognition in the Anglo-Cameroon anti-slave trade and legitimate commercial treaties with the kings and chiefs of Batanga and Malimba in 1847 and 1848. But it was not until the 1870s that French firms began to establish trading stations in the area. They concentrated their trading activities in the villages south of Douala at Malimba, Big Batanga and Campo. These villages were not far from their enclave in Gabon where they had already established firm control. The French authorities made sure that any area on the West African coast which constituted their sphere of influence was properly secured for French trade alone. They did this by introducing in such areas tariffs that were so high and so discriminatory that they resulted in the virtual exclusion of all non-French goods.

In 1883 an alarm was raised by the English missionaries and local chiefs that the French were about to annex Big Batanga and that the chiefs of the area were enthusiastically signing away their sovereignty to French officials. British and German traders, English missionaries, local chiefs and kings of the Duala ethnic group protested against the presence of the French anywhere on the Cameroon coast, arguing that they preferred British annexation which would assure the continuation of the various traditional relations among the related ethnic groups of the area. But the treaties the French had signed with the chiefs south of the Douala township established them more firmly on the Cameroon coast.

Interest in and requests for annexation

Interest in the acquisition of any part of Cameroon as a colony began to be shown at a time when European governments were least interested in taking possession of African territories. The earliest recorded date we have so far expressing such a colonial interest and attempting annexation is 1833. In that year Colonel Edward Nicholls of the Royal Navy made an arrangement with King William of Bimbia for the British to annex part of the Cameroon coast stretching westward from Bimbia to Rio del Rey, but the Government refused. Twenty-four years later, in 1857, Captain Close of the anti-slavery squadron informed the British Consul at Fernando Po that local authorities in Douala wanted their country to be taken over by Britain, but the Consul did nothing about it. After founding Victoria in the Ambas Bay enclave in 1858, the English Baptist missionaries requested the British Government to declare the settlement a colony and assume control, but the Foreign Office could not be persuaded to accept responsibility. In 1859 Alexander Innes also attempted, through an arrangement with King Akwa of Douala town, to annex on behalf of the British Government a large district extending east and south of the township, but the Government rejected the idea. In 1862 and 1864 the inhabitants of Victoria again requested formal annexation through Commodore A.P.E. Wilmot of the West African Squadron who hoisted the British flag and reported the matter to his government. In reply Her Majesty's Government instructed Commodore Wilmot to confine himself to the suppression of the slave trade and not to attempt the acquisition of colonies. The following year, the British Parliament adopted a minute stating that it was inexpedient either to obtain further extension of territory, assume government over new territories, or sign new treaties offering protection to native tribes.

Between 1865 and 1875, active interest in and appeals for British annexation of Cameroon cooled down. Attention and concern were now directed to trade, which was regulated by the Court of Equity in Douala. It was through trade and the Court of Equity that the ground for imperial rivalry for the control of the Cameroon coast in the 1880s was prepared. Some of the clauses of the treaty setting up the Court of Douala had political implications. Such clauses often allowed British officials to intervene directly in the internal affairs of coastal villages on the pretext of offering protection to both white and black traders in all kinds of transactions. The clauses establishing the Court of Equity definitely made Great Britain the sole, informal political authority on the Cameroon coast.

The British dominance of trade and politics of the Cameroon coast could only be challenged if merchants and officials of other powers joined and competed in increasing numbers in the Cameroon trade. In the 1860s and 1870s the Germans and the French came. Together with the British, their involvement and activities in Cameroon began to bring the region to notice in major European capitals. Beginning in 1875 events on the Cameroon coast began to follow the trend towards the scramble and annexation of the territory.

Between 1875 and 1880 reports reaching Europe about the political situation on the Cameroon coast implied a trend towards instability in the future. The kings and chiefs were said to be finding it increasingly difficult to govern their people. According to English Baptist missionaries in Victoria and Douala, every dispute, particularly between chiefs or local traders in Douala, Bimbia and Tiko led to war and to great loss of life. In addition, commercial rivalry between rival village polities and between white and black traders was causing instability in the region, making it difficult for chiefs to rule their people. As a result of the disturbances, chiefs began to seek the protection of a European power that would hold local passions in leash, and made frequent overtures to local British representatives to annex the territory. The missionaries expressed the hope that Britain would take control of Cameroon because it was the only way of establishing law and order in the region. In 1879 the chiefs of the Duala ethnic group wrote a personal letter direct to Queen Victoria asking that an English Government be established in Cameroon. The chiefs regretted that their earlier request through British officials in Cameroon had received no attention. They hoped that their direct appeal would now receive the attention of the Queen. They wanted all the laws of their villages replaced by English laws.

Meanwhile trade and commerce on the Cameroon coast, now involving British, German, French and Cameroon traders, became increasingly competitive. Although the greater share of the European trade continued to be handled by the British, the Germans were fast covering the gap between themselves and the British. The rivalries between European traders were directed at winning the favour of influential African middlemen, while the Africans competed with one another for generous creditors among European traders. The arrangement of trade between white and black traders often allowed for the competition among the coastal middlemen for white trade masters to become violent. The tradition was that Africans should receive goods from their trade masters on credit, and barter them inland for local products, before returning to pay their debts. Often many did not return to pay their debts in time or at all. Thus the refusal by whites to trust every middleman made the struggle among blacks for such trust unfriendly and antagonistic.

From 1880, British trade on the Cameroon coast declined drastically while German trade continued to flourish. By 1884 the volume of German trade was already superior to that of the British. Several reasons have been attributed to the progress in German trade. First, it is claimed that at this time German trade was better organised than British trade. Second, that German traders extended credit to black traders on easier terms than the British, thereby attracting more black traders to their side. It was known that while most British traders objected to the credit or 'trust' system of trade, the Germans saw it as the only way of competing successfully against British firms in the Cameroon trade. Third, it is also known that in some villages German traders bought the firms of British companies which were closing down and thereby controlled trade that was supposed to flow into British hands. Lastly, German traders were effective because they were greatly protected by the British authority in the area.

The decline of British trade and the threat posed by the French south of the Duala territory led to the belief among certain British nationals that both the economic and political situations would improve if Britain formally annexed Cameroon. Such British nationals began to pressure their home government with the economic advantages of a British protec-torate or colony in Cameroon. They listed among the advantages of formal annexation: the cultivation of coffee, cotton, tobacco, cocoa and other tropical agricultural plants on the fertile soil of Cameroon; the possibility of extending trade into the interior and the elimination of the coastal inhabitants' mono-poly of it; and the proper protection of British trade through levying customs duty on non-British goods. These advantages began to convince the British Government that definite steps towards the annexation of Cameroon should begin to be taken. But there were no tangible reasons yet for a rush.

The British decided to move slowly and cautiously towards annexation. They were convinced that the threat posed by the French was not serious enough to offset their plans in the region. They did not at any time consider the possibility of Germany annexing Cameroon, because German traders in the area cooperated very well with British traders and publicly supported the campaign for British annexation. Besides, it was common knowledge among the imperial powers that the German Chancellor, Otto von Bismarck, was least interested in acquiring colonies. But the times had changed since Bismarck declared his opposition to colonies in 1871. The British, as it turned out, were right in assessing the level of the French threat, but wrong about German colonial interests.

The German annexation of Cameroon

German traders on the Cameroon coast who had all along supported the campaign for British annexation, began to think seriously about the need for a German annexation in 1883 for several reasons. First, German annexation would give them better and more permanent protection than British annexation. Second, German annexation would upset the French plans in the region. Third, the German traders were urged by the patriotic feeling of all Germans everywhere that Germany must join the colonial race and obtain colonies. Fourth, the traders were convinced that German annexation was the only way to assure a permanent market for German products in this part of Africa. Indeed, all German merchants trading on the African coasts knew that Cameroon was the single most valuable area for German trade. Finally, German traders saw the German annexation as the only way by which large debts in money and raw materials owed to them by the coastal middle-men in the credit systems of trade could eventually be recovered. These arguments and the pressure brought to bear on the German Government from everywhere tò join the race for colonies eventually yielded fruit. Bismarck who was least interested in colonies in 1871 was persuaded to change his mind at the end of 1883, when he agreed to the establishment of a coaling station at Fernando Po, a consular service and a warship patrol on the Bight of Biafra, and trade treaties with Cameroon chiefs.

In February 1884, Dr Gustav Nachtigal was appointed by the German Government to head a mission to Cameroon and Fernando Po. The purpose of the mission was to study German trade and the prospects of a consular service and a coaling station in the area. Dr Nachtigal was accompanied by Dr Max Buchner and Mr Moebius. They were to be joined in Cameroon by Eduard Woermann, Emil Schultze and Eduard Schmidt who were already in the Bight of Biafra. When Nachtigal and his companions had reached Lisbon, Portugal, on their way to West Africa, new and definite instructions were sent to them to annex Cameroon and hoist the German flag. At the same time instructions were despatched to German traders in Cameroon to prepare for Nachtigal's arrival. They were to begin negotiations with the chiefs for the German annexation of their territory. During the negotiations which began secretly on 1 July 1884, the kings and chiefs of the Duala indicated their willingness to sign an annexation treaty with Germany, although they were afraid of their people, who continued to demand British annexation.

1 *Dr Gustav Nachtigal*

On 11 July 1884, Nachtigal and his companions arrived at the Cameroon coast where they were received with honour by their countrymen. They found out that German traders in the area had successfully concluded a number of treaties with the local chiefs which they began to study. The following day, 12 July, the kings and chiefs of the Duala summoned an ethnic meeting at which no European was invited. They discussed the annexation and prepared a statement setting out clauses which they wanted to be included in the final treaty before they would sign it. The clauses concerned important economic and social rights which were to be protected. These included: rights of the third party and the full power of treaties already signed with other governments; rights to continue to own their lands, towns and domestic animals like dogs, pigs and so forth; rights to and respect for their traditional system of marriage; rights to freedom from arbitrary arrest, beating and detention; and rights to their middleman monopoly of trade. These clauses were endorsed by Emil Schultze as acceptable to the Germans before they were submitted to Nachtigal for a final approval.

But the actual treaty of annexation which was prepared for signature by the Germans and the chiefs did not contain all the clauses which the chiefs had submitted. The provisions of the final treaty were: reservation of the rights of the third party; former treaties of friendship and commerce to remain in force; the land of the towns and villages to remain the private property of the natives; the chiefs to continue to levy their dues as formerly; the natives to retain for the present their customs and usages. The treaty which was signed on 12 July 1884 was signed on the side of Cameroon by King Bell, King Akwa and a number of their Duala subjects, and on the side of Germany by the traders Eduard Schmidt (agent of the firm of C. Woermann), Johannes Voss (agent of the firm of Jantzen & Thormahlen), Eduard Woermann (brother of the President of the firm C. Woermann), and Herr Busch. It was officially legalised by Emil Schultze, the German Consul and agent of the firm C. Woermann in Gabon. The treaty was not signed by Nachtigal, Buchner or Moebius.

On Monday 14 July 1884, Johannes Voss officially handed the treaties over to Nachtigal. Nachtigal then proceeded to proclaim the annexation and to hoist German flags at Akwa, Dido and Bell Towns. On the basis of a treaty obtained on 11 July by Woermann, Schmidt and Schultze, Bimbia was also proclaimed annexed and the German flag hoisted. Similar ceremonies were performed in Batanga. By these acts, Germany obtained the rights of sovereignty, legislation and management over Cameroon. The following day all the British nationals – missionaries and traders – were informed officially by Nachtigal about the German annexation. He also abolished the Court of Equity at Douala and established in its place the Cameroon Council under the Chairmanship of Dr Max Buchner who became the first official German representative in Cameroon.

Although the Germans had kept their plans for annexation secret, British intelligence became suspicious of Nachtigal's journey to the West Coast of Africa. In May, the British Consul, Edward H. Hewett, who was then on leave in England was asked to return to his post in the Bight of Biafra without delay. He was instructed to express to the chiefs of Cameroon on arrival the desire of Her Majesty the Queen to strengthen the relations of peace and friendship between Cameroon and England and to inform them of her willingness to extend her favour of protection over them. Hewett was also to proclaim Victoria and the Ambas Bay territory a British protectorate, and to fix his residence in the neighbourhood of Douala.

When Hewett reached the Niger Delta, then known as the Oil Rivers, British intelligence reported a German ship steering in haste towards Douala. Some British naval officials were immediately dispatched to Cameroon with instructions to try to prevent a German treaty and to inform the kings and chiefs that Consul Hewett was coming very shortly with a friendly message from the Queen. Word was then sent to Consul Hewett in the Niger Delta to hurry to Cameroon. On receiving the message he left and arrived on 19 July, five days too late. Having lost Cameroon, the British Consul was nicknamed 'Too Late Hewett'. Hewett was informed about the German annexation by the chief English Baptist missionary at Victoria, Thomas Lewis.

Reactions to German annexation

The British, the French and the majority of the coastal inhabitants of Cameroon were taken by surprise by the German annexation. Except for the French, the initial reactions were generally unfavourable and, on the African side, even violent. On being told about the annexation, Consul Hewett decided to sail straight for Douala to verify the story for himself. But before he left, he instructed the missionary Thomas Lewis to proclaim Victoria annexed as an integral part of Her Majesty's dominions, fix some notice in a public place to that effect, and hoist the British flag. At Douala he held meetings with German officials and with the chiefs, but failed to make the important King Bell change his mind. Later he addressed letters to each of the Duala chiefs expressing shock and dismay that after their application for British protection they should have accepted another power. King Bell replied that he had signed the German treaty because he and his chiefs received no definite answer to their several requests for British protection. Those who did not sign the treaty condemned the German annexation, and some of those who signed it claimed that they had been duped into signing a treaty whose nature and terms were not clearly explained to them.

British missionaries and traders strongly protested against the German annexation and called for the annulment of the annexation treaty. The missionaries argued that the whole of the Cameroon district was British, and that the Germans had acquired it by intrigue. They said that it was not too late to turn back the clock and put the district in the hands of the British Government. The traders on their part argued that the German treaty, which was negotiated in the dark, violated an Anglo-German treaty signed with the chiefs in 1883 affirming that everyone in Cameroon would be happy if the territory was taken under British protection.

Though taken by surprise, the French appear to have readily accepted the German annexation. They considered it their own victory over Great Britain. Most importantly, they had been duly informed about Nachtigal's mission and assured that nothing would be done anywhere in West Africa against French interests. The Germans had in mind, of course, French treaties with the chiefs of Malimba and other villages south of Duala country.

On the part of the indigenous population, violence erupted between those who favoured and those who were against the German annexation. Some of King Bell's people rose against him, forcing the king and his family to take refuge in the bush and to seek German protection. There was also an outbreak of hostilities towards the Germans which resulted in many wounded and a few killed on both sides. In fact in 1885 Chancellor Bismarck admitted in the German Parliament, the Reichstag, that there was fighting in Cameroon between the natives and the Germans, instigated by the British Consul, missionaries and the traders. The Chancellor warned that Germany would take her responsibility in Cameroon seriously. Some young Cameroonians who supported the German annexation, however, began to volunteer for the German army and were sent abroad for training.

The Germans decided to act firmly and forcefully to put an end to all anti-German activities and propaganda in Cameroon. They threatened to banish all British nationals if they continued to side in any way with the hostile natives. German authorities began to search and even to destroy the homes of British nationals whom they suspected of arming or inciting the natives. They tried to make the position of the missionaries and British traders as uncomfortable as possible in the hope of driving them away from the territory. They also began to make it clear that they were not only anxious to obtain Victoria, but also to extend German territory further westward, southward and into the interior. They began to talk about bringing German missionaries to replace British missionaries in the territory. This attitude of the Germans fostered the feeling among British nationals that Cameroon was definitely lost and that their days in the territory were numbered.

Attempts by the Germans and the British to increase their respective protectorates of Douala and Victoria resulted in a major scramble for possession of more Cameroon land. The affected territories included the region westward of Victoria, territory around and including the Cameroon Mountain, and the land between Victoria and Douala and including the Mungo region. While the Germans aimed at annexing the Cameroon Mountain region and limiting the British occupation to the Ambas Bay, the British aimed at signing treaties in the Mungo area and behind the German protectorate in an effort to cut the Germans off from the interior. This virtually brought the agents of the two colonial powers into a treaty contest in the same villages with the same chiefs. Because the chiefs were generally induced by gifts to sign the treaties, many accepted them from both German and British agents and then signed treaties with both powers. The British were assisted in the exercise by two Polish nationals, Stefan Szolc Rogozinski and Leopold Janikowski, who signed more than thirty-five treaties with local leaders in the region. Rogozinski and Janikowski were able to obtain the Cameroon Mountain and the whole of the coast stretching from near the German settlement to Calabar for the British. It looked as though a violent clash would erupt between the British and the Germans on the Cameroon coast, but war was averted.

Germany consolidates her position

The British authorities took the initiative in keeping the situation under control once they realised they had lost Cameroon. In January 1885 the British Foreign Office wrote to the Cameroon chiefs advising them to remain loyal to the Germans under whose protection they had placed themselves. They instructed the British Consul in the Bight of Biafra to use his influence with the natives of Cameroon to accept their new masters, and the English missionaries and traders to keep quiet and not raise difficulties between the two governments. Given the controversy over the roles of Rogozinski and Janikowski, the British Government decided not to press any territorial claims on the treaties signed by them, letting Germany have the territories in question. Despite the fact that the British held the settlement of Victoria, they pressed for the boundary between themselves and the Germans to be located on the Rio del Rey.

For their part, rather than wait and be expelled from Cameroon, the English Baptist Missionary Society began to explore ways of reaching agreement with the Germans and withdrawing peacefully from the territory. They requested the British Government to assist in negotiating compensation for their land and investments in the settlement of Victoria and other buildings elsewhere on the Cameroon coast. By January 1887 agreement had been reached and a total of £2750 was received in compensation for the transfer of the Baptist Mission lands to the Germans. On 28 March 1887, Victoria and the territory stretching to the Rio del Rey effectively passed into German control. The British withdrew with the consolation that the German annexation had kept out their arch-enemy, the French, from Cameroon.

The French, who had occupied territory south of Dualaland, had decided much earlier to withdraw from Cameroon following the German annexation. It was during the Berlin West African Congress of 1884–5, that the two colonial powers had started negotiations to establish a boundary between their spheres. The French had suggested the Campo River as the boundary. By December 1885 agreement had been reached fixing a provisional boundary on the Campo River. By virtue of this boundary, all the territory between Douala and the Campo River, including Malimba and the other villages where the French already had treaties, were incorporated into the German protectorate. With Cameroon's southern and western boundaries fixed and following the cession of French and British claims, Germany became the sole colonial power in possession of the entire Cameroon coast from the Rio del Rey to the Campo River.

Cameroon and the Berlin Conference

The Berlin West African Conference was held in Berlin, Germany, from 13 November, 1884 to 26 February 1885. The idea of the Conference came from Portugal. But the idea was quickly taken over by the famous German

Chancellor, Otto von Bismarck, who a few months earlier had laid claim to and authorised the annexation of Cameroon, Togo and other African territories. After due consultation with Belgium, Britain and France, Bismarck on behalf of Germany and France invited all the European colonial powers with interests in Africa to the Conference. The German Chancellor intended to use the Conference not only to consolidate Germany's position in Cameroon and other parts of Africa, but also to assert the leadership of his recently united country in Europe. The Conference was attended by representatives from every major power in Europe except Switzerland, and also by delegates from the United States and the Ottoman Empire. No African was present. Germany and France demonstrated practical cooperation in summoning the Conference.

The major issue that provoked and directly led to the Berlin West African Conference was the Congo basin. European interests and claims in the Congo basin had become complicated. King Leopold II of Belgium and France held longstanding and conflicting colonial ambitions in that region. Britain and Portugal also had longstanding commercial and sailing interests in the Congo basin and along the Congo River. By 1884 King Leopold's agent in the Congo, H.M. Stanley, and the French agent and explorer, Savorgnan de Brazza, had entered into a dangerous treaty-signing competition in the region, and Britain and Portugal were reacting to it. The Berlin Conference aimed at preventing the establishment of an exclusive colonial control in the basin, and attempted to guarantee freedom of trade and navigation on the Congo River. Other issues which made the Conference necessary were: the need to limit arbitrary expansion in Africa; the need to guarantee commercial freedom on the African coasts not yet under European control; and the need to assure free navigation on the Niger River.

When the Conference opened in November 1884, three major problems were listed on the agenda for discussion. These were: (a) liberty of commerce in the basin and mouth of the Congo, (b) application to the Congo and the Niger Rivers of the principles guaranteeing liberty of navigation on international rivers, and (c) definition of formalities to be observed before newly-acquired territory on the African coast could receive international recognition. Territorial questions were specifically excluded from the agenda and only dealt with in a series of bilateral agreements extending over many years. It was during the Conference that the various powers put forward their claims to African territory.

When the Conference ended in February 1885, consensus was reached on four important questions. First, it was agreed that any power wanting to claim African lands should immediately inform the other signatory powers at the Conference. Such information would enable the interested powers to make good any claims of their own. Second, it was agreed that for any claims on African lands to be valid, they should be supported by effective occupation. Effective occupation meant being present and administering the land. Third, it was agreed that there should be freedom of navigation on the Congo and Niger Rivers. These two rivers were recognised as international rivers, though no provision was made to secure the freedom of navigation on them. Finally, it was agreed that there should be freedom of trade in the Congo basin, but again no provisions were made for assuring the effectiveness of this Article.

It can be seen from the agreements that the Berlin West African Conference had tried to bring some form of order to the scramble which at the beginning looked as if it would lead to a European war in Africa. The Conference succeeded in limiting the ill-effects of the scramble upon international relations among the colonial powers in Europe. The agreement on 'effective occupation' was the Conference's international support and recognition to the partition of Africa. It resulted in colonial territories with well-defined boundaries. These colonial territories were transformed at independence into modern African states.

As far as Cameroon is concerned, the Berlin

Conference provided an opportunity for Germany, Britain and France to negotiate bilateral agreements on the territory. It was in the spirit of Berlin that the British suggested an Anglo-German boundary on the Rio del Rey and the French a Franco-German boundary on the Campo River. Both Britain and France peacefully surrendered to the Germans territories they had annexed or with which they had treaties after the coastal boundaries were defined. Through several other bilateral agreements, Cameroon's boundaries with neighbouring British and French territories were defined as far into the hinterland as Lake Chad.

Further reading

Shirley G. Ardener, *Eye-Witnesses to the Annexation of Cameroon 1883 – 1887* (Government Press, Buea, 1968).
Michael Crowder, *West Africa Under Colonial Rule* (Hutchinson, London, 1968).
Harry R. Rudin, *Germans in the Cameroons 1884 – 1914* (Greenwood Press, New York, 1968)

Questions

1. How did the British, the French and the local rulers contribute to Germany's successful annexation of Cameroon in 1884?
2. Why were the British unwilling to annex Cameroon?
3. Why was the British Consul Hewett referred to as 'Too Late' Hewett?
4. Why was Cameroon annexed by the Germans and not by the British?

Chapter three

German expansion and conquest of Cameroon

After the annexation and the cession of territory extending from the Campo River to the Rio del Rey by the French and the British, the territory occupied by the Germans was confined to the coastal region. Although the Germans had endorsed the Duala provision prohibiting European penetration inland, they had no intention whatever of thus limiting their occupation of Cameroon to the coast. The violation of the Duala provision actually began early in 1885 during the Anglo-German scramble for the control of independent villages located in the neighbourhood of Victoria, Douala, the slopes of the Cameroon Mountain, and the Mungo valley.

The decision to penetrate the hinterland

The Germans were determined to disregard almost immediately any clauses in the treaty of annexation which guaranteed the protection of the coastal middleman's trade in the hinterland from white interference. For a long time they had known that the real value of Cameroon was in the interior and not on the coast. Through explorers of the inland territories like Barth, Rolfs, Nachtigal and Flegel as well as agents of German firms trading on the Cameroon coast, the Germans had received reports of the riches of Cameroon's 'back country'. Besides this knowledge, the Germans were induced by many major considerations to penetrate into the interior and expand the territory they had occupied on the coast. The first was to conform with the 'hinterland theory' which loomed large in the background during the Berlin Conference of 1884 – 5. The 'hinterland theory' stipulated, in principle, that any power in control of any portion of the African coastland had the right to acquire the hinterland from which it derived its exports and within which it distributed its imports. The second was to conform with Article VI of the Berlin Act which stated that European traders, missionaries and other agents should have free access to the interior of Africa so that its slave trade and slavery could be finally crushed and the benefits of European civilisation made freely available to all its peoples.

There were, however, many equally important local reasons requiring immediate German penetration and expansion of Cameroon. First, early explorations of the country around the Cameroon Mountain in the immediate hinterland led to the discovery that the Cameroon soil was rich and very suitable for plantation work. This realisation made the Germans determined to penetrate and establish control in the interior and begin the cultivation of tropical commercial crops there. Second, Europeans who had ventured inland had much to say about the low costs of ivory and palm products as compared to the prices paid to the local middlemen at the coast. This revelation made the German traders resolve to deal directly with the inland producers of these products. Third, the manner in which the British-controlled foreign traffic on the Niger – Benue river system and the French over the Congo, forced the Germans to forget about them as possible routes for reaching the interior of Cameroon, although these had been declared international rivers at Berlin. They therefore decided on establishing direct overland routes and control from the coast to all parts of the interior. Fourth, when the Germans learned during the early years of occupation that a good deal of Cameroon's inland trade was flowing north and west to the advantage of the British in Nigeria and east and south into the hands of the French in the Upper Congo region, they redoubled their efforts to penetrate the interior and control that trade for themselves. Fifth, when plantations were finally begun in the coastal region in the 1890s, the shortage of labour directed the attention of the Germans inland where there were heavier populations and abundant labour. Besides, workers from inland were also needed by the traders as porters, since the African head and back were the only means of transporting goods in most parts of the tropical forest. The last principal reason for the expansion of Cameroon after 1884 was the urge to establish effective control in an extensive region, from the coast to Lake Chad, and to make the territory and its people German.

Penetration and expansion from the coast

The task of extending Cameroon from its Atlantic shores into the interior was accomplished by German colonial explorers. These explorers were instructed to study the regions assigned to them, establish relations with the local leaders, and make them subjects of the German Empire. Specifically, the explorers were advised to: hold discussions with inland chiefs and other local leaders; give them flags as symbols of German authority; recognise them as agents of the colonial administration now exercising authority over their people with the consent of the German government; inform them of their new duties as German colonial chiefs; let them know that their land and people were now German; and settle disputes as well as warn them against capital punishment and inhuman practices.

The early explorations were limited to the coastal region and the immediate hinterland. These ventures had very interesting results. They led to the discovery that the rivers flowing into the Cameroon sea were not navigable for great distances inland. The Germans also found that the Rio del Rey on the Cameroon – Nigeria border, which was at first believed to be a major navigable river, was not a river but a creek. It was also realised that the River Benue was further inland from the coast than was thought. These revelations, of course, convinced the Germans that the only way of reaching the interior and inland territories was by overland routes. The journeys inland generally commenced from one of the four major coastal stations: Douala, Victoria, Big Batanga and Kribi.

The first explorer with a well-conceived plan to travel into the interior and acquire an extensive region for Germany was Dr Eugen Zintgraff who had earlier explored areas near the Cameroon Mountain. Zintgraff had worked out a scheme for establishing stations inland which would serve commercial, administrative, military and research needs, and set his mind on obtaining the whole of the region from the Mungo to the Benue in Adamawa for Germany. He began his hazardous journey from Douala in 1888 and travelled by water through the creeks and the Mungo River to Mundame and Barombi where he established the first inland station. From Barombi, Zintgraff and his entourage followed an overland carrier-route through Mukonje, Mabanda, Ikiliwindi and Nguti to Banyang country. While in the region of the Upper Cross River, he was able to visit the villages of Defang, Fotabe, Tinto and Sabe before climbing the escarpment to Ashong in Moghamo. From Ashong he travelled to Bali Nyonga, arriving in January 1889, where he established his second German station.

Zintgraff was given a 'red carpet reception' by the Fon of Bali Nyonga, Galega I, who knew he was coming and waited for him. Galega I and Zintgraff swore 'blood friendship', and the Fon promised to supply workers and soldiers for German needs. Through a later

2   *Alfred Zintgraff*

treaty on behalf of the colonial administration in August 1891, all the ethnic groups in the western grassfields were placed under the suzerainty of Galega I and Bali Nyonga was offered German protection. Bali Nyonga was to become the headquarters of the German administration in the whole of the western grassfields until 1902 when the station was transferred to Bamenda. From his headquarters in Bali, Zintgraff visited the fondoms of Bafut, Kom, Babungo, Bambui, Mankon and Nkwen before continuing his journey to Adamawa.

From Bali Nyonga in mid-1889 Zintgraff moved on over the highlands through Beba-Befang, Bafwum, Fungom, Takum and Wukari to Ibi on the Benue River. He then continued his journey from Ibi through Bakundi and Gashaka to Yola, the Muslim headquarters of the Emirate of Adamawa. In Yola, Zintgraff was received by the Emir, Sanda, who inquired about the purpose of his visit. The Emir refused to grant Zintgraff's request to visit Banyo because the Lamido of that city was in rebellion against the authority in Yola. Having failed to establish a station or sign a treaty of any kind in Adamawa, he retraced his steps through Ibi and Bali back to the Cameroon coast, finally reaching Douala at the end of 1889. Zintgraff was the first German to get through to northern Cameroon using an overland route.

While Zintgraff was expanding the German territory from the Mungo to the Benue in the west, other explorers were at work in the south and the centre. They were Lt R. Kund and his assistant, Lt Tappenbeck, who made the first attempt to penetrate into the innermost territories of the south. Using their experiences in the Congo, these two explorers began preparing for the difficult journey inland by exploring the region behind Big Batanga, including the Ngumba country and the Nyong valley. They were accompanied by the zoologist Weissenborn and the botanist Braun. Their journey inland was started from Big Bantanga, near Kribi, on 15 October 1887, but they were held back by Bakoko resistance and the shortage of provisions. They tried again early in 1888, travelling by way of the lower Sanaga and through thick forest to the country of the Beti, arriving in Yaounde after 22 days. They opened their first German station in the heart of Cameroon at Yaounde.

The Yaounde station was soon to become important for many reasons. It was used as a post for organising and sending further expeditions to the various parts of the territory, and for exploiting the wealth and the trade of the interior. It became a centre of trade in its own right, the point for checking and eliminating the slave trade, and the inland station for organising military expeditions to put down anti-German rebellions in the central region. The Germans hoped, after establishing the Yaounde station, that Cameroon's trade which the French in the south and the east, and the British in the north and the west, were diverting into their own territories, would now flow into their hands. Yaounde was popular for its ideal climate and also because its Ewondo population had accepted the German presence peacefully, offering only a symbolic resistance to the occupation of their country.

The next team of explorers was led by Curt Morgen and Von Stetten. Morgen was commissioned by the administration to extend exploration further inland from Yaounde. After travelling to Yaounde by the safe route established by earlier explorers, Morgen's expedition began from there in 1890. The team followed the northern traditional route which led through Nguila, Yoko, Tibati and Banyo to Ibi. This expedition gave the Germans their first real knowledge of the greater part of the interior of Cameroon. Morgen found that the Muslim chiefs in the north were unwilling to sign treaties and accept the German flag without the prior approval of the Emir of Adamawa whose residence was in Yola in the British territory. Through Morgen's exploration the Germans discovered that the French were already hard at work signing treaties with local rulers and establishing territorial claims in the extensive region between the Congo River and Lake Chad. They also learned that the British and the French were already defining their respective frontiers near Lake Chad. This knowledge forced the Germans to take immediate steps to establish claims in the north, the east and the southeast in order to save a huge hinterland for Cameroon.

Between 1890 and 1894 several expeditions were prepared to capitalise on Morgen's discoveries, but these never got off the ground. Morgen himself was rendered inactive by illness in his family. An expedition to be led by von Gravenreuth in 1891 failed to materialise because he was killed at Buea in a war against the Bakweri group led by chief Kuva Likenye. Another expedition to be led by von Ramsay was aborted because he felt the military support offered him was inadequate for such a mission. These delays led to the fear in 1893 that Cameroon's eastern frontier with the French might be determined by a straight line running diagonally from longitude 15° east in the southeast to Yola on the Benue in the northwest.

However, the British decided to help the Germans acquire unexplored territory in the far north by defining their common boundary to run from the neighbourhood of Yola all the way to Lake Chad. The Germans had made only verbal claims to the land in the Lake Chad region which nevertheless the British decided to recognise. Negotiations with the French in 1894 led to an agreement defining Cameroon's eastern frontier from longitude 15° east to Lake Chad. By virtue of these agreements with the British and the French, Germany was able to lay claim to territory stretching from the Cameroon coast to Lake Chad, but this huge territory remained largely unexplored and unsubdued to German rule. It required more exploratory expeditions to achieve this.

During the period lasting from 1895 to 1910, almost very part of Cameroon became subjected to German rule, and the German might in one form or another was felt or feared by all. The method of conquest was largely military, due to resistance mounted by different groups in different parts of the country. Although the final subjection of hundreds of Cameroon groups to German rule was the work of many officers and expeditions, we can only mention a few whose achievements were remarkable.

The most extraordinary of all was Major Hans Dominik. This officer arrived in Cameroon from Germany in 1894 and was immediately commissioned to establish a military camp in Yaounde to serve as a starting point for military ventures to different parts of Cameroon. His effort to bring the Ewondo country and the central region under German rule peacefully, gradually resulted in the formation of a nucleus of young men who were recognised as having traditional authority and given greater rights in the management of the affairs of their areas. Among such young men were Charles Atangana among the Ewondo, Peter Mvemba among the Vute (Babute), Ndengue Kathou in the Sanaga district, Martin Samba in Ebolowa, and Alphonse Bagneki Tombi in Ndiki. In 1899 Major Dominik successfully put down a Bulu revolt against the Germans. He also directed several campaigns

3 *Major Hans Dominik*

Carnap Quernheimb, head of the Yaounde military station, explored the course of the River Sangha to the Ngoko and its other tributaries. He also investigated other parts of the region and collected information on its wealth in rubber and ivory. After Quernheimb's survey, a German administrative and trading station was opened on the Ngoko river for the purpose of preventing the region's trade from flowing into the hands of French, Belgian and Dutch traders in the Congo. Other explorers of the southeastern region after Quernheimb were von Stein in 1902, Engelhardt in 1903, and Scheunemann in 1904. All three made valuable discoveries of additional rubber and ivory, and populous districts that could serve as sources of labour supply for the colony.

Resistance to penetration and conquest

The penetration of the hinterland and the conquest of Cameroon were bitterly opposed by many groups at different locations all over the territory. The coastal groups which had trade monopolies to defend were the first to begin the resistance. It is said that even when these groups had been subdued, it was only with the aid of troops that the Germans kept the inland routes open. We have, of course, seen that some of the Duala chiefdoms which objected to the annexation took up arms against the Germans soon after the hoisting of the flag. The Duala forces fought bravely for many weeks, sending a fusillade of shots with their breech-loading guns, inflicting and suffering casualties, before they were finally subdued.

In the same vein, Zintgraff's penetration and attempts to subdue inland groups were resisted vehemently. The Banyang of the Upper Cross River valley opposed his use of their territory as a route to the grasslands and Adamawa. In fact he, his other German companions and hundreds of African carriers, principally Vai people from Liberia, were forced to walk quietly and rapidly through Banyang country to avoid the possibility of an open conflict or

against the Bamileke chiefdoms and the Fulbe *lamibe,* establishing a garrison in Garoua in 1901 and capturing Maroua and Mora in 1902. Early in 1902 Major Dominik's assistant, Von Pavel, led another expedition from Bali Nyonga demonstrating the German might and presence through Nso to Banyo. There it joined up with the main German detachment in the north.

Earlier, in 1900 – 1901, Herr Kamptz had led the explorations of the Gbaya, Banen and Vute countries before proceeding to the Tikar country and Adamawa. While in the Tikar country in the Upper Mbam valley, he found the chiefdom of Ngambe engaged in a seven-year-old losing battle with the Fulbe state of Tibati. In 1899 Kamptz's force was able to defeat those of Lamdo Mohama of Tibati, impose humiliating conditions on the Fulbe prince, and put an end to the siege on Ngambe.

Other expeditions were sent to subdue the southeastern region of Cameroon. In 1898 Herr

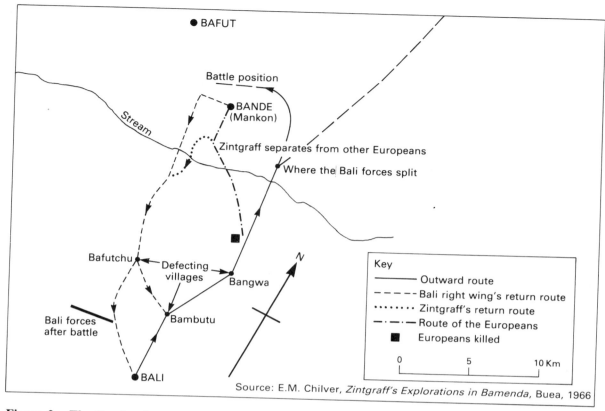

Figure 2 *The Battle of Mankon: 31 January 1891*

Source: E.M. Chilver, *Zintgraff's Explorations in Bamenda*, Buea, 1966

Key labels in figure: BAFUT; Battle position; BANDE (Mankon); Stream; Zintgraff separates from other Europeans; Where the Bali forces split; Bafutchu; Defecting villages; Bangwa; Bambutu; Bali forces after battle; BALI; N

Key
—— Outward route
- - - Bali right wing's return route
········ Zintgraff's return route
-·-·- Route of the Europeans
■ Europeans killed
0   5   10 Km

an attack from an ambush. When he arrived in the grassfields in 1890, Bafut and Mankon provoked him into a war by killing his two Vai envoys sent to them and by refusing to pay compensation for the murders. In the ensuing battle on 31 January 1891, the allied forces of Bafut and Mankon killed more than 180 of Zintgraff's Vai and Bali-Nyonga warriors and all his white companions who took part in the war on the battlefield. Zintgraff himself escaped death only by chance. Although Bafut and Mankon lost more than 600 men, they won the war and rallied the neighbouring chiefdoms of Nsongwa, Bambutu and Bafochu to their side. Having failed to obtain reinforcements and ammunitions for a counter-attack, Zintgraff sued for peace but his enemies refused to surrender the bodies of Lt von Spangenberg, H. Nehber, M. Huwe and H. Tiedt, who were killed in the war. Disappointed and humiliated

by the events in the grassfields, Zintgraff withdrew from Cameroon, leaving the 'proper' subjugation of Bafut and Mankon to the forces of Col. von Pavel in January 1902. When Zintgraff withdrew from Bali, his only remaining German companion, Von Hutter, stayed on and trained a *Balitruppe* and armed them.

In the Abo and Bassa-Bakoko country, resistance to penetration and conquest was also violent. The people readily took up arms under the leadership of chiefs Toko of Bona Ngan, Ngango of Pongo Songo and Janje of Janje village and fought several German military campaigns conducted with ferocious cruelty. Assessor Wehlan, who led the expeditions, ordered many villages to be burnt down, women, children and old people to be killed and captives to be burnt to death in the most outrageous manner. When they were finally defeated by the Germans, the chiefs were humiliated and forced to sign a harsh treaty of surrender on 14 December 1892. But the Abo, Bassa and Bakoko continued to agitate against the Germans until after 1900.

Conquest of the Gbaya, Banen and Vute countries by Herr Kamptz and his companion von Schimmelfennig in 1902 were made difficult because of local insurrection. Recalcitrant groups were organised by leaders such as Watile, Somo Mambok and Manimben, and in later years the strong forces of Major Dominik were required to quash them. The final subjugation of the groups was followed by the banishment of Chief Manimben to Douala where he died in 1909, and the imprisonment of Chief Somo and his leading warriors Bekemen, Ihumb, Belema, Kitiek, Mem, Tibagne, Endeka, Mesote and Bokwagne. These people were released in 1911 when they accepted reconciliation and payment of a ransom in ivory.

In the south, in Bulu country, where the American Presbyterian Mission had opened a station in 1895, the people continued to oppose the occupation of their land by the Germans. In 1896 and 1898 they impeded the explorations of von Kampf and von Stein in their country and frequently attacked German caravans journeying through the region. These hostile acts precipitated a major Bulu-German war in 1899 which resulted in bloody massacres on both sides. The war resulted from the desire of the Bulu to protect their trade monopoly on the route from the coast to Yaounde. The Bulu assaulted and laid siege to Kribi which was already under German control, and put the government officials in the township to flight. German reinforcements and superior weapons did not bring immediate victory. The war lasted from 1899 to 1901 before the Bulu resistance was split and one chief after another was forced to accept peace treaties. The settlement obliged each chief to provide slave-labour and deliver stated amounts of ivory and rubber to the officers of the expeditionary force.

Events in Nso in the northwest told a similar story. Subsequent to Pavel's provocative march through the extensive fondom in 1902, reports continued to describe the Nso as uncooperative, uncompromising and much-feared bloodthirsty slave-hunters who were difficult to subdue. A German report in 1905 even claimed that the paramount Fon of Nso had refused to accept a public act of submission to the German government. Aided by the Bali Nyonga who acted as scout, the Babungo who were carriers, and the more than 200 Bamum auxiliary troops, the German force of 11 Europeans and some 200 Vai soldiers under Captain Hans Glauning mounted a two-month punitive expedition and war of conquest against Nso from April to June 1906. The Nso knew from the numerous postponements of the expedition that the Germans were coming and were prepared to defend their motherland. When the Germans came, many major battles were fought. The German used machine-guns and modern small arms like rifles and revolvers and the Nso fought with flintlocks, spears and cutlasses. In the battle at Vekovi the Germans massacred over 300 Nso and sustained only a few casualties. At Nkar, a strategy to beat the Germans by a decoy led to the slaughter of scores of German troops. In the neighbourhood of the capital Kimbo and in Djottin and Dzeng, fierce battles led to heavy casualties on both sides. The Germans continued to be unrelenting and powerful. In the end, in order to save his people from total annihilation, the Fon, Sembum II, surrendered to his white enemies. He was now forced to perform a public act of submission to the German Kaiser, pay a ransom of seventy ivories for the release of his men in German custody, and supply free labour for the road linking Bamenda and Banyo, and 150 men for work in the south.

It took ten years from 1893 and several expeditions under different military officers to bring the extensive region of northern Cameroon under German authority. In 1893 – 4 an expedition led by Lt Edgar von Uechtritz and Herr Siegfried Passarge, which found it difficult to use Zintgraff's route, was helped by the British to reach Garoua by way of the Niger and Benue rivers. It encountered major resistance from the local forces in the district and as far south as Ngaoundere. In the ensuing battles, Uechtritz and his 'protective force' inflicted a severe defeat on the force from Babandjidda, sacked and set fire to the towns of Djurum and Assali, and induced several rulers to sign treaties of friendship recognising German rights in the area. The Fulbe ruler of Ngaoundere was forced to sign a treaty of protection with Germany. But as soon as Uechtritz and his mercenary force returned to the coast, the defeated groups regained their independence and reorganised their armies.

The final subjugation of the important Fulbe state of Tibati was undertaken in 1899 by Major Hans Dominik, whose forces had also defeated the Bamileke chiefdoms. The Lamdo of Tibati who had earlier refused to recognise German suzerainty was seized, dethroned and exiled to the coast, where he died shortly after. But his people continued to resist European aggression and within a year they rose against his successor and the Germans who appointed him. In the course of a long war which lasted until 1901, Tibati was devastated and crushed and the principality lost its economic and political importance. The Germans made their military station in Tibati the base for the wars against neighbouring Fulbe states and the reconquest of Ngaoundere. In their second encounter against Ngaoundere, the Lamdo was shot and killed and another treaty of protection was forced on his successor.

In the rest of the north, from Adamawa to Lake Chad, resistance to German forceful penetration continued and was broken down ferociously. In and around Garoua in 1901, a German force of five Europeans and about 120 auxiliary troops equipped with machine-guns, artillery and rifles defeated a Fulbe force of several thousand armoured horsemen under Lamido Zubeiru, the Emir of Adamawa, recently forced out of his official palace in Yola in the British territory. At the end of this encounter the Germans counted 300 of Zubeiru's warriors killed on the battlefield. This heavy defeat prompted many lesser rulers in the region to submit to German authority.

Zubeiru, who escaped unscathed, quickly assembled another force of militia from loyal districts for the defence of Maroua, the most powerful Fulbe principality in Adamawa. On 20 January 1902, this new force too was overwhelmed by a well-drilled, well-equipped and heavily reinforced contingent under Major Hans Dominik. The German commander ordered that enemy soldiers wounded and left behind should be slaughtered. More than 500 of the Emir's fighting men were killed and Maroua town was violently plundered. Dignitaries loyal to the Emir were either executed, jailed, replaced or exiled to the coast. The defeat suffered by the Fulbe in Maroua virtually settled the fate of the remaining Muslim districts in northern Cameroon. German presence and control were accepted. Only the non-Fulbe groups, in their isolated and hidden settlements, continued to defend their freedom and to resist subjugation.

Although the absence of powerful ethnic units in southern Cameroon did not allow for the fierce and durable opposition witnessed in the grassfields and the north, some groups, like the Bulu already discussed and the units in the Upper Cross River region, did put up effective and sustained resistance. Revolt in the Upper Cross River valley, often referred to as the Anyang or Ejagham Resistance, began in 1899 and reached its peak in January 1904 with a successful attack on a German military expedition and the murder of the commander, Graf Puckler, six of his soldiers and 120 carriers. This resulted in the utter defeat and disorderly retreat of the expeditionary force. The people of the region – Anyang, Ejagham, Keaka, Banyang and Boki – were united in a general uprising. Within 18 days all trading posts and the administrative station in the region were destroyed and all the German and African employees and troops were killed or driven away. It took the greater part of the colonial force almost six months to reimpose German authority in the Osidinge district. The campaign ended with the demobilisation of the groups and the execution of the leaders of the uprising.

Collaboration with the forces of penetration and occupation

A balanced story of the resistance to penetration and conquest of Cameroon requires that something be said about the groups that collaborated with the Germans and embraced their rule from the outset. Among those who collaborated were small and weak states like Ngambe and Ndu in the central grasslands who preferred German to Fulbe rule. More significant are the few large and powerful groups such as Bali-Nyonga, Bamum and Ewondo, who were in a position to resist but who realised the futility of confronting the Germans and instead chose to collaborate.

Bali-Nyonga provide an extraordinary example of the cooperation which the Germans received. On the orders of their king, Galega I, the Bali not only enthusiastically welcomed the German explorer Zintgraff and his white and black companions, but also built his administrative station themselves and asked that German rule be established in their country. In the ensuing friendly talks and treaty (the terms of the treaty are set out below), Galega freely transferred the sovereignty of his country and his personal power as king to the German government, and entered into a blood-brotherhood relationship with the German envoy. In so doing, the Fon of Bali Nyonga claimed that it was more beneficial to his people to have the Germans as friends and to obtain their knowledge than to have them as enemies. On this unprecedented friendly gesture Zintgraff, on behalf of the German Government, recognised and promised to protect Galega's position as the paramount chief of the surrounding groups in the western grasslands. Thenceforth, the Bali collaborated fully and provided the majority of fighting men for the German wars against the groups that resisted the Germans in many parts of the western grasslands.

The Galega – Zintgraff treaty of August 1891, which had only five articles, was set out as follows:

In order to bring the Bali tribe to such power and influence as will enable it to lead the tribes in Northern Kamerun, the following persons, namely Garega as an independent Chief speaking for himself and his people and Dr Zintgraff as Commissioner of the German Government, make the following treaty subject to the approval of the latter:

1 Garega will transfer to Dr Zintgraff such powers as he at present exercises in the lands, namely the right over life and limb and the final decisions as to war and peace.

2 Accordingly Garega undertakes to give effect to such orders as may be given by Dr Zintgraff in the interest of the Bali and secure their acceptance, likewise to carry out penalties inflicted by Dr Zintgraff himself or to comply loyally with their execution by other means, and finally to hold his forces in unconditional readiness for any war Dr Zintgraff may consider necessary and not to undertake war for his own advantage and without Dr Zintgraff's concurrence.

3 In consideration of this the establishment, recognition and protection of Garega's position as the paramount Chief of the surrounding tribes of the northern Kamerun hinterland will be secured.

4 The proceeds of regular tax to be raised from the neighbouring tribes and a fixed duty payable by caravans passing through the Bali districts from the hinterland will be divided between Dr Zintgraff and Garega to defray the costs of administration in North Kamerun, the part due to Dr Zintgraff to be used for direct Goverment costs such as road and bridge building, supplementation of weapons and ammunition, provisioning of the station, etc., and the part due to Garega to be regarded as an official payment for loyal compliance with the terms of the treaty now concluded.

5 The regulation of the incidence of these taxes, the establishment of customs stations and appointment of customs officers and connected regulations are to be decided in accordance with the wishes of Dr Zintgraff.

When the treaty was concluded and the terms carefully explained to the king, his retainers and subjects, the Bali demonstrated, in the market-place, that their power of fighting now belonged to the Germans. The treaty was eventually acknowledged by the German Foreign Office.

In Bamumland, the German expeditions reaching Foumban led by Captain Ramsay on 6 July 1902 and of Lt Hitler on 13 April 1903, were well received. Ramsay's expedition, which included Lt Sandrock and the trader Habisch, was accompanied by 20 or so riflemen, although other sources mention 117 persons including carriers, servants and riflemen. The Bamum had heard that the Germans were coming and were prepared to resist in defence of their homeland. But their monarch, King Njoya, refused to give sanction to a war against the Germans, saying that such a confrontation would not only be disastrous for the country, but would also end with only a few Bamum remaining. He called on the Bamum to welcome and obey rather than resist the Germans, and hoped that a cordial relationship would be established between the colonial administration and his country. King Njoya immediately took steps to solicit German cooperation by sending envoys to Buea with gifts of ivories, a colt and samples of trade items for the governor. He also requested protection and permission to establish commercial links with the coast. The former request was immediately accorded, and Bamum was attached to the German station at Bamenda for the purpose of administration. Thereafter, Njoya's relations with the Germans went from strength to strength, and the administration frequently consulted him on African policy. The Bamum also began to constitute the main fighting force for the various expeditions against resistant groups in the west-central grasslands and southern Adamawa. In 1906, King Njoya personally accompanied the German military expedition (made up principally of Bamum fighters) against Nso, and was decorated by the administration for his total support and cooperation.

In Ewondoland the collaborators were men of noble rank who easily influenced the masses to follow suit. Essono Ela and Onambele Mbazoa set the scene when they welcomed, entertained and offered a hand of friendship to the German explorers, Kund and Tappenbeck, the first Europeans to tread on Ewondo soil. This was a happy surprise for the two colonial officials who had received only total opposition and hostility from the Bakoko as they tried to penetrate the forests and reach the hinterland. Kund and Tappenbeck immediately saw the Ewondo as friends of Germany and they resolved to build a German station in the real hinterland, at Yaounde in the heartland of Ewondo country. The collaboration which Essono Ela and Onambele Mbazoa offered the Germans in their enthusiastic reception soon elevated the two noblemen to the rank of *minkukuma* (chiefs), although one needed to be a good warrior, a just and impartial judge, and a talented, experienced, influential and wealthy person to become a *nkukuma* in Ewondoland. The rise of Essono Ela and Onambele Mbazoa soon encouraged other well-placed people in Ewondo society to establish friendly ties with the Germans. Indeed, it soon became a mark of nobility to be honest and loyal to the Germans. The overwhelming support of the leaders and the willingness of the masses to work for the administration, made the Ewondo highly desirable as plantation workers in the coastal districts and as riflemen in the military expeditions to southern, eastern and northern Cameroon. Before the end of the second decade of German rule, the administration began to think seriously about removing the administrative capital of Cameroon from Buea and establishing it in Yaounde where the population was enthusiastic about the German presence.

Cameroon's international boundaries

An international boundary is an actual line of division between neighbouring independent states or countries. Cameroon's international boundaries were the object of negotiations between Germany and Great Britain, Germany and France, and Great Britain and France. Each negotiation was usually concluded by a treaty or joint agreement establishing the particular boundary or section of it.

There were generally three stages adopted by the colonial powers in the establishment of international boundaries in Africa. The first stage was the *definition stage*. At this stage the colonial powers concerned allocated adjacent territories to themselves by defining a common boundary line on paper, using pencil and ruler at a joint meeting summoned for that purpose in one of the European capitals. The allocation of territory and the definition of the boundary were done without full or actual knowledge of the inhabitants of the region being divided. The second stage was the *delimitation stage*. At this stage, officials of the concerned colonial powers were sent to Africa to actually study the boundary zone noting carefully all the natural features, ethnic settlements, the movement of people and trade, and possible hindrances on the boundary line as defined. Such studies led to further negotiations and modifications in the boundary. The third and final stage was the *demarcation stage*. At this stage, the parties concerned established a joint boundary commission which marked or demarcated the final boundary line on the ground, using permanent and easy-to-identify landmarks or cairns at uniform distances. The present-day Cameroon's international boundaries followed these stages of evolution. A demarcated boundary could still be a subject for negotiation if new facts requiring modifications later emerged.

The establishment of Cameroon's international boundaries began with the definition of the limits of the Cameroon coastline. It was the result of the attempt to separate the coastal claims of the British, the Germans and the French in the Bight of Biafra. The idea of a boundary between the German and British spheres came from the British during the winter of 1884–5. During the negotiations that followed in London, the British surrendered claims they were making on territories based on Rogozinski's treaties and then suggested that their coastal boundary be established on the Rio del Rey. The Germans accepted this generous suggestion, knowing that the British were still holding on to Victoria. When the British eventually withdrew from Victoria in 1887, the Cameroon western coastline extended from Douala to the Rio del Rey. The southern coastal boundary between the German and French spheres was also suggested at the end of 1884. The French, who were claiming territory in Malimba, surprisingly suggested the Campo River on the southern coast as the boundary. The Germans accepted the suggestion and the Cameroon coastline, the boundary with the sea, was now defined as running from the Rio del Rey to the Campo.

In March 1885 the Germans and the British decided to extend the Rio del Rey boundary inland to follow the course of the Rio del Rey creek to its source. From the source of the creek, the line was proposed to continue straight to a point 9° 8′ east longitude, marked 'Rapids' on the British Admiralty map, on the Cross river. From November 1885 to the summer of 1886, the two colonial powers negotiated and prolonged the line from the point 'Rapids' to a point on the right bank of the Benue river, east of the Adamawa capital of Yola. In 1893 negotiations recommenced to extend the line from the Benue River to Lake Chad. Agreement on this section concluded the allocation of territories in the west and the definition of Cameroon's boundary with Nigeria from the Atlantic Ocean to Lake Chad in the extreme north. What remained to be done on this line were delimitation and demarcation, processes which could only be accomplished much later.

Negotiations to establish the southern and eastern boundaries of Cameroon were held between Germany and France. The two powers agreed to extend the Campo river line inland to longitude 10° east on the river, and from there latitudinally to the Ngoko river, terminating where it forms a confluence with the Sangha river. Following this agreement, the

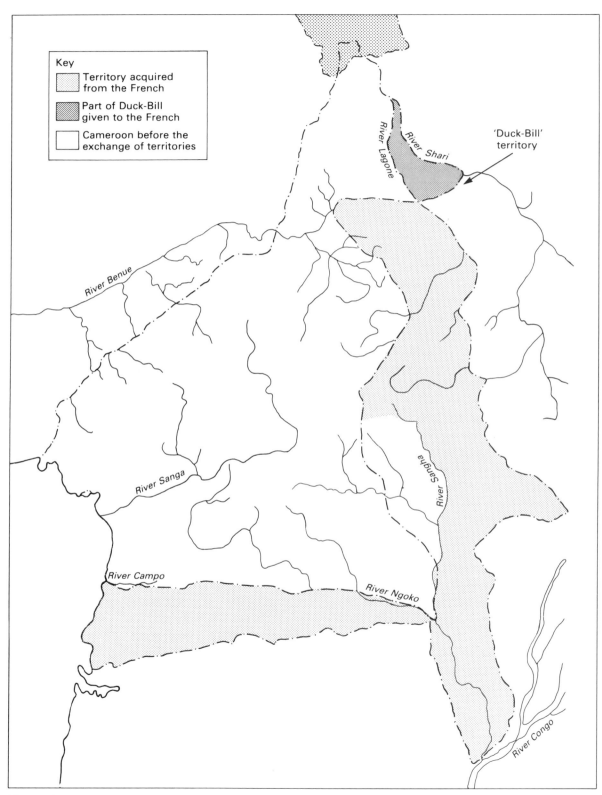

Figure 3 *Cameroon after exchange of territories in 1911*

Germans took steps to establish the boundary in the eastern hinterland. These steps brought Germany into competition with Britain and France for a foothold on Lake Chad. Germany, like Britain and France, wanted the territory she had acquired in the hinterland to extend uninterruptedly to Lake Chad. Serious talks with France began in July 1893 and ended with a treaty on 15 March 1894. This treaty, which defined Cameroon's eastern boundary from the Ngoko – Sangha confluence in a zigzag fashion northwestward to Lake Chad, gave the German protectorate its final form and size. There was, however, an incident which led to the shortlived exchange of territories in 1911. This incident led to the southern and western boundaries remaining undemarcated for a long time to the inconvenience of the colonial governments concerned.

'Duck bill' and exchange of territories in 1911

Following the Franco-German accord of March 1894, the term 'duck-bill' was applied to a peculiar geographic conformation in the extreme northeast of Cameroon, between the Logone and Shari Rivers, just below Lake Chad. It seems probable that the term 'duck-bill' was applied to the region because the curve in the boundary between the Logone and the Shari had the shape of a beak like that of a duck.

The story of the 'duck-bill' territory in Cameroon is linked closely with what is known as the Agadir Incident. Agadir was a tiny territory in Morocco claimed by the French but contested by the Germans. The French wanted the Germans to surrender their existing rights in Agadir and to recognise French claims to the whole of the Moroccan territory. In order to do so, Germany requested as compensation the cession of large territories of French Equatorial Africa, including the whole of Gabon and French Congo as well as territory in Ubangi-Shari, present-day Central African Republic. After lengthy negotiations, a formal agreement on the exchange of territories was signed on 4 November 1911. Germany agreed not only to surrender her existing rights in Agadir, Morocco, but also to cede to the French a small portion of the 'duck-bill' territory in north-eastern Cameroon. In return, Germany obtained from the French the extensive territory in Gabon, Rio Muni, and parts of French Congo and Ubangi-Shari. The territories were officially exchanged on 1 October 1912, the day the 'duck-bill' officially became French territory. The French cession enlarged the area of German Cameroon by about fifty per cent. The circumstances of the exchange and the exchange itself were considered by the French as humiliating.

But the newly-acquired territories of Cameroon lasted only a few years. In February – March 1916, following the Allied victory and the expulsion of the Germans from Cameroon, the French quickly reannexed to their Equatorial African possessions all the territories ceded to the Germans in 1911. In doing so, however, they failed to return to Cameroon the 'duck-bill' territory which the Germans had ceded to them.

Following the conquest of German Cameroon, the British and the French negotiated the establishment of the boundary which partitioned the territory.

Further reading

E.M. Chilver, *Zintgraff's Explorations in Bamenda, Adamawa and the Benue Lands 1889 – 1892* (Government Printer, Buea, 1966).

Harry R. Rudin, *Germans in the Cameroons 1884 – 1914* (Greenwood Press, New York, 1968).

Helmuth Stoecker, *German Imperialism in Africa* (Akademie Verlag, Berlin, 1986).

Questions

1. Why did the Germans decide to expand their territory of Cameroon from Douala along the coast and into the interior?
2. How was the expansion of the territory of Cameroon from the coast into the interior organised?
3. Why was Yaounde, which became the first German station in the centre of Cameroon in 1888, immediately important?
4. Discuss the resistance mounted against the Germans by: (a) Bafut and Mankon (b) the Bulu (c) the Nso (d) Tibati.
5. Why did Bali-Nyonga, Bamum, and the Ewondo decide to cooperate and collaborate with the German colonisers?
6. How were Cameroon's international boundaries determined and established?
7. Discuss the exchanges of territories between the Germans and the French involving the 'duck-bill' in 1911.

Chapter four
Germans in Cameroon: 1884-1914

The Germans acquired the right to administer Cameroon from the treaties signed by their agents with traditional rulers in different parts of the territory, beginning with the Duala treaty of July 1884, and from military subjugation of groups that resisted their presence. During the thirty years of the Cameroon Protectorate the Germans laid the foundation of a colonial (modern) administration and established the bases of modern economic, educational, judicial and fiscal developments. This chapter is devoted to the study of the German administration from 1884 to 1914.

The beginnings

The German Chancellor, Prince Otto von Bismarck, had approved the annexation of Cameroon in 1884 in the hope that the administrative machinery would be run and financed by the German business companies whose firms were operating on the Cameroon coast. The companies concerned were the C. Woermann Company and the Jantzen & Thormahlen Company. But the two companies, which had actually influenced the annexation, flatly refused to run the administration and to contribute towards the cost of running it. Yet by the urging of Adolf Woermann, president of the C. Woermann Company, an Imperial Commissioner was appointed to take over from Nachtigal as the representative of the German Government in Cameroon. The man appointed was Dr Max Buchner who found it difficult to establish any form of government in the territory for one year. The following year a colonial administration with a governor at its head was formed in Cameroon.

On 3 July 1885, Julius Baron von Soden arrived in Douala as the first colonial governor of the German Protectorate. He had the authority to establish a government and appoint administrative officials. The territory to be administered by von Soden in 1885 was confined to the Duala estuary, small strips of land on both sides of the River Wuri in the Douala township. It did not take long for the governor to realise that his authority in the township could not reach much further than the guns of the German warships which he called in whenever there were signs of resistance among the people whom he governed. Governor von Soden began his administration by appointing a law official, a 'chancellor' to handle legal matters, and an advisory council of three to give him advice in all administrative matters. He also set up a court composed of three persons including himself as president to replace the abolished British Court of Equity. All the officials appointed by the governor were responsible to him. His own appointment by the Kaiser conferred on him the authority to rule by decree. He did not immediately attempt to extend governmental control into the interior, preferring to do so gradually. This is how the actual German administration was established in Cameroon.

During the six years of von Soden's governorship, German authority was extended along the entire Cameroon coast and to settlements in the immediate hinterland easily accessible from the coast. After 1886 Douala and Victoria were the two most important administrative centres for a very long time. Real extension of authority inland did not begin until after the various explorations and subjugation of ethnic and regional resistances. Until then the number of German administrative officials in Cameroon remained small. Indeed, there were only between ten and fifteen officials when Governor von Soden's term came to an end in 1891.

The evolution of the colonial administration

There were three stages in the evolution of colonial administration in Cameroon from the time of Governor von Soden to the end of German rule. The first stage can simply be referred to as the early years. During this period of exploration, expansion and occupation, explorers and heads of expeditions were authorised to make treaties with native rulers, give them flags or other symbols of German authority, and to urge them to recognise and accept German rule. The treaty was also a sign that the administration had recognised the position of the local ruler in the traditional society. The traditional rulers so recognised were instructed not to interfere in German trade in their districts. They were also required to supply workers for the plantation and other projects. If there were any local difficulties or disputes which might lead to instability in the region, the German treaty makers were to resolve them.

The second stage in the evolution of German administration was the creation of stations with garrisons of troops at critical points to protect the whites, control trade and subdue rebellious groups. These military stations were run by heads of station who exercised military, administrative and judicial functions. The head of station had legal jurisdiction in cases involving Africans only and in cases involving whites and blacks. In the event that the litigant (usually the white) was unsatisfied with the judgement of the head of station, he could appeal to the District Commissioner based in Victoria.

Death-penalties imposed on the natives required the approval of the governor. The head of station had to furnish the administration with information concerning the geography and climate of his area, road conditions, local products, missionary and school work, health and commerce. He also advised the administration on the recruitment of labour for government and plantation work in the area under his control. Heads of station were required to put an end to the smuggling of local products out of and foreign goods into the territory. They were to impose and collect tariffs on non-German goods and on native products exported to neighbouring foreign territories. When peace was assured in the region under the station, a civilian administrator was appointed as the station master. It was then that the soldiers in the area were succeeded by the police.

The third stage (the last) was the creation of large administrative districts under district commissioners. The duty of the district commissioner was to advise heads of stations and local rulers in areas where the authority of such local rulers was strong and extensive. The district commissioner was also to protect the enslaved groups or people in his district and to use them as a source of labour supply for government and plantation work. Yaounde, which was one of the earliest inland stations, became the head of an administrative district in 1905. The centres of other administrative districts were Victoria, Dschang, Banyo, Bamenda, Douala, Doume, Edea, Ebolowa, Kribi, Loumie, Mora, Ossidinge, Ikelemba, Ojem, Ukoko, Yabassi, Yokadouma, Logone, Mbaikie, and Garoua. An administrative district was under a civilian administrator. As soon as an administrative district was created in an area, telegraph, telephone and postal services were introduced, and the network of roads serving the outstations was developed.

The administration of Adamawa and other areas of the north where Muslim rule had been established was entirely different from that of other areas. There, unlike elsewhere, the Germans found a well-organised, unified and extensive traditional administration under Fulbe leaders and decided not to destroy it. Here they decided to leave the affairs of the region in the hands of the Fulbe chiefs who were, however, to be advised on government policy by the German resident commissioners. The resident commissioners were charged with the responsibility of maintaining peace in the area. They were to administer the region indirectly through the traditional authorities, who were to be treated with respect, prevent anyone opposed to the Germans from coming to power, give as much attention as possible to the economic life of the region, and refrain from the use of military force except with the governor's approval.

Local traditional rulers in northern Cameroon played a large part in local affairs under German supervision. They organised and collected taxes imposed by the administration and in many places adjudicated disputes in native courts according to customary and Muslim law. They were paid a small percentage of the government taxes they collected.

Colonial officials and the administration

The most senior and most powerful colonial authority in Cameroon was the governor. His authority as head of the administration was conferred on him by the German Government and his powers were derived from those delegated to him by the Kaiser and the Chancellor in Berlin. He ruled by issuing decrees which touched upon every phase of colonial activity – general administration, taxes, tariffs, appointments, labour, and so on and so forth. The governor controlled the colonial courts and was in his person the highest court of appeal in the territory. He was also head of the colonial military force. But since it was difficult for the governor to exercise his authority personally in every part of the territory, he appointed local officials and conferred on them part of his powers. Those to whom the governor delegated his powers were heads of exploratory and military expeditions, heads of administrative stations and districts, administrative commissioners and residents.

During the thirty-two years of German rule in Cameroon, there were altogether six governors. The first, as we have seen, was Julius Baron von Soden whose term of office lasted from 1885 to 1891. Von Soden was an advocate of gradual rather than rapid and military expansion inland. During his term the German flag was hoisted at Buea on the slopes of the Cameroon Mountain, and stations were opened in Barombi, Bali and Yaounde. The Germans also acquired Victoria from the British and consolidated their position on the entire Cameroon coast during von Soden's governorship.

The second governor was Eugen von Zimmerer, 1891 – 1895. Under von Zimmerer the exploration of the hinterland of Cameroon and the establishment of stations was carried on in earnest. His administration succeeded in opening up a large part of the interior of Cameroon to German trade and administration. Like von Soden, Governor von Zimmerer did much to safeguard the interests of German traders in Cameroon, particularly the interests of the firms of C. Woermann and Jantzen & Thormahlen at whose request the territory had been occupied. His administration also subdued the Bakweri, Bassa and Bulu anti-German rebellions.

The third governor was Jesko von Puttkamer whose term ran from 1895 to 1906. He encouraged penetration into northern Cameroon and gave sanction to ferocious military campaigns. Under von Puttkamer all the inland parts of the territory were conquered step by step by a military unit known as the 'protective force', made up of African mercenaries recruited outside Cameroon. Governor von Puttkamer was instrumental in getting plantations started on a large scale. In 1898 and 1899 he created two private trading corporations, *Gesellschaft Sudkamerun* and *Gesellschaft Nordwest-Kamerun*. The first succeeded in establishing a German monopoly in rubber and ivory trade in southeastern Cameroon and

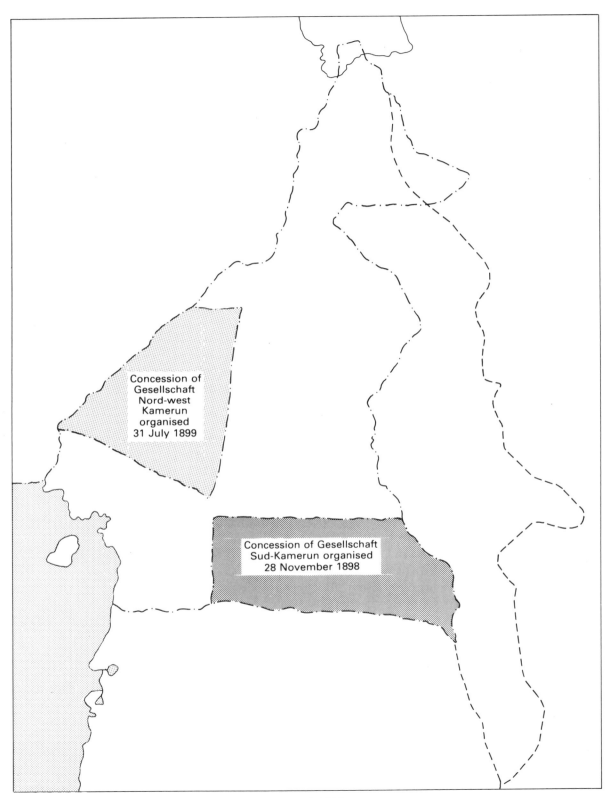

Figure 4 *Trading concessions created in 1898 and 1899*

the second established a commercial monopoly in the northwestern grasslands. The great government mansion known as the *schloss* at Buea and other important administrative buildings and forts in other parts of the territory were constructed during von Puttkamer's governorship.

But too many scandals occurred in the colonial administration during his rule and with his encouragement. Since von Puttkamer believed that the officials must be allowed every comfort in a territory which must be fully exploited for the benefit of Germany, he paid little attention to the way these officials treated the local inhabitants while achieving their objective. He encouraged and defended the practice of giving troops captive women as wives. He was dismissed from his post in 1906 after he was convicted of unjust behaviour toward and physical abuse of Cameroonians. Von Puttkamer was the longest-serving German governor in Cameroon.

The fourth governor was Theodore Seitz, 1907–1910. Governor Seitz was sent to correct the mistakes made by Puttkamer's administration. He was a humanitarian administrator who favoured an increased participation of Cameroonians in the administration. He also favoured the abolition of forced labour and was opposed to flogging as a better form of punishment for the African. Governor Seitz began the negotiations with France over the exchange of large parts of French Equatorial Africa for a part of the 'duck-bill' in Cameroon and the cession of German rights in Morocco.

The fifth governor was Otto Gleim, who was in office from 1910 to 1912. During Gleim's short rule the question of the local administrator's plan to dispossess the Duala from their land came up. The Duala land problem resulted from a decision by the local administrator in 1910 to move the local population from Douala town to a new location about a kilometre away. This act was intended to improve the health conditions of the European population in the town and also to prevent the indigenous Duala from speculating in land in the town. By an act of expropriation the African inhabitants of

4　*Jesko von Puttkamer*

Douala were to lose their land and the German Government was to become the owner. Of course the scheme met with great resistance from the indigenous population. Governor Gleim was opposed to the scheme and supported the strenuous Duala objections to it.

Under the leadership of King Manga Bell the Duala population sent a telegram of protest and, later, a long petition against the expropriation to the German Parliament, the Reichstag, in November 1911 and March 1912 respectively. In 1912 the actual moving of the Duala from the town was begun. Duala resistance hardened, and the local administrator warned seriously that if they did not give up their land freely and choose lots in the new area by a certain date, the government would act with force. Even after a change of governor, King Bell continued to lead the Duala protest and in 1913 he was sacked from his government job, which earned him 3000 marks a year, and threatened with exile from Cameroon. With the King's encouragement, the Duala raised a large sum of money and sent a delegate, Ngoso Din, to Germany to put their case in person to the German Government and to the Reichstag. In 1914 the Cameroon administration discovered that King Bell was trying to incite traditional rulers in other parts of the territory to support an uprising against the Germans. It was also revealed that the King and his people were already soliciting British and French assistance in a rebellion against the Germans. King Bell was arrested on these charges and executed at the outbreak of the First World War in 1914. Governor Gleim's term came to an end when the Duala land problem was still unresolved.

The sixth and last German governor in Cameroon was Karl Ebermaier, 1912–16. During Ebermaier's governorship, the Duala land problem became an issue of major concern. It was under his administration that King Manga Bell was charged in 1914 with high treason and sentenced to death and execution after a summary trial. The execution of King Bell and his secretary, Ngoso Din, made the Duala particularly bitter and rebellious. The Governor even rejected pleas for mercy from the high authorities of the Catholic and Protestant missions. With the fall of Cameroon to the Allies in 1916, Governor Ebermaier was interned, along with the remaining German forces, by the Spanish in Rio Muni.

There were by 1914 more than two hundred administrative officials under the governor in Cameroon. From a mere handful, including a chancellor and some secretaries under Governor von Soden in 1885, the number of administrative officials rose to about 240 in 1912, excluding officers in command of the army. These officials were predominantly young people between the ages of 23 and 30. Most of them lacked both administrative experience and training. It was not until 1908 when a Colonial Institute was founded in Hamburg for the purpose of training people for the colonial service that Cameroon began to have trained personnel. Until then the situation was chaotic and frequently scandalous.

The regular colonial administration was organised in the form of an advisory council. The first two councils, from 1885 to 1903, were formed at the discretion of the governor, who selected its members from the trading firms in the territory. In 1903, a decree in Germany officially created Advisory Councils in the German colonies, to be composed of official and non-official members. Traders, planters, missionaries and other non-colonial officials appointed to the Council were non-official members. The members were to be named by the governor from among German settlers near the administrative centres. The function of the Advisory Council was to consider the administrative budget laid before it by the governor as well as decrees to be issued by him. The governor was not bound by the advice of the Council even if it was given unanimously.

Members of the new Advisory Council in Cameroon were named in November 1904. They included three traders, two planters, one Catholic and one Protestant missionary, and some administrative officials. The native inhabitants of the territory were not represented. Although in theory the Council had only an advisory role to play, in practice it became more and more like a legislative body. It met several times a year, each session lasting three to four days. Its discussions touched upon every aspect of colonial activity, including the budget, administration, transportation, communication, taxation, native welfare, land, health, education, missions, exploitation, trade and commerce.

The difficulty in sending enough officials for administrative work forced the colonial administration to rely on the traditional authorities of the territory for certain services. Cameroonians were recruited and used as interpreters and increasingly in minor administrative positions. In the region of Adamawa and other areas of the north, the entire local administration was in the hands of traditional rulers who were advised by two resident commissioners. Elsewhere, chiefs ran traditional courts, collected the administration's taxes when these were introduced, and advised on the recruitment of labour.

Colonial revenue

The colonial administration in Cameroon depended on two major sources for governmental revenue or income. These were grants from the home government and inland revenue or taxation within the protectorate. Of the two taxation (direct and indirect) was considered a vital source because it reduced the burden of colonial costs on the shoulders of the German taxpayer. But direct taxation was not introduced in Cameroon until after 1900 and did not constitute a major source of income until 1908. Until then the administration was almost totally financed from Germany through grants.

Proposals for introducing direct taxation in Cameroon were made as early as 1885 but after serious consideration the scheme was rejected as premature. In 1900 the first form of direct taxation was introduced in Victoria as a rental requirement of Africans using what was technically government land acquired through purchase from the English Baptist Missionary Society. In 1901 another form of direct taxation was introduced in the Douala township known as the 'dog tax' to be paid by native owners of dogs in the town. In 1902 the issue of a head-tax to be levied on every adult native was again seriously considered and approved on the grounds that it would offset annual deficits in the budget and induce natives to cultivate a habit for remunerative work. In 1902 the first real direct taxation was imposed on the Duala in the form of a head-tax at the rate of 3 marks for every man, unmarried woman and child

who could perform paid work. Married men with more than one wife paid an additional tax of 2 marks per additional wife.

The idea of a head-tax became general for the colony in 1908. In that year every adult male in the parts of the territory completely under German control was obliged to pay a tax of 6 marks a year in cash, or perform tax work of 30 days on public works. In many places (for example, in the inland fondom of Nso where direct head-tax was introduced in 1909), the tax was a poll-tax in theory only. Often, the Germans issued tax tickets in numbers which bore no close relation to the number of taxable males. Such a method turned the head or poll-tax into a district quota, and the traditional rulers collected the required money from their subjects on the basis of ability to pay. In the Muslim region of Adamawa where German rule was indirect, Fulbe rulers were required to pay tribute to the government treasury instead of a general head-tax on their subjects. In 1913 the head-tax was increased to 10 marks for those whose annual income was estimated at more than 400 marks or who had more than one wife.

The introduction of the head-tax, as mentioned earlier, resulted in a major increase in government income from 1908 onwards. Statistics show that the increase in income from taxes from 1908 was generally between fifty and one hundred per cent.

Indirect taxes came from import duties, sales of franchise and tariff on foreign goods. There were also similar taxes collected on plural wives,

Year	Income	Increase
1908	100 000 marks	—
1909	300 000 marks	200 000 marks
1910	562 000 marks	262 000 marks
1911	900 000 marks	338 000 marks
1912	1 245 000 marks	345 000 marks
1913	2 210 000 marks	1 035 000 marks
1914	2 300 000 marks	590 000 marks

Table 4.1 Increases in colonial income from 1908 to 1914

Year	Total Budget (marks)	Grant in Budget (marks)	Loan in Budget (marks)
1887-88	89 400	40 000	—
1888-89	178 000	11 000	—
1889-90	?	none	—
1890-91	?	none	—
1891-92	?	1 425 000	—
1892-93	566 000	none	—
1893-94	580 000	none	—
1894-95	610 000	none	—
1895-96	1 230 000	620 000	—
1896-97	1 318 000	678 000	—
1897-98	1 270 300	690 300	—
1898	1 394 100	814 100	—
1899	1 713 400	983 400	—
1900	3 245 000	2 163 000	—
1901	3 775 800	2 179 800	—
1902	4 236 000	2 205 100	—
1903	3 665 500	1 582 600	—
1904	4 086 000	1 404 800	—
1905	5 108 449	2 380 249	—
1906	5 624 995	3 252 095	—
1907	6 158 054	3 104 354	—
1908	6 610 239	2 780 139	4 000 000
1909	7 208 366	2 292 107	5 000 000
1910	8 550 615	2 390 588	3 200 000
1911	9 281 013	2 321 566	12 400 000
1912	9 584 680	5 228 222	8 050 000
1913	13 194 624	2 803 696	2 000 000
1914	17 260 409	3 166 318	15 230 000

Table 4.2 Revenue, grants and loans from 1887 to 1914

land sales, fees and licenses of many kinds. Some income came from the health and agricultural establishments and from the sales of acquired gifts. In 1914 income from the varied sources of indirect taxation was expected to stand at 1 735 000 marks in the budget.

Grants from the German Government formed the principal source of revenue. Even after direct taxation had been introduced and had begun to yield substantial amounts of money in the budget, grants and loans continued to be the main source of revenue. In fact, the administration was financed almost entirely from grants and indirect taxes from 1895 to 1907, and from grants and loans thereafter. Harry R. Rudin supplies the figures in Table 4.2 for the total budget of Cameroon and the grants-in-aid and loans in it from 1887 to 1914.

Development of German education

The German annexation of Cameroon in 1884 led to the closure of all the English Baptist Mission schools on the Cameroon coast by 1886. In that same year the new colonial administration of Governor von Soden asked for German schoolteachers to establish German education in the protectorate. While the teachers were awaited, efforts were made to suppress the English language and English culture and to encourage German. In January 1887 the first German teacher, by name Christaller, arrived in Douala. Christaller quickly studied the Duala language and within a year produced a book of stories for use in teaching the Duala their own language.

The first German school was opened in Bell Town, Douala, in 1888 by Christaller. The subjects taught were arithmetic, reading and writing. Some instructions were also given in moral and religious education. The second school was opened in Dido Town, still in Douala, in 1890 and a third a few years later in Victoria. The Victoria school is said to have opened at the request of the Cameroonian Pastor Joseph Wilson who was greatly liked by the Germans for trying to win support for Germany among the pro-English inhabitants of his community. Some of the English schools that had been closed down after the departure of English missionaries were taken over and transformed into German schools by the Basler Mission which also assumed temporary control over the schools in Douala and Victoria in 1897.

Both the administration and the missions continued to open more schools as the Cameroon Protectorate expanded from the coast into the interior. But it was not until after 1900 that schools began to be established in the distant hinterland. In 1906 the first German school was opened in the Muslim centre of Garoua in Adamawa. The creation of the Garoua school was opposed by the Muslim community of Adamawa who saw it as a colonial trick for teaching Christianity rather than Mohammedanism. In order to allay Muslim fears, both the German and Arabic languages were taught and the pupils were compelled to attend Islamic religious services in the local mosque every Friday.

In December 1907, Governor Seitz convened an important educational conference at Douala. It was attended by representatives of government and mission schools. The purpose of the conference was to review the educational system in the colony and to draw up a standard curriculum for Cameroon. The conference was presided over by the governor himself. The administration expressed its opposition to the use of any European language other than German in the colony. It was also announced that a German language examining board would be set up to visit schools and keep up high standards in the German language. A course of study lasting five years was worked out as necessary for proficiency in reading and writing German and knowing other subjects. Of course, the German language and arithmetic were the two most important subjects on the new curriculum. Emphasis was also laid on the teaching of nature study, the geography of Cameroon and (later) the geography of the world, the history of Germany after 1870, and general science involving the knowledge of minerals, products of plant and animal life, rainfall, barometers, thermometers and simple machines.

One of the major concerns of the Douala Conference was school attendance, although it was aware of the difficulties of enforcing it. The Conference decided to make school attendance the concern of both the parents and the pupils. It recommended that chiefs who asked for schools to be opened in their villages must see to it that attendance was regular for all who enrolled. It was also recommended that students, particularly those in the fifth year who

required employment after graduation, must attend school for at least 150 days in a year. In 1910 a decree to enforce attendance specified that students had to remain in school until the end of the term or pay for the costs. Parents or guardians keeping children away from school would be fined. At the time education was free although in 1911 a fee of 6 marks a year for tuition was introduced in Douala. The decree of 1910 also stated that Christian missions wishing to benefit from government appropriation (which averaged 20 000 marks a year) must follow the school programme worked out by the Douala Conference. Such aid would be based on the percentage of students passing the official examination in German. It was recommended that school age be set at five or six although older children, some in their teens, were also admitted.

In 1910 a government higher agricultural school was established in Victoria. The purpose of the school was to train selected indigenous graduates with good knowledge of German from government or mission elementary schools for agricultural work in the colony. The course lasted two years. Instruction was not only free, but first-year students were also given free board and second-year students a monthly pocket allowance of 5 marks. The student bound himself by contract not only to complete the course, but also to work for the administration for five years after graduation. A student who breached the contract was fined 200 marks for each year of training. Similar agricultural schools were established in Dschang, Yaounde, Douala and Garoua within a very short time.

In terms of statistics, enrolment in government and mission elementary schools was very high. In fact, one of the greatest achievements of German rule in Cameroon was in the field of education. By 1911 there were, besides the numerous government schools, 413 Protestant and 112 Catholic schools with 22 000 and 10 000 pupils respectively. By 1913, according to Rudin, the number of all the mission schools was 624, broken down as shown in Table 4.3 overleaf.

Enrolment in government schools was

Denomination	No. of schools	No. of pupils
Baptist Mission	57	3 151
American Presbyterians	97	6 545
Catholic Mission	151	12 532
Basler Mission	319	17 833

Table 4.3 Number and enrolment in German mission schools, 1913

limited to the number thought necessary to work in the service of the administration. In spite of the limitation, the regular schools at Douala, Victoria, Yaounde and Garoua had, in 1913, an enrolment of 362, 257, 160 and 54 pupils respectively.

Missions under German administration

Before they withdrew from the Cameroon coast at the end of 1886, the English Baptist missionaries handed their work, property and congregation over to the Basle Mission. But the Basle Mission found it extremely difficult to control the lively pro-British indigenous Baptist congregation based principally in Victoria and Douala. Relations between the Basle and the German Lutheran missionaries on the one hand and the indigenous Baptists on the other became strained over matters of organisation, not doctrine. It was soon clear that the English Baptist missionaries shortly before their departure had arranged for the indigenous members of their Mission to continue their denominational practices independent of German missions. The Native Baptists insisted during their negotiations with the incoming Basle missionaries that only blacks would be head of their church and that their missionaries would work under the same conditions as German religious bodies. Disagreements over church organisation and policies led the Native Baptist and the Basle Mission to agree to operate separately. In 1889 the Native Baptist

Church in Victoria broke away from the Native Baptist Church in Douala. An attempt by the German branch of the American Baptist Mission to work together with the indigenous Church in Victoria also failed. In 1898 the German branch of the American Baptist Mission began to establish its own separate mission stations. Their first station was at Great Soppo on the slopes of Buea Mountain, and later others were established at Ndongongi, Njambtang and Ngambe.

The German branch of the Protestant Basle Mission which began work in Cameroon in December 1886 was the most important missionary denomination during the German period. Despite the initial disagreements with the indigenous members of the English Baptist Mission, during the following two decades the Basle missionaries extended their influence far into the interior and the distant grasslands and enjoyed a favoured position with the colonial administration. Their first mission station was established at Tokoto on 5 August 1888, under the catechist Johanness Deibol who was ordained as the first Cameroonian Basle Mission pastor in 1901. In 1899 a second station was opened at Bonaberi, to be followed by those at Mungamba, Buea and Lobetal in 1891, Nyasoso in 1896 and Bombe in 1897. Other stations were established at Edea, Ndunge, Sakbayeme, Ndogbea, Logkwo, Bali, Foumban, Bagam, Bangwa, Bandjun, Bana and Babungo. There were several outstations attached to these main stations.

At the beginning of 1889, the Basle Mission had only ten workers, 160 converts and several hundred pupils in its daily and Sunday schools. By 1912 it had 12 main stations, 89 white missionaries and teachers, 13 176 converts, and 17 833 pupils. By the time of the outbreak of the First World War in 1914, the Mission could boast of having more than 15 000 converts in Cameroon. But the distinguished work of the Society was interrupted and almost completely destroyed during the war as a result of the arrest and internment of all German missionaries. At the time of the commencement of hostilities, there were only three Cameroonian Basle

Mission pastors, namely, J. Ekollo, J. Kwo Isedu, and J. Modi Din. When the war ended and Cameroon was partitioned by Britain and France in March 1916, none of the three indigenous pastors was resident in British Cameroon.

When the German Government invited the Basle Mission in Switzerland to take over the work of the English Baptists in Cameroon, the Swiss organisation immediately established a German branch of their mission with headquarters in Stuttgart. From here they negotiated conditions for work in Cameroon with the German Government. It was agreed that their missionaries would have a broad degree of control in regulating their church and community affairs without government interference and that the importation of liquor into areas where they would be established would be prohibited. The administration agreed to allow the Basle Mission a free hand in the hope that it would also use the missionaries to serve administrative interests. Indeed, the Basle Missionaries were nominated to sit on the local councils and land commissions, and some even sat as judges on cases between natives and between blacks and whites. The missionaries invariably took the side of the local inhabitants and defended their interests fully. For example, they totally supported the Duala in 1912 when land was being taken away from them. They also helped to maintain peace between indigenous groups. The educational work of the Basle Mission was also very important in the period before the war. In 1913 they had 319 schools and 17 833 pupils spread all over southern and central Cameroon.

The second most important missionary enterprise in Cameroon from 1884 to 1914 was Catholic. The coming of this mission to Cameroon was accompanied by a great deal of controversy. The first Catholic Order that requested to work in Cameroon shortly after the German annexation was the French Congregation of the Holy Ghost and the Holy Heart of Mary. The German Government refused to grant this Order permission, first because it was French and would work against German interests and, second because it had the Jesuit tendency of unquestionable and total obedience to their superior.

In 1889 another Catholic Order, the Pallotine Missionaries, requested to come to Cameroon. After a very careful investigation and a thorough study of the Order's constitution, the government reluctantly granted permission. This consent came after Chancellor Bismarck had visited East Africa and learned to appreciate the work of the Catholics there. The German Government might also have been influenced by the publicity given the first Cameroonian Catholic, Andreas Mbangue from the Duala ethnic group, who was baptised in Germany in 1889. In granting permission to the Pallotine missionaries, the government listed several conditions under which they were to operate in the colony. The conditions were that: the Basle Mission should not object to their coming; only German missionaries of the Order would be sent to the colony; the Order must keep out of the Basle Mission territory; there must be no foreign control or interference in the Order's work in the colony; and the Order must use the German language in the colony. The Pallotines accepted these conditions and were immediately ready to establish a Pallotine mission house and a training school at Limbourg, in Germany. In 1890 the Basle Mission removed their objections to Catholic missionaries coming to Cameroon, so long as they agreed to work only in regions not under their own control.

The pioneer group of Pallotine missionaries arrived in Cameroon on 25 October 1890, and soon opened their first mission station near Edea and named it Marienberg (Mount Mary). The Pallotines established other stations and schools at Kribi and Edea proper in 1891, Bonjongo in 1894, Douala in 1898, Batanga in 1900, Yaounde in 1901, Ikassa in 1906, Sasse and Minlaba in 1907, Victoria-Bota in 1908, Dschang in 1910, Ossing (Mamfe) in 1912 and Deido-Douala in 1913. On 28 November 1912, missionaries of the Society of the Sacred Heart of Jesus arrived in the colony to cooperate with the Pallotines and to carry the Catholic faith to the interior and the grasslands of Cameroon. Accompanied by two grasslanders, Peter Wame and his wife Elizabeth Yadiy who had just been baptised in Douala, the Sacred Heart missionaries trekked to the consolidated kingdom of Nso where they established a station and school at Shisong. The Sacred Heart missionaries later took over the station in Mamfe from the Pallotines and opened another in Kom in July 1913. By the time of the outbreak of the First World War in 1914, the two Catholic Mission Orders had made thousands of converts and educated as many pupils in their schools all over central and southern Cameroon.

The last religious group that worked in Cameroon during the German rule was the American Presbyterian Mission. American Presbyterians were allowed to operate on the conditions that they would use the German language in their schools, avoid conflicts with other denominations, and have in Cameroon representatives authorised to control mission work and deal with the local administration. The American Presbyterians accepted these conditions, although they expressed doubts about ever having German-speaking missionaries to recruit in America. In 1890 the Mission began work in their old stations at Batanga and eventually opened other important stations at Elat, Lolodorf and Sende. They concentrated their missionary activities in Bulu country. In the course of time they succeeded in getting a very few German-speaking missionaries for work in their missions and schools. By 1913 the American Presbyterian Mission, one of the smallest foreign Christian enterprises in Cameroon, had on roll 2796 communicants and 9213 pupils in their schools. The mission was not as badly affected by the World War as were the missions run by German missionaries.

Economic development under the Germans

The major areas of economic development during the German period were plantations and agriculture, the transportation and communication networks, and trade.

Before the annexation in 1884, the agents of the Woermann Company trading on the Cameroon coast had taken note of the fertility of the volcanic lands around and up the slopes of the Cameroon Mountain, and discussed the possibility of establishing plantations if the territory was annexed. Thus the establishment of plantations was given the first priority after the annexation. But it was not until 1895, after the defeat of the Bakweri and the expropriation of their lands on the slopes of the Mountain north of Victoria that the first German plantation was opened by the newly-founded Victoria Plantations Company. Its capital was 2.5 million marks. In 1896 another plantation company, known as the Bibundi Company, was formed and began work with a capital of 2.1 million marks. Twelve more plantation companies were formed by 1902, and by 1913 there were altogether 58 German plantations in Cameroon with 195 European employees and 17 827 African workers.

The vast majority of the plantations were situated in the present-day Fako and Meme Divisions and in the region of the Mungo. A few of the plantations were established south of Duala country at Ngulemekong east of Kribi and at Sangmelima. In 1905 cocoa cultivation was begun in Ebolowa and Yaounde, and extended to other areas in the interior. These plantations specialised in the production of oil palm products, cocoa and banana which was introduced in 1907. In 1912 the banana plantation in Tiko covered 2000 hectares.

Cameroonians, too, cultivated in their own farms the cash crops grown in the white-owned plantations. In 1905 they began to cultivate cocoa and their production in 1912 amounted to 715 metric tons compared with 3796 metric tons produced by the plantation companies. All in all, the plantations were much valued because they produced at cheaper costs tropical commodities which were being imported from other countries at exorbitant prices. Because they were owned and supervised by German planters, the quality of production and processing of commodities was much higher than those obtained from natives and other countries.

Efforts were also made to improve agriculture and farming in the territory. African soldiers were required to have gardens at their garrisons to raise their own food. This arrangement served the many purposes of economy, botanical experimentation at different altitudes and with different soils, and the training of the local inhabitants of the district in agriculture. At Buea, European crops and vegetables were grown on the government farm, and cattle was raised for milk, meat, butter and cheese. Cameroonians were also given training in agriculture in both mission and government schools. The principles of agriculture featured prominently in the tilling of the soil. There were also higher schools of agriculture at Victoria, Yaounde, Dschang and, eventually, Garoua where students who had graduated from elementary schools received advanced training in agriculture.

Another effort directed at developing agriculture and forestry was the establishment of the botanical garden in Victoria. The garden was founded for experimentation with hundreds of various tropical plants in an effort to discover which ones had values that allowed for exploitation. Apart from the famous Victoria Botanical Garden, there were between 20 and 40 similar but smaller gardens attached to military posts and administrative stations in different parts of the territory. Experiments were also carried on by experts in the cross-breeding of local cattle with those imported from Europe. When experiments were successful, seeds or cuttings for sale or distribution to planters and to Cameroonian farmers were produced in large quantities.

In the area of transport and communication, roads were a great necessity from the very beginning of German occupation. The construction and maintenance of roads was an obligatory tribute by the defeated groups to the colonial administration. It was not until after 1900 that roads of a permanent character began to be constructed from the coast inland. Difficult terrain made necessary the construction of an unusually large number of bridges on the roads. In 1905 the first motor-car was used in Cameroon and in 1913 the first long journey by automobile was made from Kribi to Yaounde, a distance of 280 km, in 11 hours. Much attention was also devoted to water transport. Some rivers were made navigable after they were cleared of dead trees, sand bars and other hindrances. River routes were connected at some points to roads.

Railroads were also introduced in the transport system during the German period. In Victoria, a narrow-gauge railroad was built by the Victoria Plantations Company in 1901. In 1904 the actual survey of a major rail route from Bonaberi to Nkongsamba started, and the construction of the 160 km railway line began on 25 May 1911. Another line was constructed from Douala to Widimenge on the Nyong River, towards Yaounde. There were plans to extend the railway lines to Adamawa and beyond to Chad, but the plans were cut short by the war and the expulsion of the Germans from Cameroon.

In the area of capital investment and territorial development, it can be said that the grasslands and northern Cameroon were neglected by the Germans. No economic development was undertaken north of the forest region. The problem of 'developing' the high grassfields and the north was, and remained throughout the colonial period, communications. The wealth resulting from colonisation steadily grew in the south at the expense of the centre and the north which were far away from the centres of communication. A large part of the imports represented capital invested in railroads, roads, bridges, public buildings, plantations, schools, hospitals, and so on. These were long-term investments for which the period of German rule was too short to determine Cameroon's real economic value to Germany. Cameroon had about 19 per cent of the German capital invested in all German colonies in 1913. There were 39 companies with an estimated total capital investment of 96 million marks.

The Germans realised from the very beginning of their rule that the labour required for the exploitation or development of Cameroon would have to be supplied by the Cameroonians themselves. Workers were needed by the planters for their plantations, by traders for the transportation of goods, and by the government for public works. The expansion of trade and plantations and the construction of roads, railroads and public buildings increased the demand for labour, which was always in short supply. Thousands of workers were engaged on the various public projects and on the plantations. In 1914 there were more than 18 000 workers in the plantations and about 80 000 as carriers of trade-goods on the Yaounde – Kribi road alone.

The difficulty of getting sufficient manpower within the territory led to its importation from neighbouring colonies. However, every possible means was always used to obtain labour from within Cameroon. These means included: force, use of prisoners, exaction (excessive and enforced demand) of workers from subdued groups, contracts with chiefs for the supply of specified number of workers for a specified period, and the imposition of tax to force people to work to earn the money for it. The majority of workers employed from within Cameroon came from the interior and from the grasslands. Great attention was directed to improving the health of the worker. This was due probably to the very high mortality in the early plantation camps and the critical reports made about it by the Basle Mission and German parliamentary delegations in the Reichstag. Government doctors were required to visit plantations and other labour camps regularly to keep the workers in the best physical condition for work. Of course they could do nothing until the plantation companies were pressured into better sanitary and feeding arrangements. Health centres and/or hospitals were established in several places in the country to combat such diseases as malaria, smallpox, sleeping sickness, leprosy, dysentery, worms and venereal diseases. Plantations were required to have trained medical personnel to look after their workers. Hospitals and medical supplies were also made a requirement.

The judicial system

The earliest courts of justice in Cameroon were the famous Douala Court of Equity and the Victoria Court of Justice run by English traders and missionaries respectively. Both were abolished when the Germans annexed Douala and later acquired Victoria from the British. Beginning in 1885 when a governor was appointed, both the German law and local customs and practices were to be given consideration in settling European and African disputes. It was found necessary at the beginning to establish separate courts for blacks and whites. For fear that whites would lose respect among the Africans, fines were the commonest punishment imposed on Europeans. Any jail sentences were served in Germany rather than in the colony.

The enforcement of law among the blacks was different and elaborate. While jurisdiction over Europeans was kept as far as possible in the hands of professional judges, blacks were adjudicated in the early years by German officials who were assisted by interpreters so that local languages could be used and local customs considered. In 1892 a Court of First Instance for Africans was established at Douala and kept in the hands of local chiefs. Similar courts were opened in other places as the colony expanded. The chiefs were to adjudicate according to native law and custom in civil cases where the object of contention was valued at not more than 100 marks, and in criminal cases where the penalty for the crime was not more than 300 marks or six months imprisonment. From the Court of First Instance appeals could be made to a second tribunal composed of chiefs appointed by the governor. Appeals from the second tribunal as well as cases like murder and manslaughter which were beyond the powers of the two courts were heard by the governor or a judge appointed by him. The penalties inflicted on convicted Africans included whipping (which was the commonest form of punishment), jail sentences, and death penalties with the consent of the governor.

Further reading

John Bridgeman and David E. Clarke, *German Africa* (The Hoover Institution, Stanford, 1965).
Evans Lewin, *The Germans in Africa* (Cassell, New York, 1915).
Harry H. Rudin, *Germans in the Cameroons 1884 – 1914* (Greenwood Press, New York, 1968).
Helmuth Stoecker, *German Imperialism in Africa* (Akademie Verlag, Berlin, 1986).
Mary Evelyn Townsend, *The Rise and Fall of Germany's Colonial Empire* Columbia University Press, New York, 1930).

Questions

1. How was the German colonial administration in Cameroon organised?
2. Discuss the contributions made by the administrations of each of the six German governors to the development of Cameroon.
3. How did the German colonial administration in Cameroon get its revenue or income?
4. How was German colonial education in Cameroon organised?
5. Discuss the coming and expansion of Christian Missions in Cameroon during the German period.

Chapter five

The wartime situation in Cameroon and the peace settlement: 1914-22

The First World War broke out in Europe in August 1914. Shortly after hostilities began, the British, the French and the Belgian forces based in neighbouring West and Equatorial African colonies launched an attack on German Cameroon. The Cameroon war lasted 18 months and ended with the defeat and expulsion of the Germans from the territory in 1916.

Preparations for the European war in Cameroon

The First World War resulted from purely European quarrels which did not concern the Africans. The decision to spread the war into Africa was therefore taken by the belligerent powers and not by Africans. The actual responsibility for expanding hostilities into the African continent was that of the Allied Powers, principally the British and the French. The British invasion of Togoland almost immediately the war was declared in Europe meant that fighting had definitely extended to Africa. The Central Powers, particularly Germany, were against the Allied decision to spread hostilities to the African colonies because they would be at a disadvantage in the face of an Anglo-French military combination. The Germans even approached the United States Government through its ambassador in Berlin urging it to dissuade Britain, France and Belgium from waging war in Africa. The Allies rejected the German plea because, according

to them, Germany had violated the neutrality of Belgium in the war. It would appear, however, that the fundamental reasons for the extension of the war into Africa were more strategic for the Allied Powers.

The British took the lead in spreading the war to Africa. Their naval supremacy was greater than that of any other power or possible combination of powers against her in the world, and they were determined to use that supremacy to cut the German colonies off from sources of military supplies. It was therefore in the British interest to drive the Germans out of Cameroon and her other African possessions as quickly as possible. It was already an established British tradition, according to *The Times* of London in August 1914, that in a major war against a European power possessing territories overseas, such territories should be occupied by British forces as soon as practicable. This was in order to have in British hands something with which to bargain in case the enemy conquered territory in Europe and refused to release it at the end of hostilities. It would also appear that this British establishment was an outcome of the spirit of territorial acquisitiveness. Besides, in the case of the First World War, the British were aware of the fact that the Germans whose naval armament was really strong, given less of an area to defend, aimed at winning the war speedily, and were therefore determined to occupy her colonies as fast as possible before she destroyed her enemies.

As already mentioned, in the invasion of

Cameroon, the British decided to combine their forces with the French. The two powers expected a short campaign but this turned out not to be the case. It was at the end of August 1914 that the British and the French reached agreement on a joint Anglo-French military expedition against German Cameroon. The joint expeditionary force was commanded by a Briton, Brigadier-General Charles McPherson Dobell. Initially, General Dobell commanded a joint force of 7000 men made up of 3000 from the French West African colonies and 4000 from the four British West African colonies. In July 1915, the forces under General Dobell were increased to 9700 men.

5 *Major-General Sir Charles M. Dobell*

Besides these, there were two other Allied forces not under General Dobell's command. There was a French force of 3000 men under General Joseph-Georges Aymerich, outside the joint expedition. This force was increased from October 1914 by three companies of Belgian troops commanded by three Belgian captains from the Belgian Congo. Another French force of 1000 was organised under General Largeau and Colonel Brisset in Chad. This force was eventually incorporated into the British

Nigerian force under General Frederick Cunliffe in 1915. General Cunliffe's own force operating on the Cameroon – Nigeria border from the latitude of Ekok in the south to Fatoko in the north, numbered 2224 men made up exclusively of the Nigerian Regiment. In the course of the war the (British) Indian Army was involved, the largest source of military manpower available to the British in the First World War. German Cameroon was completely encircled.

Facing these Allied forces were 2000 German troops and 2200 policemen with para-military training. The troops were led by 185 whites, while the police had 30 white officers. From June 1895, the German administration had decided on having a well-trained and well-equipped colonial army, *Schutztruppe*, in Cameroon. There was already formed in 1891 the police force, *Polizeitruppe*, which was given para-military training. The strength of the German force in Cameroon before it was increased at the outbreak of hostilities in 1914 was 1650 troops and 1550 police, officered by 200 whites.

The Commandant of the German force, Lt-Colonel Zimmermann, was determined to make the best of a bad situation in the war. Colonel Zimmermann relied on a number of advantages available to his troops in Cameroon. In the first place, the German forces, in addition to their establishment, had the services of German reservists who, like all Germans, had had one or two years' military training under the German system of universal military service. These – planters and traders and technicians among them – often had good local knowledge and contacts. Secondly, the German troops had an excellent knowledge of the terrain. Thirdly, their command, unlike the Allies, was unified. Fourthly, their African soldiers were superior to the Allied troops because of better and longer battle training. Fifthly, many African groups like the Ewondo under their chief, Charles Atangana, and some Fulbe Ardo and Lamibe backed the Germans militarily, some using spears and poisoned arrows against the Allies. This was in spite of the fact that some other groups, principally the Duala, were disloyal and hostile. Sixthly, the Germans had available local levies and prepared positions for the war. Finally, German troops received support from the Spanish subjects in Rio Muni and Fernando Po in the form of ammunition which they smuggled into Cameroon from Spain. This attitude of the Spanish eventually forced the British and French navies to blockade Fernando Po and Rio Muni towards the end of 1914. On the other hand the Germans lacked what the Allies had in abundance, namely, soldiers and ammunition. They were also cut off by the Allied navy and by land from Germany and from other German colonies in Africa.

The outbreak of the war in Cameroon

The signal for the war against Cameroon was given in Nigeria on 5 August 1914. On that date the Nigerian colonial administration received instructions from the Colonial Office in London to expel all German and Austrian consular officers from Nigeria. They were also to arrest and intern all German naval and military reservists in the country. Shortly after these instructions, the British Nigerian regiment, commanded by Colonel Carter, hurriedly mobilised and was ready to attack Cameroon even before they were asked by London to do so. An attack was prepared even before a joint expedition with the French was agreed upon and organised.

While arrangements for a joint Anglo-French expedition were still being worked out, the Nigerian troops were moved to the frontier with Cameroon. On 29 August 1914, they launched an attack on Garoua and succeeded in capturing one of the forts there. The Germans quickly counter-attacked, recapturing the fort and inflicting severe blows on the Nigerian detachment, killing the commanding officer, Lt-Colonel Maclean. A similar fate befell another Nigerian detachment hurrying to capture Mora.

But the worst disaster was experienced by yet another detachment which attacked and captured Nsanakang temporarily between 30 August and 6 September 1914. In that Nsanakang encounter, according to Professor Akinjide Osuntokun of Nigeria, the Germans inflicted severe losses on the Nigerian detachment, killing three officers, capturing one, and wounding another fatally. The Germans also killed 71 soldiers and 18 carriers, wounded 24 soldiers and gun-carriers, and captured 29 soldiers and gun-carriers. A considerable amount of British ammunition as well as 7 machine guns, two of them quick-firing, were lost to the Germans in that confrontation. Colonel Carter's troops had attacked without precaution, undermining the Anglo-French cooperation in the invasion, and met with disaster. Colonel Carter was immediately recalled and replaced by Lt-Colonel Frederick Cunliffe who was promoted Brigadier-General in 1915.

French troops from French Equatorial Africa had also started invading Cameroon before the joint expedition was agreed upon. The Governor-General of French Equatorial Africa had ordered a general mobilisation as early as 1 August 1914, and French troops had started moving into areas which France had ceded to Germany in 1911. French troops had also advanced towards the strategic points of Bonga and Zinga before serious fighting began.

After the initial reverses, the British and French invading forces were properly organised and began to make progress. A three-pronged attack was mounted on Cameroon from the sea at Douala, from southeastern Cameroon, and from the north. Allied troops scored their first major victory when the British navy and the forces commanded by General Dobell attacked and captured Douala-Bonaberi on 27 September 1914. General Aymerich followed by attacking from the French Congo, and participated in the assault and submission of Douala. General Cunliffe attacked from northern Cameroon.

The defeat of the Germans was slow but steady. At one time between 10 and 13 April 1915, a strong German raiding unit broke through the Nigerian defences and reached the emirates of Muri and Yola inside Nigeria. This surprise-raid resulted in the burning-down of government headquarters in Mutum Biu, the destruction of the telegraphic line in the area, and the fleeing of the Emir of Yola, his Native Administration and the British District Officer from the district. It took about two months before the Germans were completely driven from Nigerian soil. Demoralised and tired, short of food, ammunition and reinforcements, the Germans in Cameroon under Governor Ebermaier surrendered to the Allied forces and evacuated the territory on 17 February, although Mora in the far north was still held by troops commanded by Captain von Raben. Mora finally surrendered on 20 February 1916. By the time the war in Cameroon was over, the British casualties numbered 1668 and 2567 French killed or wounded.

Shortly after the cessation of hostilities, Britain and France reached final agreement on the return to France of the parts of French Equatorial Africa ceded to Germany in 1911. The two powers also agreed to a provisional division of the remainder of Cameroon between them. France received four-fifths of the territory and the British received one-fifth, mostly territories along Nigeria's eastern frontier. Each country at once proceeded to establish an administrative structure for the newly-acquired territory.

The wartime administrative arrangements

Douala fell to the Allied forces of General Dobell and the British Navy on 27 September 1914. The immediate concern of the Allies in that economically important city was to work out a system of joint administration for all the areas of the territory jointly conquered by the Anglo-French force. While such an arrangement was being negotiated, steps were taken to establish a workable system for Douala. General Dobell's force had been accompanied from Nigeria by people ready to assume administrative roles in the city. These included finance and treasury staff, transport and requisition agents, engineering service staff, naval service staff, customs service staff, information staff, and staff for administering property and commerce. Frightened by the thorough preparations of the British and determined not to be outdone, the French rushed their own administrative personnel from Gabon and French Congo to assure joint administration of areas captured by both forces. These officers were to salvage the enormous German capital invested in Douala and other parts of Cameroon.

The first task of the administrative staff was to restore peace, law and order in Douala. This objective was made easier by the full cooperation of the Douala population, who welcomed the downfall of the Germans. The second aim was to keep essential services functioning. In order for commercial houses to begin trading activity again, the British and the French reached an agreement to redeem the German mark at one shilling for the British and 1.25 francs for the French per mark. Efforts to restore the health services led to the opening, renovating and re-equipping of the five German hospitals by British doctors. The prison quarters were reopened and their 47 Cameroonian warders were re-employed. Postal services were also restored and postal links between Douala and the British and French territories re-established. Customs services were reorganised and Nigerian customs officials were stationed at Douala and Victoria (Limbe). This administrative arrangement for Douala lasted until 4 March 1916, when the two powers decided on the division of Cameroon. The head of the Douala administration was always a Briton.

The major question unresolved since the very beginning of the joint expedition concerned the greater territory of Cameroon captured from the Germans. The British wanted General Dobell to have responsibility for the administration of the conquered area. Such an arrangement did not work. Instead the tendency was for each to take over in areas where their own troops dominated.

In the month of December 1914, the French suggested that the two powers, Britain and France, should establish a joint administration or condominium over all the territories captured from the Germans. The administrative condominium would be provisional until the end of the World War when a final decision about what should be done with each former German colony would be taken. The French pointed out that an Anglo-French condominium would assure the Allies of the unity of Cameroon under one administrative control and a common sense of direction. This very attractive French proposal was quickly and easily accepted by the British who described it as the only reasonable thing to do at the time. The British added in support of the French idea that the division of the territory into spheres of influence should be avoided because such an action might become permanent.

After accepting the idea of a condominium the British laid down their initial conditions for its establishment. Their first condition was that the General Officer commanding Allied forces in Cameroon, General Dobell of Britain, should be the head of the condominium. Secondly, the British wanted General Dobell to have full powers not only of administration but also the power of appointment and dismissal of French and British officials serving under him. Thirdly, the British demanded that General Dobell should have a free hand in dealing with all matters civil and military. Fourthly, the condominium could be established only if the French accepted that in the event of the death or transfer of General Dobell from Cameroon, his successor should be a senior British military staff officer acceptable, of course, to the French and suitable for the job. This condition was necessary, they explained, in order not to create an anomalous situation that would result if he were to be succeeded by a French officer. A French successor would necessarily require a change of staff and cause discontinuity in civil affairs. Fifthly, the British demanded that the general expenses of the administration should be shared in the same proportion as the eventual parti-

tioning of the country. All expenses of pay, allowance and maintenance of troops should fall on the government to which the troops belonged. This requirement meant that the French would shoulder a greater share of the financial burden since they not only had more troops than the British in Cameroon but were also likely to obtain a greater share of Cameroon in the case of partition. Finally, it was the wish of the British that the areas of Cameroon along Nigeria's eastern frontier occupied solely by British troops who were not directly under General Dobell should be administered by the Governor-General of Nigeria. Similarly, areas near the eastern and southern frontiers formerly ceded by France to Germany in 1911 should be administered by adjacent governments under the Governor-General of French Equatorial Africa. These areas would be handed over to General Dobell only when circumstances permitted such an action.

These capricious and despotic British conditions were rejected by the French. Thus the chance for agreement and a condominium in Cameroon was wrecked. On 19 March 1915, the French bitterly criticised both the British policy in Cameroon and General Dobell's attitude towards French troops. They complained that the British wanted to be masters in Cameroon in spite of the fact that their forces in the campaign numbered less than the French. They also complained that General Dobell's reports about the campaign were biased against French troops although the greater burden of conquest was borne by France. The French lamented that General Dobell had adopted the attitude of assigning to the French contingent a task too great for its strength. Finally, the French complained that the value of their cooperation in Cameroon was completely ignored in General Dobell's dispatches to London. The British replied that the French were forgetting that their statement on military effort in Cameroon did not take into account the role played by the British navy. They pointed out that the French were only able to act because the British navy kept Cameroon cut off from fresh supplies of ammunition from

Germany and that this British action was the deciding factor in tilting the balance of power in favour of the Allies.

In July 1915 the British instructed the Nigerian government to assume the administration of all areas of Cameroon captured solely by British troops. In December 1915, and again in January 1916, the Nigerian officials appointed administrators to the areas of Cameroon controlled by British troops and contiguous to Nigerian districts and provinces. These administrators were instructed to assist the military forces operating in their areas in every way, avoid friction with French troops, and refer difficulties to the nearest provincial Resident or Commissioner in Nigeria. In matters of local administration, they were to hold courts with full jurisdiction in civil matters in which Cameroonians were concerned, administering the laws of Cameroon insofar as they were known or the laws of Nigeria as applied in the area from which the officer came. This policy of the British brought to an end the idea of a condominium in Cameroon. It is evident that except for the partial French administrative assistance in the city of Douala, a condominium was never established in Cameroon during the First World War.

The Anglo-French partition of Cameroon

Failure to establish an Anglo-French condominium resulted in the division of Cameroon. The idea of partition loomed large in the minds of both the British and the French from the very beginning of the Cameroon war. Indeed, France and Britain held major territorial grudges against the Germans in Cameroon. The principal object of the British was to regain all territories lost to Germany during the period of the scramble and delimitation of the boundary separating British Nigeria from German Cameroon between 1884 and 1894. These territories included the area between the Rio del Rey and the Wouri river in the south and parts of the emirates of Yola

and Bornu in the north. The French on their part yearned to recover all the territories of French Equatorial Africa lost to the Germans in the humiliating concessions of 1911. Besides, the French saw the Cameroon war as their best opportunity to obtain the greater part of the original German territory in order to possess land in Africa stretching uninterrupted from Algiers in Algeria to Brazzaville in the Congo. The Anglo-French ambition to partition was demonstrated at the beginning of the war in 1914 in the British rush to set up a separate administration in captured areas contiguous to the Nigerian border, and in the French haste to incorporate recovered territories into French Equatorial Africa where they had formerly been assigned.

The idea of a formal partition of Cameroon began to be discussed by Britain and France from as early as September 1914. The British had three possible scenarios for partition. The first was that except for parts of the emirates of Yola and Bornu and the Cameroon Mountain region, the whole of Cameroon should go to France. In return Britain would ask for the whole of Togoland and Dahomey so that British possessions should stretch uninterrupted from the Gold Coast to Nigeria. The second possibility was that except the pieces including Victoria, Buea and the Cameroon Mountain and parts of the emirates of Yola and Bornu, the British should give up their share of Cameroon in exchange for the French half of the condominium in the New Hebrides. The third possibility was that Cameroon be partitioned into two equal sections from the sea up along the Sanaga River so that Britain would obtain the western half and the port of Douala and the French the eastern half and the port of Kribi.

The idea of giving up an equal share of Cameroon for concessions outside Africa was very unattractive to senior British administrators in Nigeria who saw Cameroon as the only direction in which Nigeria could expand. The idea of acquiring Dahomey and Togoland and keeping pieces along Nigeria's eastern frontier was acceptable to the Nigerian administration. But the British were not agreed on which of the three possibilities was the most attractive and which should first be introduced for discussion with the French. On 14 December 1914, the British government sounded French opinion on the possibility of an equal partition. The French rejected the plan.

The French, unlike the British, had not given thought yet to the possibility of a formal partition of Cameroon. They did not want discussion on the future of Cameroon to begin until the end of the war, when the global situation would be clear to the two powers. They were therefore neither interested in the idea of equal partition nor in that of the administration of each half by British Nigeria and French Equatorial Africa. They suggested that instead of partition there should be established a condominium which would see to a provisional administration of the territory until the end of the war. The condominium idea effectively shelved the discussion on the partition for some time. But the British continued to assume that although they might not need nor would usefully occupy more than one quarter of Cameroon, they were entitled to half of the territory.

Negotiations with the French were only resumed in February 1916. The British had reduced their possibilities of partition and exchange of territories to two. They were ready to offer to France three-quarters of Cameroon instead of one-half, plus a share of Togoland, in exchange for the French share of the condominium in the New Hebrides and the French settlement of Jibuti, opposite Aden, which controlled the mischievous arms traffic to Abyssinia and Central Africa. Alternatively, they were ready to offer all of Cameroon except Mount Cameroon and Douala, their share of the New Hebrides or even the Gambia in order to retain all Togoland and Dahomey.

Forced to accept the idea of partition, the French made known their opinion of how Cameroon should be partitioned for the first time. They explained to the British that they very much wanted all of Cameroon particularly as the British had not been friendly with them in the occupation of East Africa. They suggested that Britain should hand over Douala and the larger part of Cameroon since Douala was the only possible port for French Equatorial Africa. France was ready to allow Britain to incorporate Dikwa into Bornu and to drop their demand for a share of German East Africa. The British agreed to the French suggestion, taking into consideration the fact that German South West Africa was already British and in the possession of the Union of South Africa. The partition would, however, be provisional until the final decision at the peace conference at the end of the war.

The Anglo-French accord to divide Cameroon was reached on 4 March and effected on 6 March 1916. The provisional boundary was fixed after conferences between General Dobell and General Aymerich in Douala. The boundary line was traced by the two Generals from Lake Chad to the Mungo River on the bases of river courses, watersheds, hills, mountains, villages and ethnic groups. The French received the bulk of the territory, less the territories ceded to Germany in 1911 which were returned at once to the administrative aegis of French Equatorial Africa. The British obtained two disconnected pieces of territory along Nigeria's eastern frontier, estimated at only one-fifth of the original German territory.

On 1 April 1916, officials and troops of each power withdrew to their own side of the frontier. Shortly after effecting the partition accord, a French decree named General Aymerich as Commissioner of the French Republic with authority to institute a military administration in French Cameroon. A similar British Order in Council named General Dobell to take charge of the administration in British Cameroon. Details of the boundary on the ground would be worked out after the peace conference, at the end of the war.

Between 1916 through the Paris Peace Conference of 1919, to the application of the League of Nations mandates in July 1922, the

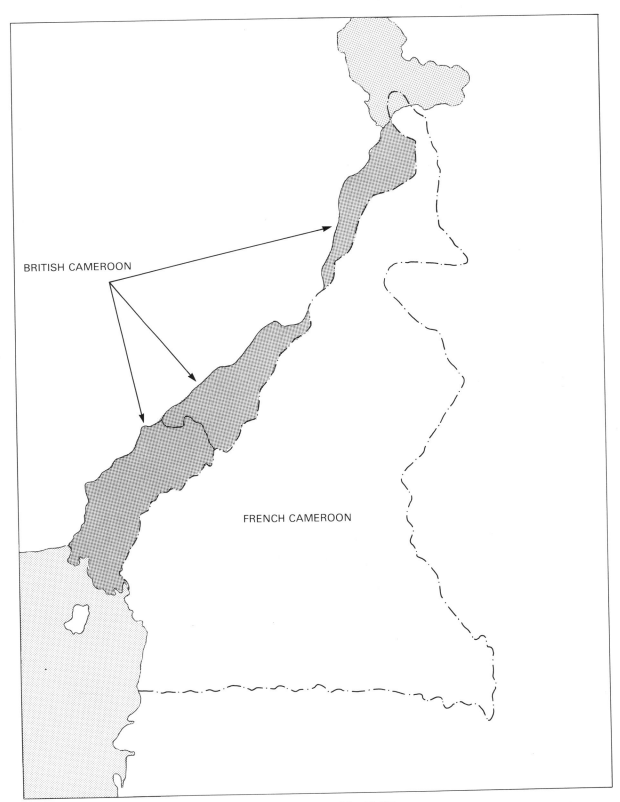

BRITISH CAMEROON

FRENCH CAMEROON

Figure 5 *The partition of Cameroon after the First World War*

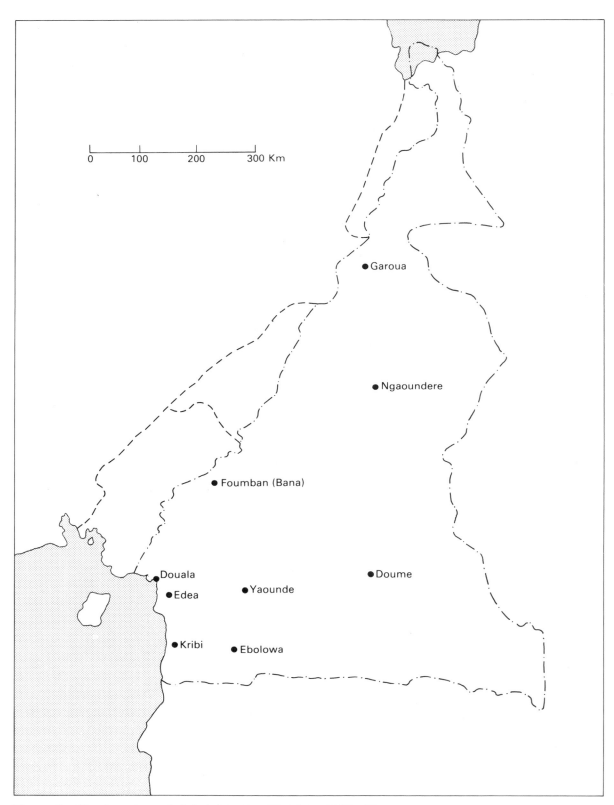

Figure 6 *Headquarters of Administrative Districts, 1916–23*

58

French and the British established transitional governments in their spheres of Cameroon. General Aymerich went ahead with astonishing rapidity to create administrative districts and to appoint heads of districts and administrative services. On 14 May 1916, he issued a decree creating nine administrative districts in French Cameroon with headquarters in Douala, Doume, Ebolowa, Edea, Foumban (Bana), Garoua, Kribi, Ngaoundere and Yaounde. Later in the year the General was replaced at his own request by Mr Lucien Fourneau who was appointed by decree on 5 September and arrived in Cameroon on 8 October 1916. In 1918 Mr Fourneau issued a decree opening thirty French schools in the nine districts. He continued with efforts to maintain peace and essential services and to win the confidence of the Cameroonians for the French Government.

On behalf of the British, General Dobell was replaced by Mr K.V. Elphinstone, formerly Chief Political Officer under General Dobell in Douala. Mr Elphinstone became the first British administrative Resident in the Cameroons Province at Buea. The British had decided to create only one independent administrative province in Cameroon to bring it in line with the division of Nigeria into administrative provinces. The northern territory of British Cameroon was shared by the three contiguous Nigerian provinces of Bornu, Adamawa and Benue. These districts continued to be administered provisionally as integral parts of the Federation of Nigeria.

The British and French mandates in Cameroon

The First World War ended at 11 a.m. on 11 November 1918, when Germany requested and signed an armistice based on President Woodrow Wilson's Fourteen Points for world peace. Following this formal cessation of global hostilities, a peace conference was called and formally opened in Paris on 18 January 1919, with delegates and experts representing twenty-seven of the victorious Allied and Associated Powers. Representatives of Germany and the Central powers were excluded from the Conference until the peace terms were ready for submission to them. When the principal peace treaty was signed at Versailles on 28 June 1919, between the victor and the vanquished, Germany renounced in favour of the principal Allied and Associated Powers all her rights over her overseas possessions, including Cameroon. Following this renunciation by Germany, the Allied and Associated Powers agreed that the governments of France and Great Britain should make a joint recommendation to the newly-formed League of Nations as to the future of Cameroon.

When France and Britain began discussing the joint recommendation to be submitted on the future of Cameroon, they had before them the articles of the covenant or constitution of the League of Nations adopted only two months earlier at Versailles on 28 April 1919. Article 22, paragraph 5 of the Covenant stated that the peoples of former German colonies in Central Africa, including Cameroon, were to be placed under mandatory powers which should administer the territories on behalf of the League of Nations. The mandatory power should render to the Council of the League an annual report in reference to the territory committed to its charge. Yet France was vehemently against the idea of converting Cameroon into a mandated territory. She wanted the territory to be purely and simply annexed. In fact, the French Minister of Colonies, Monsieur Henri Simon, argued that since France had won Cameroon by force of arms, she was not obliged to place the territory under the League's control. The French Minister even referred to Cameroon as a colonial Alsace-Lorraine which must remain under the full sovereignty of France. Monsieur Simon said France was ready to accept the general conditions of Article 22 of the Covenant to administer Cameroon in the spirit of a mandate, but without a mandate. In other words, France would fulfill all the obligations of a mandatory administration without being responsible or accountable to the Council of the League of Nations.

While France continued to resist the idea of administering Cameroon as a mandated territory, France and Britain reached agreement on the final partition of Cameroon. With only minor adjustments which were worked out by the two governments, the line of the provisional partition of 1916 was accepted as final. The minor adjustment the French wanted was that Britain should cede pieces of land in and around Dschang as they were needed for an eventual extension to Garoua of the Bonaberi – Nkongsamba railway. For their part the British wanted the boundary of 1916 to be readjusted in the extreme south so that the frontier should coincide with the upper waters of the Mungo River and then to run from there to the sea. Having agreed on these adjustments, the two powers set up commissions of experts in their colonial ministries to work out in detail where the boundary should be. On 10 July 1919, the British and French Colonial Ministers, Alfred Lord Milner and Monsieur Henri Simon, signed the famous Milner-Simon Declaration recommending the adoption by the League of the final partition of Cameroon. By the end of January 1921, local officials from the British and French spheres had completed delimitation and minor territories in Dschang and the Mungo had been exchanged.

Concerning the future of Cameroon, the only agreement reached between Britain and France by June 1919 was that they would make a joint recommendation to the League to that effect. The two powers did not indicate the nature of the recommendation they would make, nor when it would be made. During the lengthy negotiations that followed, the French government changed its mind and agreed with the British that Cameroon should be held under the League of Nations mandates. The two powers then jointly recommended that a mandate to administer Cameroon in accordance with Article 22 of the Covenant of the League of Nations should be conferred upon them. The two governments then formulated and proposed two separate but similar terms of the mandate for their spheres.

There were twelve articles in the mandates which Britain and France proposed should be conferred on them to administer Cameroon. They had the following significant provisions. Britain and France declared that they should be responsible for the peace, order and good government of their respective territories, and for the promotion to the utmost of the material and moral wellbeing and the social progress of their inhabitants. They also proposed, in agreement with Article 22, clause 5, of the Covenant, that they should not establish in their respective territories any military or naval bases, nor erect any fortifications, nor organise any native military force except for local police purposes and for the defence of the territory.

The third significant provision concerned the suppression of all forms of forced or compulsory labour, emancipation of all slaves and speedy elimination of slavery and slave trade, protection of the natives from abuse and measures of fraud, and the exercise of a strict control over traffic in arms and ammunition. Another article stipulated that native laws and customs should be respected in the framing of laws relating to the holding or transfer of land, and that the rights of the native population should be respected and safeguarded. There was an article providing for the assurance of complete freedom of conscience and the free exercise of all forms of worship. Britain and France also asked for full powers of administration and legislation and for liberty to constitute their territories into a customs, fiscal and administrative union or federation with their adjacent territories. The last significant provision called on each mandatory power to submit to the Council of the League annual reports of its administration to the satisfaction of the Council.

With hindsight it is clear that the British and French mandates were inadequate on several counts. First, there were no provisions for the League of Nations to supervise the administration of Cameroon by the mandatories. Second, there were no provisions in the mandates for the future reunification of the British and the French Cameroon. Third, there were no provisions for political advancement or the eventual emergence of either mandated territory as an independent unit in its own right. Fourth, there were also no provisions in the mandates for local inhabitants of the mandated territories to petition the League of Nations against obnoxious policies of the mandatory. Finally, there were no provisions in the mandates for the inhabitants of divided Cameroon to continue to relate socially, culturally or economically as formerly across the frontiers.

Since, however, the proposals were a typical product of current colonial attitudes, the Council of the League of Nations accepted them without amending a single article. On 20 July 1922, the British and French spheres of Cameroon were assigned to their respective administering powers as mandates in the 'B' category. And so the 1916 arbitrary partition of Cameroon was confirmed by the League of Nations and given the sanction of international law.

Further reading

Joseph G. Aymerich, *La Conquête du Cameroun* (Payot, Paris, 1931).

Lovett A. Elango, *The Anglo-French Condominium in Cameroon 1914–1916: History of a Misunderstanding* (Navi-Group Publications, Limbe, 1987).

Jean Ferrandi, *la Conquête du Cameroun-nord 1914–1915* (Charles Lavanzelle, Paris, 1928).

E.H. Gorges, *The Great War in West Africa* (Hutchinson, London, 1927).

F.J. Moberley, *History of the Great War, Based on Official Documents: Military Operations: Togoland and the Cameroons* (HMSO, London, 1931).

Akinjide Osuntokun, *Nigeria in the First World War* (Longman, London, 1979).

Engelbert Mveng, *Histoire du Cameroun,* Tome II (CEPER, Yaounde, 1985).

Questions

1. What preparations were made by the Allies for the invasion of Cameroon during the First World War?
2. When the Allies decided to invade Cameroon in 1914 they expected a short campaign, but they were to be disappointed. Discuss.
3. Why were the Germans defeated in Cameroon during the First World War?
4. Why was Cameroon partitioned by Britain and France after the expulsion of the Germans in 1916?
5. What were the terms of the British and French mandates for Cameroon?

Chapter six
Cameroon under French mandate: 1922-39

As we have seen, Cameroon was one of those territories which as a consequence of the First World War ceased to be under the sovereignty of Germany which formerly administered it. As a result, and in conformity with Article 22 of the Covenant of the League of Nations, the tutelage or guardianship of the people of the territory was entrusted to Britain and France which had invaded, occupied and partitioned Cameroon during the war. The two powers exercised control as mandatories on behalf of the League of Nations to whose Permanent Mandates Commission they agreed to render annual reports in reference to the territory under their control. France administered Cameroon as a mandated territory from 1922 to 1939.

The administrative arrangement

The period of the French mandate began officially on 20 July 1922. A year earlier, in March 1921, in anticipation of the confirmation of the mandates, the French Government named a High Commissioner of the Republic with the status of Governor-General as head of the administration in Cameroon. The man appointed was Jules-Gaston Henri Carde who had been head of the provisional administration since 1919.

Although Cameroon was a mandated territory, the system of administration which the French established there from 1922 onward was practically identical with the system they applied in the French colonies of Equatorial Africa. The High Commissioner in Cameroon had practically the same powers as the Governor-General in French Equatorial Africa. Both were invested with the powers of the French Republic and they represented, on the spot, the unconditional power of the French Government which nominated and recalled them.

The only differences between the French mandatory administration in Cameroon and that in her neighbouring colonies arose from the international obligations implied in the mandate status. France was required to comply with the formal duty of submitting an annual report on the administration in Cameroon to the League of Nations. She was also expected to respect the 'open door' policy in matters of customs tariffs and foreign religious missions. She was prohibited from military recruitment and conscription in the mandated territory.

The structure of the French administration reflected the hierarchy of officials appointed to administer it. The only superior to the High Commissioner in Cameroon was the French Minister of Colonies in Paris, to whom he was directly responsible. Any law or decree emanating from Paris with reference to Cameroon reached the High Commissioner officially through the Minister of the Colonies.

On the spot in Cameroon, and from below, there was no limit to the High Commissioner's power and authority. The administration he controlled was direct and unitary, with a direct progression to the top. He nominated and dismissed all employees and every official, military or civil, was responsible to him. He drew up the general estimates. He decided on assignments of officials placed at his disposal by the Government in France, and could freely return them without having to justify his action.

During the period from 1922 to 1939, there were altogether six High Commissioners of the French Republic in Cameroon. These were: Jules-Gaston Henri Carde (1919 – 23), Theodore-Paul Marchand (1923 – 32), Auguste-François Bonnecarrère (1932 – 34), Jules Repiquet (1934 – 36), Pierre Boisson (1936 – 38), and Richard Brunot (1938 – 40).

6 *M. Carde*

Beneath the High Commissioner were the secretary-general of the Administrative Council and heads of administrative services who were resident in Yaounde, the administrative capital. The secretary-general assisted the High Commissioner and in case of need took his place. Heads of administrative services were considered to be experienced French civil servants. Each was in charge of an administrative service such as health, education, agriculture, judiciary and postal services. Each head of administrative service directed the affairs of his service and also advised the High Commissioner when need arose. The administrative head of the financial service was in charge of the budget and its supplements. The treasurer directed the treasury service. The head of public works controlled the ports, roads, public buildings and other important technical services. The economic service dealt with general economic questions such as trade and prices and directed specialised economic services such as agriculture, stock-raising, forests, fisheries and so on. Below each head of administrative service and directly under his control were scores of workers occupying various positions in the service.

Also beneath the High Commissioner and answerable to him were heads of administrative districts or *circonscriptions* into which the territory had been divided. Administrative districts which were later retitled regions were thirteen in number in 1923, although the administration continued to create new districts as need arose. In 1935 when the districts were renamed regions, there were already seventeen.

The head of an administrative district was responsible for the local administration of the area under his jurisdiction. His principal duty was to maintain law, order and good government. He reported to the High Commissioner about developments in his district. The High Commissioner consulted the district heads on most important administrative questions. Each district was divided into sub-districts (later sub-regions) and placed under the control of heads of sub-districts. In 1923 there were 37 sub-districts in Cameroon.

One important administrative institution which the French introduced in Cameroon in anticipation of the mandate's confirmation was the Administrative Council (*Conseil d'Administration*). The Administrative Council was a sort of cabinet. Its membership was composed of important personnel, heads of administrative districts and eminent European persons or notables resident in Cameroon. The High Commissioner appointed the members of the Council and removed them from it. He consulted this body on such matters as the budget, land questions, taxes, expenditure, creation of new administrative districts, and public works. The Council gave its opinion on all questions submitted to it by the High Commissioner. It met not more than once a year over a period of several days. As a consultative body, the Administrative Council could not in any way oppose the High Commissioner, who was not obliged to accept its advice. It met only when the High Commissioner convened it. The Council's membership was periodically renewed and expanded. In 1927 two indigenous eminent Cameroonians were nominated by decree and given seats in the council.

Another administrative institution which the French established in Cameroon, this time in the administrative districts, was the Council of Indigenous Notables or *Conseil de Notables*. Although the institution was introduced in French Tropical Africa by decree in May 1919, it was not until 1923 that its establishment in Cameroon was authorised. In that year the French decided to curb the power and authority of the traditional ruler, the Sultan of the district of Ngaoundere who, apparently, was unwilling to cooperate fully with the administration. The French levied several accusations against the young Sultan and followed this up with his deposition. They replaced him with someone who was willing to work cooperatively with the French. But fearing that the Sultan of their choice might eventually try to wield the power and authority of his predecessor in office, they set up a local council of notables to work in conjunction with him. The new council of notables had no traditional powers and represented only the official French policy. In 1925 the French decided to establish similar councils in all the other administrative districts of Cameroon.

The Council of Notables played a purely con- sultative role. It was made up of notables from the district who included chiefs of various grades and representatives of the major ethnic groups. These notables were selected as members of the Council by the administrative head of district from a long list of nominees submitted to him. The number of notables selected was on the basis of one representative for every five thousand inhabitants. The Council was summoned and presided over by the district administrator. Its main function was to examine problems involving farming, animal husbandry, the improvement of human capital and all other issues concerning the administration and to advise the head of the administrative district accordingly. The introduction of the Council of Notables soon led to a major reorganisation of the traditional institution of chieftaincy in Cameroon. We will look into that later in this chapter.

French colonial policies in Cameroon between the wars

Cameroon was classed as a category 'B' mandate, that is a territory inhabited by peoples not yet able to stand by themselves. Unlike territories in the 'A' category, Cameroon was not considered to have reached a stage of development where her existence as an independent state could be provisionally recognised until such a time as she would be able to stand alone. But the mandate system did not state any explicit political goals for the territory, and France did not commit herself in the Mandate Agreement to prepare Cameroonians for the management of their own affairs in the future. As a result, the administration which France established in Cameroon followed the policies that were applicable in adjacent French colonies.

By the time of the outbreak of the First World War, France had experimented with several colonial policies all of which were tried in Cameroon during the mandate period. These policies included assimilation, paternalism, association and differentiation.

Assimilation was a policy which had as its object the gallicising of the colonies to the point of turning them into political divisions of the French state. The policy aimed at assimilating or absorbing France's colonial subjects to the point where they would actually be Frenchmen linguistically, culturally, politically and legally. The bases of these policies were the beliefs held by French statesmen and others that France and her colonies were indivisible, that French civilisation was superior to African civilisation which must be suppressed, and that the doctrine of the equality of man left no doubt about the fact that the African had an equal capacity to learn and to progress. These statesmen associated the idea of spreading French civilisation to Africa with that of French citizenship which they sometimes conferred with all its rights and benefits on those Africans who had fully acquired the French language and customs. Thus, if fully pursued, the policy of assimilation would involve both the turning of Africans into Frenchmen and the incorporation of their territory into the French state.

The origin of the French idea of assimilation can be traced as far back as Louis XIV, King of France from 1643 to 1715. Louis is claimed to have remarked publicly to a prince from the Ivory Coast who had spent a year at his court that there was no longer any difference between the prince and himself, except that one was black and the other was white. In 1795 the policy of assimilation was outlined in the constitution which, however, was not applied, because of the wars of the French Revolution. In 1848 the policy was embodied in the constitution under Article 109 which stated that the colonies were French territory and enjoyed the same rights in private and public law. It fitted in well with the republican ideals of Liberty, Fraternity and Equality. Earlier, the French-speaking Africans of St Louis and Goree in Senegal usually described themselves as Frenchmen and enjoyed the political rights of French citizens. After 1848 when France abolished slavery and the slave trade, the three minute French trading-stations in Gabon and the Ivory Coast and the two settlements of St Louis and Goree were given representation in the French National Assembly.

There were many criticisms levied against the policy of assimilation. Some Frenchmen did not believe that black Africans could be equal to Europeans or had equal capacity to learn and to progress. They doubted if most Africans could really absorb the benefits of French civilisation. Others argued that the great cultural gap between France and her black African colonies made the policy of assimilation unrealistic. They pointed out that the social standards of black Africans were too far removed from those of Frenchmen for assimilation to be practical. Besides, between the end of the nineteenth and the beginning of the twentieth centuries, scholars developed a new interest in cultures and societies outside Europe and began to insist that African societies and their institutions be respected.

Although these objections to assimilation were gradually accepted and the policy became less definite, assimilation was never officially abandoned. It instead became a selective policy that was applied only to those Africans who proved worthy of it by demonstrating that they had the attributes of French citizenship. The attributes of course were the mastery of the French language and culture. The assimilationists decided that France should try to create in each colony a thoroughly gallicised elite which would help to spread French civilisation amongst the African masses and would some day be able to participate in the administration of their territory. The members of the gallicised elite might individually apply for French citizenship.

Paternalism was a policy advocated by the critics of assimilation who wanted France to relate as a 'father' to her African colonies. Its advocates were those critics of assimilation who held the belief that the African did not have the equal capacity with the European to learn and to progress. The advocates of this policy who came to prominence and held power in the period 1799 – 1875 showed no eagerness to extend the benefits of French civilisation to Africans. In their opinion, France had a responsibility to provide Africans with an administration run entirely by French officials, which would ensure peace, order, stability and efficiency. Such an administration must be free from ideological conflicts. In carrying out their tasks of administration, the French officials need not seek the opinion of the Africans of the territory they were administering because the Africans could not know what was best for them. The administration would be direct, and no attempt would be made to utilise African political institutions. Such a policy, if fully pursued, would make direct rule and the subordination of Africans to French control permanent features of French administration. The paternalist ideas were surely more in terms of successive development.

Advocates of the policy of paternalism undid certain of the measures of the advocates of assimilation, and tried to prevent the application of the policy outside the Senegalese communes. When the policy of assimilation eventually became selective and limited in scale, the policy of paternalism prevailed by force of circumstances. As far as Cameroon was concerned, French rule in the mandate era can better be understood by reference to the policies of assimilation and paternalism.

Association was France's colonial policy advocated by the critics of assimilation and paternalism during the two decades before the outbreak of the First World War. This policy, which sought practical and functional collaboration between the French rulers and the indigenous elite, was France's official policy in Black Africa from 1922 on. Association assumed that the great majority of the indigenous Africans could only develop slowly toward eventual assimilation to French culture and must not be rushed. There would be respect for traditional African institutions which could be utilised for administrative purposes or serve the general policy of association. Such respect, it was believed, would lead to cooperation between colonial administrators and native political bodies and to an administrative decentralisation in the colonies to permit a greater adjustment of French legislation to local situations. There would be a planned economic development French by which the economic potential of each colony would be developed along lines most profitable to both France and the colony in question.

In practice, the policy of association contained a great many elements of assimilation and paternalism. Like assimilation, the policy of association called for the formation of a gallicised elite who, as leaders of their people, would remain within the framework of African society and serve as an intermediary group between the French officials and the traditionally orientated masses. As it turned out, the elite selected had to accept so much of the French civilisation that they lost touch with their own culture and with the unassimilated populations they were supposed to lead. Like assimilation, association implicitly assumed the superiority of French civilisation over African and expected that Africans in their colonies would gradually abandon their cultures and adopt the superior French models. Like paternalism, the policy of association did not envisage colonial independence or even self-administration. Also involved in the policy was a dual system of law and administrative separation which operated to distinguish between the indigenous elite and the masses.

Differentiation was a feature of both the policies of assimilation and association. This policy had as its object the administrative separation of people who had advanced closer to assimilation, from the rest of the traditional African masses. Individual Africans who had acquired French citizenship or good education and who were considered gallicised came to be identified as 'assimilated' or as 'evolved', while the rest who were still subject to native law and customs were identified as 'subjects'. The 'assimilated' and the 'evolved' who were ripe for assimilation had the civil, political and legal rights of citizens or persons of French origin. The 'subjects' had no 'civilised rights' of any kind and were subject to native treatment, compulsory labour, and the *indigénat* or disciplinary penalties which could be summarily administered by any French official.

The judicial system

The French colonial system of justice distinguished between persons subject to native law and customs, *les sujets*, and those assimilated to European law, *les citoyens*. The 'citizen' had civil, political and judicial rights identical with persons of French origin; the 'subjects' had only their local traditional rights. There were, therefore, two systems of justice, the French and the native systems.

French justice comprised a hierarchy of courts: courts of first instance, assize courts, and courts of appeal. These courts, presided over by French magistrates who passed judgements according to French law, were used in all cases involving a French citizen.

Indigenous justice applied in all other cases, and was based on the 'native penal code'. The judicial powers which traditionally belonged to chiefs and leaders of traditional communities were gradually taken away from them. Native courts were set up. There was the native court of first instance (also known as 'tribunal of races') presided over by the administrative head of the district. He was assisted by two 'notables' designated by the High Commissioner. In 1924 the chairmanship of the native court of first instance was entrusted to the administrative head of the sub-district or some other European designated by the High Commissioner.

The native court of second instance was presided over by the head of the administrative district or someone designated by the High Commissioner. He was assisted by two 'notables', designated by the High Commissioner. This court dealt with first appeals in civil cases or commercial matters, and only exceptionally with criminal cases. In criminal cases two European assessors were required.

Judgement from the higher 'tribunal of races' or native court of second instance went to the 'court of homologation'. This court, which was later designated as the 'chamber of homologation', was presided over by a French professional judge. The judge was assisted by two assessors recommended by the procurator-general and appointed by the High Commissioner of the Republic. The 'court of homologation' received and studied the record of judgement submitted to it by the native court of second instance and could reduce, increase or annul the sentence passed by the lower court.

In 1927, the indigenous judicial system in Cameroon was slightly modified to give traditional rulers the power of 'reconciliation' in civil cases. Traditional chiefs were encouraged to persuade their litigants to always try to settle their disputes at home and not rush them to the courts.

At the level of both the sub-district and the district, the head of the administration held a plurality of powers. He had prerogatives in matters of the *indigénat*, and total judicial powers in indigenous matters. The local notables recommended by him as assessors could do nothing against his will. The administrator was a judge with discretionary powers because he was, at one and the same time, policeman, examining magistrate, public prosecutor, judge, and in charge of the execution of the sentence. This was what gave justice its arbitrary aspect, the more so since the law administered was customary law, unwritten and therefore open to every kind of interpretation. Indigenous justice extended the administrator's powers completely over the mass of the Cameroon population.

Since the French administrator was likely to be ignorant of local custom, the notables who were appointed as assessors were expected to help him. But, as was often the case, either these notables were not fully competent themselves or were corrupt. They could very easily be tempted to give opinions advantageous to their friends, particularly as the administrator did not understand the language of the accused. In both the presentation and the discussion of the case, the administrator could only follow what the interpreter translated for him. If the interpreter was dishonest and in connivance with the assessors, the judge could be manoeuvred to the advantage of the richer or more open-handed of the litigants.

The Indigénat

The *indigénat* was the name given to the group of provisions in the criminal code which permitted French administrators to impose punishments on African subjects without reference to a court of law. It was a system of summary disciplinary punishment applied to Africans who had not acquired French citizenship. Exempted from the *indigénat*, although not put at the same level with citizens, were regional chiefs, indigenous agents of the administration receiving fixed salaries, assessors serving in native courts, indigenous persons who had received French decorations, and indigenous persons who had served in the French colonial forces, together with their families. Unlike citizens, these people might still be subject to the *indigénat* if the High Commissioner found it necessary. Traditional notables not exempted from the penalties included quarter heads, village chiefs, and a wide variety of northern Muslim and Kirdi rulers who were neither regional chiefs nor members of the Council of Notables, nor receiving salaries from the administration. These notables did not, according to the French, constitute the elite.

The *indigénat* permitted the administrative authorities to impose penalties on subjects without having to justify their action before any judicial authority. A French decree of 8 August and the High Commissioner's *arrêté* of 4 October 1924, which officially made the *indigénat* applicable in Cameroon, gave the administration the right to inflict disciplinary punishment on subjects. These punishments were originally limited to a maximum of 15 days' imprisonment and/or a 100-franc fine. The authority to inflict punishment was limited to administrators and their white clerks, and to officials representing the public powers.

Offences which justified the imposition of summary penalties were spelt out in the decree of 1924. Although they were limited to 34, their variety was such and their definition so loose that the effect was arbitrarily to cover anything. Moreover, the decree gave the administrator a list of 'motives', among which he could always have an offence for people he wished to punish. Some of the offences listed in the *arrêté* of the High Commissioner of the French Republic in Cameroon (see the Appendix) were: acts of disorder, organising games of chance, circulating rumours likely to disturb public peace, making seditious utterances or showing disrespect for a duly authorised officer, giving aid to malefactors, illegal wearing of official insignia, hindering traffic, destroying administrative property, vagabondage, leaving an administrative district without authorisation, practising sorcery, reluctance in paying rates and taxes, failure to appear at official meetings, allowing animals to stray, possessing contraband, refusal to work a food plantation, allowing relatives suffering from mental and contagious diseases to stray, failing to declare human or animal contagious diseases, and burial outside consecrated burial grounds. The *indigénat* was even used to punish natives who failed to take off their hats in the presence of the local administrator. It was used as a means of bullying the Maka of the East Province into growing cash crops and resettling them.

The *indigénat* was in general use whenever there was a shortage of manpower. According to official statistics in 1935, there were 32 858 prison sentences under the *indigénat*, as against 3512 of common-law prisoners in Cameroon. The administration of the *indigénat* in Cameroon and other French African colonies was roundly condemned at the end of the Second World War, particularly at the Brazzaville Conference of 1944. It was abolished in the various territories in 1945 and 1946.

Reorganisation of chieftaincies

When the French acquired their own portion of Cameroon after the partition of 1916, they decided to give temporary recognition to the judicial powers of the traditional chiefs. This recognition lasted until 1922, when a full-scale reorganisation of the chieftaincies was begun. Earlier, in 1921, native courts presided over by the traditionally uninstitutionalised chiefs in the south had been suppressed on the grounds of confusion, and the judicial powers of the chiefs were vested either in the administrative heads of district or in the official native courts. In the areas of the grasslands and the north where the traditional judicial powers of prominent institutionalised chiefs were maintained, official native courts were set up by the administration as better alternatives where real justice and fair treatment could be had, to lure natives away from traditional courts. It was hoped that this would lead to the reduction of both the judicial power and authority of traditional chiefs. When it was realised that the inhabitants of the traditional chiefdoms were very strongly attached to their chiefs, the French decided to reorganise the chieftaincies in their own way.

Thus in 1922, the French created a number of local districts in which several traditional chiefdoms or ethnic units were grouped together and placed under a single chief, *chef de région*, appointed by the administrative head of district. These regional chiefs, who were recognised by the administration as the most senior traditional administrative authority in their districts, nevertheless exercised powers that were clearly circumscribed by the administration. Indeed, they were chosen not because they were senior in the traditional hierarchy, but on the basis of their intelligence and eagerness to serve the French authority. Those who qualified for appointment included the traditional chiefs of the villages of the region and any other person the French felt they could trust. The person appointed became the official chief. Eventually the French realised that their official chiefs were not being respected by the people and decided to take into consideration local opinion before such appointments were made.

One major example of an 'official' French chief during the reorganisation of chieftaincies in Cameroon was the Beti man, Charles Atangana. This man, who had served the German administration faithfully and followed them into exile in Fernando Po at the end of the Allied campaigns, returned to Cameroon in 1919 and was employed by the French to

7   S.M. Charles Atangana

direct a road-building project in Dschang. He completed the project using forced labour and gained the admiration of the French, who found him a devout supporter of French colonialism. In 1921 he was recognised as Chief of the Ewondo and permitted to return to Yaounde. In his new position under the French, Atangana helped the administration further by recruiting labourers for the continuation of the Duala – Yaounde railway project. In 1922 he was appointed regional chief over the Ewondo and Bane groups. During the mandate period Atangana continued to serve the French well and was taken to Paris several times as a recompense for his loyalty to the administration. But some of his people felt he had abused his powers and accused him of having developed among the Ewondo a spirit of servitude and passivity which rendered them the scapegoats for all the drudgery in every workyard. He died in 1943 and is honoured by a national statue in his name in Yaounde.

A major victim of the exercise of reorganisation of chieftaincies was Njoya of the extensive Bamum kingdom. Njoya, a traditional intellectual and one of the most notable monarchs in Cameroon history, had maintained his power and authority over his subjects and territory from the time of the Germans until the early years of French rule. At first the French were reluctant to disturb his position..But Njoya's near-supreme authority under French administration soon conflicted seriously with the French effort at suppressing traditional African institutions in favour of French institutions and civilisation. In 1924, the French took the first step towards making Njoya a nominal chief. They created over fifteen local chieftaincies in Bamum land and appointed persons as chiefs who were to be responsible directly to the administration and not to Njoya. Angered by this attempt to destroy him and his kingdom, Njoya tried to provoke a confrontation with the administration. The French reacted by cutting Njoya off from his traditional tribute monies and putting him on an annual official allowance. These measures failed to topple Njoya. The struggle between the two authorities continued unabated for six years until the stronger, the French, deposed the weaker and exiled him to Yaounde, where he died in 1933.

Several modifications of the 1922 statute of chiefs were made during the mandate era. In these modifications, the French created several types of chiefs and arranged them hierarchically according to their importance. Three classes of chiefs were distinguished. There were 'first-class' chiefs who included the *lamibe, sultans* and superior chiefs. Below these were 'second-class' chiefs who included chiefs of sub-districts, ('groupings'), and those appointed by the *lamibe* as their assistants. Finally there were 'third-class' chiefs who included village and quarter chiefs. In the whole reorganisation exercise, the traditional institution acquired a fundamentally new character. The traditional chiefdom gave way to the administrative chiefdom. Anyone could be appointed as chief and could also quickly be removed from office if he proved insufficiently docile or when it suited the whims of the administrator.

Education during the mandate period

The peoples of French Cameroon made remarkable progress in the field of education during the mandate period. Compared with other French colonies, Cameroon had the best educational system in French Black Africa. The reasons for such progress are many. First, the French government inherited a territory in which the German administration and the German Christian missions had laid an excellent educational foundation on which they could continue to build. Second, the French continued the German policy of relying on missions for early primary schooling and also recognised and subsidised schools which taught the approved curriculum. In 1929 the French government granted a subsidy to raise the salaries of the staff at private mission schools by two-thirds on condition that the medium of education was French. Third, the Mandates Commission of the League of Nations studied the progress of education in Cameroon each year and brought pressure to bear on the French to do more. Fourth, the French allowed non-French schools to operate in the territory in order to present the best educational record possible and to demonstrate that they could maintain as good a record as the Germans. As a result, missions like the American Presbyterian and the American Adventist which taught in the vernacular and not in French were allowed to run their own schools. Finally, many early educated Cameroonians were very eager to assist in the education of their peoples under the auspices of either the administration, established missionary societies, or separate native churches. For these reasons, schooling continued to flourish and the number of children enrolled in 1939 was more than double the number in 1914. Cameroon had a considerable number of private schools, although most of them were of an extremely low level.

Public primary schooling was organised differently in form and content, in the villages compared to the district and urban schools. Primary elementary education was given in three types of schools. The government village school, usually with one teacher and always poorly equipped, gave pupils elementary knowledge in French. In the more advanced of such schools, some instruction in agriculture and sanitation was given. Beyond the village schools were district schools where pupils enrolled at the age of six and graduated at the age of thirteen, although there were often much older children. During the last two years in the district schools pupils learnt history, geography and arithmetic. French was both the principal subject in the school curriculum and the medium of learning. The French regarded children who attended district schools as constituting the elite of the districts. It was hoped that, at the end of schooling, district school graduates would return to their villages and act as agents for the propagation of French civilisation. In the main towns, principally in Yaounde and Douala, there were urban primary schools whose curriculum was almost entirely academic. Graduates from urban primary schools hoped to be employed as clerks in government offices, business establishments, railways and ports.

Post-primary education in the interwar period was given in the higher primary school, *école primaire supérieure*, which was located in Yaounde and in some training schools. Admission into the Yaounde higher primary school which opened in 1927 was restricted to graduates of district and some recognised mission schools who had to sit and pass a competitive entrance examination. The duration of study in the school was three years. The standard of education in the school, which had only European teachers on the staff, was high. There were technical sections in the school where artisans for posts and telegraphs, survey, public works, railways, ports and commercial

houses were trained. The first head of state of Cameroon, Ahmadou Ahidjo, attended the Yaounde higher primary school where he trained as a radio operator for the post and telegraph services. The French generally considered their higher primary schools as the 'growing-points' of their civilisation in Black Africa. There was also an agricultural training school at Ebolowa, the ex-pupils of which could be engaged either by the administrative authorities or by private persons; or, if they so chose, they could settle on state lands with a view to establishing horticulture and plantations. Proper secondary schools were not established in Cameroon until after the Second World War.

The leading aim of French education was to spread a slight knowledge of the French language throughout Cameroon and to limit real education to the number needed by the administration or commercial houses. The French were against the idea of producing a class of educated unemployed. Thus, the number of Cameroonians who benefited from the upper-level education was not as impressive as the general record of French education in the territory. For example, out of a total of 680 students who attended the Yaounde higher primary school from 1927 to 1937, only 118 were beyond the third year of education. Considering the primary position Cameroon enjoyed in education in French Equatorial Africa, these numbers are very disappointing indeed. Yet, in all, Cameroon children had more opportunities to go to school during the mandate period than children in any other French colony in Black Africa.

Medical and health services

The French administration in Cameroon made great strides in medical and health services and surpassed any other French territory in Black Africa. But the history of the development of medical and health services during the mandate era is almost exclusively the story of the work of Dr Eugène Jamot. It is the story of how he

8 *Dr Eugène Jamot*

strived to eradicate the murderous epidemic of sleeping sickness. While in Brazzaville and Ubangi-Shari, he became interested in studying the typanosomes which invade the blood stream and then the cerebro-spinal fluid, and carried on laboratory research in the parasitic disease.

Dr Jamot was appointed to direct the fight against sleeping-sickness in Cameroon in 1921 after initiating the setting up of specialised sectors of preventive medicine in the territories of French Equatorial Africa. Sleeping-sickness was already a serious disease which the Cameroon campaign, the departure of the Germans and the Allied occupation aggravated.

In certain districts the population was even threatened with extinction within a short time by the disease. In other districts, the mortality rate among those suffering from the disease ranged from 25 per cent to 50 per cent per annum. On arrival in Cameroon, Dr Jamot took immediate steps to control and to eradicate the disease.

First he established specialised mobile teams. Mobile treatment centres for the systematic protection and registration of sufferers were then created. After limiting the focal points, mass treatment with atoxyl injections was begun. In the name of efficiency, Dr Jamot favoured the use of force in medical matters. To summon the people to the treatment centres, register them and then proceed to isolate the disease, the mobile teams employed methods that resembled those used for military recruitment. The mobile teams and their helpers literally searched everywhere for patients in the same way as a criminal is hunted down.

When Dr Jamot and his specialised mobile teams launched their campaign, the mortality rate dropped dramatically to between 5 and 15 per cent. By 1939 his system had succeeded in lowering the incidence of the disease in the affected areas from more than 25 per cent to less than one per cent.

In 1926, Dr Jamot succeeded in bringing about the establishment of a permanent sleeping-sickness mission in Cameroon. The medical personnel attached to the mission rose from 10 doctors, 20 European assistants and 150 nurses in 1926 to 18 doctors, 36 European assistants and 400 medical orderlies in 1931. Credits allocated to the mission amounted to 10 700 000 francs in 1929; 14 590 000 francs in 1930; and 15 900 000 francs in 1931.

High-level medical training became available in the territory in 1932 with the opening of one school to train nurses and another to train high-grade health assistants. Those who qualified for training in these two medical schools were graduates of the higher primary school in Yaounde. An intense scientific interest in Dr Jamot's methods of preventing and curing sleeping-sickness resulted in graduates of the colonial medical school in France seeking positions in Cameroon, with its model programme. In consequence, the rural population in the affected areas received better medical care because of the frequent visits of mobile units.

Dr Jamot's organisation to combat sleeping-sickness was transformed into a multi-purpose service against endemic diseases in Cameroon. Attention was soon directed to diseases such as malaria, yellow fever, intestinal diseases and leprosy. Dispensaries and maternity clinics were established in towns and villages so that diseases were diagnosed and drugs prescribed, and minor operations and delivery of babies performed. In 1937 Cameroon had fifteen maternity clinics and twenty-one paediatric clinics. Hospitals were also built in the main urban centres. In 1935 government hospitals had a total of 50 European beds and 3000 African beds. Although health care was almost entirely provided by the government, there were a few mission hospitals and centres with about a dozen doctors and a few junior medical workers.

Despite Dr Jamot's success in establishing an excellent medical service in Cameroon, he was abruptly relieved of his post in 1931 because of a medical scandal caused by one of his subordinates whom he tried to protect. His protégé's assistants had prescribed injections of tryparsamide at a dosage two or three times as high as that normally prescribed, causing blindness to about 700 patients who had received the treatment in the Bafia area. When informed about it, the protégé did nothing and considered the matter closed. The scandal soon broke out and Dr Jamot went to the affected region to investigate. But out of a spirit of loyalty and devotion to his profession, he covered up for his subordinate. He refused to testify before the board of inquiry set up to investigate the matter. When the board of inquiry imposed a reprimand on his subordinate, he threw all the responsibility on Dr Jamot, his protector. Dr Jamot was arrested on his way to France on a ministerial decision and with the approval of his superiors. Eventually he was released and sent to work in West Africa. He retired from medical practice and returned to France where he died a few months later on 24 April 1937. The service which he had set up in Cameroon was attached to the management of health services after his departure.

Economic development

Various studies of the economy of French Cameroon during the mandate period show that the territory made only modest economic progress as compared with developments in education and health. By the time of the outbreak of the First World War and the assumption of French control, Cameroon had already made considerable economic advance, especially in the coastal and southern districts. There was a well-established money economy through long contact with European traders, and through the German administration. The Germans had established plantations, built roads and railways and set up public works. These developments had made further inroads into the traditional economic activities and techniques, through appropriation of land, employment of labour, and the introduction of taxation. Although the disorders of the world war in the territory had forced the German merchants and technicians to leave and temporarily destroyed the trading networks and markets, it left largely intact economic buildings, a number of all-season roads, plantations, railway lines and ports.

As soon as the French occupied Cameroon, their new administration pre-empted some of the former German plantations and sold others to non-Germans. Efforts were made to prevent the return of the German businessmen to their trade and farmers to their plantations. Efforts were also made to alter the territory's allegiance to Germany for all time by substituting French values, markets, products and techniques for the Germans'. By 1925 the French administration had liquidated 116 German firms holding 366 different properties. Of these, 219 properties were sold at public auction, 107 were pre-empted, and 40 simply passed to the government because they originally belonged to the German state. The French administration also acquired the tobacco plantation in Dschang and turned it into a private company. Disposal of German property to non-Germans almost completely precluded the return of German citizens to French Cameroon. A few Germans did return after 1926 with various French and British trading companies.

In the early years of French occupation, much effort was directed at improving the infrastructure, increasing the agricultural production of the peasants and plantations, and extending commercial activity. Many more new roads were built and the existing railway lines extended some 128 km to Yaounde, with a branch of 37 km from Otele to Mbalmayo. By the time the Second World War came to an end, the Douala port had been enlarged and air services introduced. Production of cocoa, bananas, palm products and rubber was increased on the plantations. New methods of stepping up agricultural output were introduced. Timber began to be exploited on a large scale, with more than 200 000 hectares of forests being used for commercial purposes before the outbreak of the Second World War. Coffee became an important export commodity with the production of the *arabica* variety largely in the hands of smallholders and indigenous peasants, most of them in the western grassfields. The *robusta* variety was produced in the south. As a result of these developments, Cameroon's foreign trade increased by nearly 500 per cent during the interwar period, from 96 000 000 francs in 1922 to 467 171 000 francs in 1938.

Yet the economy of French Cameroon had not advanced very much, given the excellent foundation laid by the Germans by 1914. Several factors influenced whatever effort the French put into the economic development of the territory. First, the League of Nations mandate conferred something less than full French sovereignty over Cameroon whose eventual, though remote, goal was self-government. The possibility of Cameroon ever being assimilated to France's Equatorial African colonies was non-existent. Heavy investment in a territory with such an international status was considered by the French as too risky. Second, for a long time after 1918, France was more preoccupied with recovery from the First World War than with heavy investment in their African mandated territories and colonies. Third, France was also unwilling to make generous grants or loans to Cameroon because it was not certain that as a mandate the territory would remain French. A state-guaranteed loan of 10 000 000 francs, authorised in 1930 to extend the railway line from Nkongsamba to Chad, was never granted, apparently because of Cameroon's international status. Fourth, the worldwide economic depression of the late 1920s and the early 1930s also limited France's economic activities in Cameroon. During the depression, the prices of the principal African products dropped by as much as 60–70 per cent. Finally, the admission of Germany as a member of the League of Nations in 1926 and her strong campaign to regain Cameroon and her other former colonies thereafter made France unwilling to consider concessions. For these reasons, Cameroon made only modest economic progress during the mandate era.

The French were not interested in setting up industries in the territory. By 1939, the only industries established by the French were a latex plant, a palm-oil factory, a few sawmills and tin mines. There were only a handful of Cameroon salaried workers. The lack of adequate port facilities and of a good network of roads greatly limited the exportation of Cameroon products. Effective transportation for export crops, even when they could be produced, presented serious problems.

In order to effect certain aspects of economic development, especially the building of roads, railways and other public projects, the French administration in Cameroon resorted to the widespread use of forced labour. The practice of forced labour, followed much earlier by the German administration, was an almost inevitable result of the chronic shortage of funds from which the French administration in Africa suffered during the interwar era. Forced labour was introduced in the form of a labour tax known as *prestation*. Under *prestation*, all male Cameroonians of *sujet* status were obliged to furnish the administration with ten days of conscript and unpaid labour a year. After ten days, if the worker remained on the project he would be paid a minimal fixed rate for estimated portions of work finished. Commutation of *prestation* at the rate of two French francs per day of labour was made possible in 1925, although it was accepted only in exceptional cases. Initially, the recruitment of workers for *prestation* was done through the local chiefs, who were paid a lump sum for the work done. But when the chiefs began to abuse the system, the government gave the task of recruitment to local administrative officials.

The French used forced labour most extensively during the extension of the railway line from Njock, where the German line had stopped, to Makak and Yaounde. The extension line was to pass through an extremely unhealthy forest region that was practically unsettled. The lack of both proper health conditions on the project and proper medical attendance resulted in excessive mortality rates. Between 1922 and 1926 when the Njock – Yaounde railway project was accomplished, the mortality rate from forced labour was estimated by the League of Nations to range from 50 to 60 persons per thousand, although French estimates were always low. As a result of the high death rate, poor feeding, poor housing, general mistreatment, and the hard work that each person had to perform for the ten days of free labour, many Cameroonians began to evade conscription. Many fled from their regions and groups usually tapped for forced labour, going into British Cameroon, Gabon, Spanish Rio Muni and Fernando Po.

The administration decided to trap the escapers before they had time to migrate to neighbouring territories. Able-bodied men were captured during the night in their villages by 'mysterious agents' and led to work camps in faraway regions unknown to their wives, children and relatives. Recruitment took the form of manhunting. Even when the Njock – Yaounde rail project was completed, forced labour continued to be used extensively in the construction of a number of trunk-roads linking principal urban centres in the south and the building of the roads linking the south with the towns in the north. In 1931 it was reported that forced labour in Cameroon had assumed revolting proportions. By 1933, however, the use of forced labour had diminished, although the practice was not abolished until 1952.

Missions during the French mandate

The Allied campaigns of 1914 to 1916 completely disrupted Christian missionary activity and isolated all the Christian missions in Cameroon. By 1916 all the German missionaries had been expelled, together with the German administrative officials and other German nationals. The partition of Cameroon by France and Britain in 1916 was soon followed by the arrival in the French sphere of French Protestant and Catholic missionaries as replacements of the German missionaries in the territory. Following the international agreements governing mandated territories at the Paris Peace Conference of 1919, the French government which had hitherto admitted only French missionaries to their colonies was bound to allow foreign missionaries – Americans, for example – to continue their evangelical work of conversion and education in Cameroon alongside French missionaries. All the former German missions, Catholic and Protestant alike, were 'nationalised' and put in the hands of French missionaries.

Missionaries of the Protestant Missionary Society in Paris entered Cameroon to care for the congregations of the Basel Mission, the German Baptists, and the Gossner Societies. The Basel Mission, which had inherited the work of the English Baptist Missionary Society at the time of the German occupation of Cameroon, had developed a network of stations extending into the hinterland of the territory. The efforts of the first group of French Protestant missionaries who arrived in Cameroon in February 1917 were directed at uniting in a federation the three Protestant missions which they inherited. During the mandate period, they founded new mission stations at Bafoussam, Ndikinimiki, Bangwa and Bangante. The French Protestant missionaries also established a centre where apprentices were trained in various trades, a printing press, a school of theology at Ndoungou in 1926, a teacher training college, an evangelical college at Libamba, a hospital at Bangwa, and a youth hostel in Douala.

The American Presbyterians who began work in Cameroon in 1871 were the fourth important Protestant mission in the territory until 1917. The Allied campaigns did not halt the activities of this mission, which were concentrated in the south in the Bulu and Bassa lands, because all their missionaries were Americans. After the war it opened a teacher-training college at Foulassi in 1916 and a hospital centre at Enonga near Ebolowa in 1922. The American Presbyterian mission continued to expand, although at one time a large proportion of its Bulu congregation were converted to Roman Catholicism. The American Presbyterians also worked in the evangelical college at Libamba in collaboration with the French Protestant mission.

There were five other minor Protestant missions and also the Jehovah's Witnesses, who entered and began to operate in Cameroon during the period of the French administration. The first of these was the Fraternal Lutheran Mission in 1919. Of American origin, it began work in northern Cameroon where the German authorities had forbidden evangelical activities. Before long the Fraternal missionaries established a Bible School at Garoua, opened another station at Kaele where they established a printing press and a leprosy settlement, and at Yagoua where they opened another Bible School. The second minor Protestant Mission to enter Cameroon was the American Lutheran Mission of Sudan in 1922. This mission concentrated its missionary work among the Gbaya. They eventually extended their work of conversion to Meiganga, Betare-Oya, Poli and Tchollire near Rey-Bouba.

The next to arrive was the Norwegian Lutheran Mission which was established in Ngaoundere in 1925. It founded other stations at Tibati, Yoko, Bankim in Tikar country, Banyo, Galim and Mbe. Their principal church house was inaugurated in Ngaoundere in December 1934. Then came the United Church of Sudan in 1938 in the region of Maroua. This mission expanded its work of evangelism much later to Mora and Soulede near Mokolo, and continued to work among the Matakam and the Sara. Thirdly came the Adventist Mission in 1928. It began work first at Nanga-Eboko and later at Yaounde and the Bulu country. The Jehovah's Witnesses who, properly speaking, are neither in the Protestant or Catholic camp, began their door-to-door distribution of religious leaflets, Bible readings, preaching and campaigns for followers in the principal urban centres before the outbreak of the Second World War. Their principal centre was Ebolowa.

The giant of all the Christian missions in French Cameroon during the mandate era was the Catholic Church. At the end of the war in Cameroon, the Commander of the French troops, General Aymerich, who wanted only French missionaries to continue the work of the expelled German missionaries, addressed a letter to the Superior General of the Holy Ghost Fathers in Paris requesting missionaries for Cameroon. The answer was immediate and favourable. On 9 October 1916, the first contingent of seven French Holy Ghost Fathers arrived in Douala to salvage the abandoned church. Although their number was insignificant for the vast work left behind by German missionaries, their arrival was an assurance that many more would come. Rev. Father Douvry who had been the French military chaplain during the Allied campaigns and was now at Douala, was at hand to help the new Fathers on their arrival, and was soon named the Apostolic Administrator in Cameroon. In 1920 he was replaced by Father Mallessart. Two years later, the Catholic Church in French Cameroon had its first bishop in the person of His Lordship François-Xavier Vogt, a native of Alsace in Europe which, like Cameroon, had earlier passed from German to French sovereignty. The headquarters of the Cameroon Church was soon established in Yaounde.

Under Bishop Vogt, the Catholic Church in French Cameroon grew very rapidly, surpassing in its number of converts and catechumens all the Protestant Churches put together. The suddenness and massiveness of conversion to Catholicism, especially in the extensive centre-south-littoral region and the southwestern grasslands, was nothing less than miraculous. The Catholic Church, which in 1923 had only 14 priests, 6 brothers, 1227 catechists and 79 000 baptised Christians could, in 1931, boast of having 38 priests, 14 brothers, 24 religious, 2390 catechists, 192 444 baptised Christians, and 54 796 catechumens.

In 1931 the Vicarage of Douala was created and detached from the Diocese of Yaounde. His Lordship Le Mailloux was appointed the Vicar. Under him were 17 priests, 7 brothers, 6 religious, 1090 catechists, 62 444 baptised Christians, and 27 529 catechumens. In 1932, an assistant to Bishop Vogt in the person of Bishop Graffin was appointed. In 1934, the Diocese of Nkongsamba was established and given to the priests of the Society of the Sacred Heart of Jesus, with His Lordship Boucque as Bishop. The Church in northern Cameroon had its first diocese in Garoua after the Second World War, in 1947, with Bishop Plumey as the first Vicar.

Earlier, in 1923, Bishop Vogt had opened at Mvolye, Yaounde, a junior seminary with 12 students. The seminary was later transferred to Nlong and then to Akono, where it was made permanent. In 1927, a senior seminary was opened in Yaounde. In December 1935 the ordination of the first indigenous Cameroon priests took place in the dioceses of Yaounde and Douala. Those ordained were Fathers André Manga, Tobie Atangana, Theodore Tsala and Jean Oscar Awue in Edea. From 1935, indigenous Cameroonian priests began to be ordained each year. By 1940, the Catholic Church in French Cameroon had 16 African priests, 16 African brothers, and 360 031 baptised Christians. Fifteen years later, on 30 November 1955, the first Cameroonian Bishop, His Lordship Paul Etoga, was consecrated.

Protests and revolts against the French mandate

During the period of the French mandate, many groups responded in different ways against what they considered were the failures or injustices of the administration. While some groups responded by either writing petitions to the League of Nations to suppress the French mandate, defying such colonial requirements as the supply of forced labour and payment of head-tax, or massively removing themselves from the territory in order to avoid French rule altogether, others simply rebelled against the French administration. Some of the groups whose grievances led to vigorous protests or revolts were the Duala, the Gbaya, the Bulu, the Guider and the Bamum.

The Duala perhaps staged the longest and most publicised anti-French protests during the period between the two world wars. Their grievances began when they unsuccessfully demanded the reversal of the German expropriation and an adequate redress for their confiscated lands. During the 1920s and the 1930s, Duala complaints included failure to restore their land rights, failure to develop the territory economically, restrictions placed in the way of relations between Cameroonians in the British and French territories, attempts to impose European missionary control over the independent United Native Baptist Church, non-recognition of the rights and liberties of Cameroonians, and attempts to extend the head-tax to women. Thus, besides numerous petitions and memoranda submitted to the League of Nations and some European and the American governments, several public demonstrations and revolts were staged against the French.

One of the most remarkable of the Duala revolts was that of the women against the extension of head-tax to them in 1931. The decision of the administration to impose the same rates of head-tax as men on women led to the revolt. The women demanded that the decision be annulled, pointing out that it was taken without due consideration for their real financial situation and to the current economic crisis. The French responded by arresting and detaining some leaders of the protest. The other women quickly congregated in front of the Metropolitan Police Station in Deido Quarters where they suspected their leaders were being held. They wanted to know what was happening to them. The head of the Station, Thieband, perhaps with the intention of frightening and dispersing the women, fired gunshots, wounding several women who were rushed to the hospital, some of them with shells of bullets in their feet. This attitude of the white metropolitan gendarme led to passive protests on July 22 and 23. Public demonstrations were staged in different parts of the city, but more particularly in Deido, Bali and Bonaberi quarters. Petitions were written against the French administration, which was forced to arrest and sentence Gendarme Thieband to ten days' imprisonment and a fine of ten French francs. The Douala wanted the suppression of the French mandate and the transformation of Cameroon into a republic.

The most intensive single reaction against the evils of the French administration was staged by the Gbaya of Adamawa, in the border area of east-central Cameroon and west-central Ubangi-Chari (present-day Central African Republic). The uprising, known as the Carnot Rebellion, erupted in July 1928 near the town of Carnot in Ubangi-Chari. The Gbaya were reacting against years of forced labour, railways recruitment, misrule through the use of the officials of the Lamido of Ngaoundere, considerable Fulbe extortions, and practices of slavery and child-theft. They were more particularly angered by the apparent French condonation of Fulbe overlordship in Gbaya-land.

The Gbaya rebellion was declared and led by a traditional war-leader and diviner known as Karnou (Karinou, Karno or Kano). His principal objective was to drive out the French and the Fulbe from the territory and to re-establish Gbaya autonomy. The unrest spread rapidly, leap-frogging considerable distances and moving in all directions until most of east-central Cameroon as well as the western parts of Ubangi-Chari were involved. Unable to quell the rebellion through casual warfare, the French decided in January 1929 to mount a major punitive expedition against the Gbaya. After one pitched battle, Gbaya resistance

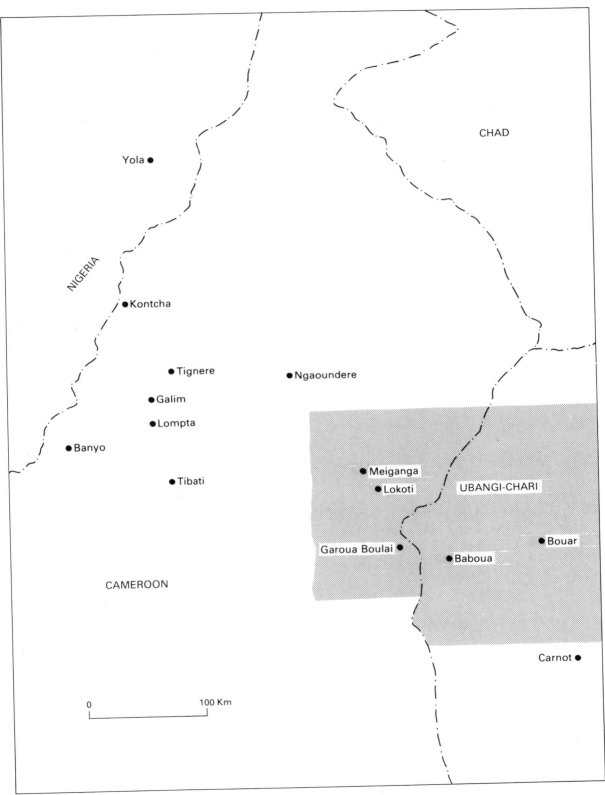

Figure 7   *The Gbaya of East-Central Cameroon*

weakened and completely collapsed when Karnou was killed. The French continued to bring more troops into the area to hunt down those responsible for the rebellion. Calm was soon restored, although the search for the rebel leaders continued until the early 1930s.

Although the revolt failed, it did hasten the founding of a sub-prefecture in Gbayaland at Meiganga, the introduction of direct administration, the adoption of reforms which removed local (Fulbe) abuses, and the establishment of closer French supervision. The French also forced all the Gbaya living in scattered and isolated hamlets to join larger villages where they would be easily controlled. Those who were unwilling to comply with the order risked having their homes and farms burnt down by the administration.

The Bulu, Guidder and Bamum protests were particularly against the local French administration and administrators. The Yevol clan in Bululand staged a long campaign in 1928 – 29 against the injustices of the local administration. The Guidder of north Cameroon who had taken to the hills against Fulbe rule in the nineteenth century, revolted when they were pursued by the French. Throughout the 1920s small wars occurred between them and the Fulbe and French military detachments. The Bamum, whose political activity revolved around their powerful monarch, King Njoya, revolted when the French began to curtail Njoya's traditional powers. The rebellion was intensified in 1924 when the French arrested and imprisoned leading Bamum notables in Dschang, and in 1931 when they dethroned and exiled Njoya to Yaounde where he died in 1933. The rebellion began in the form of contempt for the local French officials and extended to Bamum migration in thousands to neighbouring chiefdoms in British territory. The French found it difficult to put an end to these migrations until the period of trusteeship, after the Second World War.

Further reading

Robert Delavignatte, *Freedom and Authority in French West Africa* (OUP, New York, 1957).
David E. Gardinier, *Cameroon: United Nations Challenge to French Policy* (OUP, London, 1963).
Lord Hailey, *An African Survey,* Revised Edition (OUP, New York, 1957).
Victor T. LeVine, *The Cameroons From Mandate to Independence* (University of California Press, Berkeley and Los Angeles, 1964).
Engelbert Mveng, *Histoire du Cameroun,* (Tome II, CEPER, Yaounde, 1985).
Jean Suret-Canale, *French Colonialism in Tropical Africa* (C. Hurst & Company, London, 1971).

Questions

1. Discuss the various French colonial policies tried or applied in Cameroon and other African territories.
2. What was the *indigénat* and how was it applied in Cameroon?
3. How was French colonial education organised in Cameroon during the mandate period?
4. Who was Dr Jamot? Why is he important in the history of development of medical and health services in Cameroon?

5. The economy of French Cameroon between the two world wars did not advance very much, given the excellent foundation laid by the Germans by 1914. Discuss.
6. Why did the Catholic Church succeed more than other denominations in French Cameroon during the mandate period?
7. Why was it difficult for German nationals to return to French Cameroon after the First World War?

Chapter seven
Cameroon under British mandate: 1922-39

British Cameroon was made up of British Southern Cameroons and British Northern Cameroons. We are more concerned in this chapter with British Southern Cameroons which formed an administrative unit during this period. In 1961, British Southern Cameroons was reunified with the former French Cameroon, and today constitutes the North West and the South West Provinces of the Republic of Cameroon. British Northern Cameroons, on the other hand, integrated with Nigeria and is today part of that federation. British Southern Cameroons was administered during the mandate period as one of the provinces of Southern Nigeria.

The administrative arrangement

Following the Anglo-French partition of Cameroon in 1916 the Governor-General of Nigeria, Lord Lugard, ordered that, until other definite arrangements were made, the British sphere of Cameroon should be administered according to the laws of (German) Cameroon so far as these were known, or according to the laws of the part of Nigeria in which the administering officer had previously held his appointment. The administering officers, who were all drawn from Nigeria, were authorised to apply either the laws of Southern or Northern Nigeria. Until 1922, it was not definite which system of administration would be followed in British Cameroon.

On 20 July 1922, the British mandatory administration in Cameroon officially commenced. A few months earlier, in April of the

same year, the Resident in Buea was informed by the Nigerian Government that the Secretary of State for the Colonies had approved the policy of indirect rule as a system of native administration to be adopted in the mandated territories. Thus the arrangements made from 20 July when the mandate system came into force officially applied the Nigerian laws of indirect rule in the territory and, by the British Cameroons Order in Council of 1923, placed the Cameroons Province under the governorship of the Lieutenant-Governor of the Southern Provinces of Nigeria.

The general administration of the Colony and Protectorate of Nigeria and the mandated territory of Cameroon was headed by the Governor-General who was resident in Lagos, the capital of the Federation. The Governor-General had supremacy in matters both political and departmental, and was directly responsible to the Secretary of State for the Colonies in London for the administration in the Federation.

Under the Governor-General were two Lieutenant-Governors at the head of the administration of the Southern and Northern groups of provinces. In Southern Nigeria, the legislation for the colony and provinces was enacted through the Legislative Council which was established in 1923. Under the Lieutenant-Governor were senior provincial Residents, each at the head of the provincial administration. British Southern Cameroons constituted the Cameroons Province during the mandate period.

The Resident was the principal executive officer of government in the province. He was

Figure 8 *Administrative Divisions of the Cameroons Province, 1916–39*

directly responsible to the Lieutenant-Governor under whom he served for the peace, tranquillity and good order of his province, and for the efficient execution of all public business which at any time was being carried on within the province. During the period of the British mandate up to the outbreak of the Second World War, seven Residents served in the Cameroons Province. These were: Major F.H. Ruxton (1921 – 25), Mr E.J. Arnett (1925 – 8), Mr H.G. Aveling (1928 – 9), Mr E.J. Arnett (1929 – 32), Mr J.W.C. Rutherfoord (1933 – 4), Mr O.W. Firth (1935 – 8), and Mr A.E.F. Murray (1939 – 42).

Immediately under the Resident were the District Officers (DO) who really represented the British administration to the people. The DOs headed the administrative districts or divisions into which the provinces were divided. There were four administrative divisions in the Cameroons Province during the mandate period, namely Victoria, Kumba, Mamfe and Bamenda. The DOs in the Cameroons Province were directly answerable to the Resident in Buea for the local administration in their districts. From 1922 on, these administrators and their assistants were instructed to make very thorough studies of the administrative divisions and to collect information about ethnic groups, their distribution and political systems, customary law and land tenure in preparation for the organisation of the system of indirect administration in the province.

The results of ethnic assessments revealed that Victoria and Kumba Divisions were inhabited by chiefless peoples, although the Germans had created artificial chiefs who had acquired a substantial degree of popular support. Mamfe had only village chiefs who shared power with the elders. Only in the Bamenda grassfields and Bangwa were strong chiefs known as *fon*s found at the head of larger villages and ethnic groups. Armed with this knowledge, the British authorities proceeded cautiously to establish the system of indirect rule, making sure that only traditionally acknowledged or rulers popular with the governed were associated with it.

The organisation of indirect rule

The bases of indirect administration that the British applied in Cameroon from 1922 were the Nigerian Native Courts Ordinance of 1914 and the Nigerian Native Authorities Ordinance of 1916. By the provisions of the Native Courts Ordinance, four grades of courts, designated A, B, C and D were organised. The Grade A courts in the larger traditional states were the most senior while the Grade D courts were the most junior.

Grade A courts had full judicial powers in all civil and criminal cases, except death sentences, which could not be carried out without the governor's confirmation. Grade B courts had jurisdiction in civil actions in which the demand or debt did not exceed £50, and in criminal cases where the crime was punished by not more than two years' imprisonment, 24 lashes, or a fine of £50 or its equivalent in native law and custom. Grade C courts had civil jurisdiction where the claim did not exceed £10, and criminal jurisdiction where the punishment did not exceed six months' imprisonment or a fine of £10. Grade D courts had civil jurisdiction of from £5 to £10, and criminal jurisdiction of up to three months' imprisonment, 12 lashes or £5 fine. Native Courts were principally for chiefs and other leaders of the district to continue to administer the law according to the prevailing pre-colonial system shorn of those aspects that were distasteful to the British. The chiefs provided the police and prisons to enforce their administration of justice.

By the provisions of the Native Authorities Ordinance, a 'Native Authority' was defined as a chief or other 'native' formally recognised by the government. Such a recognised Native Authority was allowed executive powers to maintain law and order, and to appoint native police to assist him for such purpose. He was also empowered to prevent offences being committed, and to arrest and compel those doing so to appear before the court of law. Native Authorities could issue orders on such subjects as tax collection, labour recruitment, public health, and community development. Chiefs and other indigenous persons exercising power under the Native Authorities Ordinance were arranged in five grades based on the size and importance of their ethnic groups or chiefdoms, the traditional rules of succession, and the wish of the people.

In the 1920s and 1930s, the British established three administrative Native Authorities in Victoria, nineteen in Kumba, eight in Mamfe, and fifteen in Bamenda. The three Native Authorities of Victoria Division, each aided by an advisory clan council, were Chief Endeley of Buea, Chief Manga Williams of Victoria, and Chief Mukete of Muyuka. In Bamenda, four of the Native Authorities, the paramount Fon of Nso and the Fons of Kom, Bali-Nyonga and Bum, were aided by councils which had only advisory powers. In some areas quite big chiefdoms were thought to be too close together to offer a convenient and financially viable unit of administration, as in the Bafut Native Authority area. In others the British found no paramountcies to lean on, and were confronted by chiefdoms of different size and scope. In others again the units were almost all small and kin-based, often relying on ritual leaders. Thus in Ndop, Bafut, Fungom, Wum, Ngemba, Meta and Ngie where there was no single recognised paramount or senior chief, a composite Native Authority and Native Court were created, while in others such as Moghamo and Ngunu where the unit of organisation higher than the clan did not exist, the Native Authority was the Native Court. The Mbembe district in present-day Donga-Mantung Division was left under direct British administration until the outbreak of the Second World War. By 1936, the administration had created or recognised a wide variety of Native Authorities in the Cameroons Province, most of them based on a fairly accurate evaluation of the nature of the socio-political structures in the territory. The Fon of Bangwa (Fontem) was the only Native Authority in his own right in Mamfe Division.

Indirect rule was a system of administration in which the British administered their colonial territories through local authorities and their traditional institutions. The DOs, the Native Authorities and the Native Courts formed an integral part of the machinery of a single administration in which each had well-defined duties to perform. It is said that the British adopted the system of indirect rule because of the extreme shortage of European officials to administer the colonies directly, and because they were convinced that there could be no identity between the divergent cultures of Africa and Europe. This appears to have been the case because, as far as the Cameroons Province was concerned, there were rarely more than twelve British administrative officers throughout the mandate period.

The overall authority of the DOs in the administration in their divisions was very clear. They advised and exercised general supervision over the Native Authorities and the proceedings of the customary or Native Courts under them. The DOs sat as magistrate to hear criminal and civil cases, endorsed the execution of murderers condemned to death, directed and controlled the work of local prisons, and settled boundary and other disputes between neighbouring clans, villages and chiefdoms. They also supervised the construction of roads, persuaded the chief to supply labour for government projects, and received revenue and paid wages to government employees. They recommended the appointment of Native Authorities, taking into consideration, as best as they could, the political structures they found and what they were told of traditional dynastic and clan links and alliances. The systematic series of assessment and intelligence reports undertaken in each community helped them to discover the scope of the traditional groups and the foci of political power. In matters that concerned the overall policy of the mandated territory, as distinct from local policy, the Native Authorities received direct instructions from the British administrative authorities.

The main source of revenue for the administration was direct taxation. Local treasuries into which all the taxes of the Native Authorities were paid were established in each district. Part of the tax collected by Native Authorities was given to the colonial administration and part was retained for the day-to-day administration of the district. Taxation and budgeting of expenditure of the revenue collected constituted very important characteristics of indirect rule. Other sources of revenue were court fees and fines and payments for various licences.

In general, indirect rule was applied with a great deal of success in the Cameroons Province. This was particularly true of the extensive Bamenda grasslands most of which was under the rule of *fons*, the natural (and often very efficient) rulers of the fondoms which derived their dynasties from the same source as Bamum, or those set up by the Bali invaders, or the Nggemba-speaking groups of the central plateau. It worked well in all the areas where explicit authority structures existed, although there was a puzzling display of clan groupings, chiefdoms, ethnic units and other traditional political arrangements in the Province. Some of these had, as we have seen, explicit hierarchical authority, complete with chiefs supported by a palace staff; and others, with or without titular chiefs, had diffused authority systems in which an ethnic council, a council of elders, or an informal assembly of family heads constituted the only visible government. All the groups maintained their forms of political organisation under the system of indirect rule.

Economic development in the Cameroons province

One of the major concerns of the British upon assuming control of their portion of Cameroon in 1916, was to re-establish the economy of the territory which had collapsed as a result of the war and the expulsion of German raw material exporters, planters and traders. The Anglo-French partition of the same year had left about ninety per cent of the total plantation acreage in the former German protectorate in the hands of the British. Upon assuming control, the British appointed an agricultural expert to supervise the plantations. Medical officers and civil police were also appointed to control the sanitation of the estates and the health of the employees, and for police duties on the estates.

Under the Germans the western coastal and forest zone which constituted Victoria and Kumba Divisions under the British became the main centre of a highly capitalised plantation industry. The major problem facing the inherited plantations and other properties of the enemy nationals was to maintain their prewar productive capacity. Labour was required in abundance. In order to acquire labour, the administrative officers in the Bamenda grassfields were instructed to go on a recruitment tour of the division and to urge the chiefs to supply workers for the plantations. The administration also embarked upon the importation of labour from Nigeria. Some 2000 workers consisting of Hausas and inhabitants of the southern provinces of Nigeria were recruited. To encourage free labour from Nigeria, the grasslands of British and French Cameroon and other distant areas, the rates of pay were set at 4½d. a day for local workers, 6d. for workers from the grassfields, and 9d. for workers from very distant places.

From 1921 on, British efforts to turn over the plantations into the hands of private British enterprise failed. In 1923 the estates were put up for sale in London, but almost all of them failed to find buyers. In 1924 the second auction was organised in London with restrictions against German buyers removed. The Germans repurchased almost all the plantations, the buyers being original owners of the estates. Within two years of the return of German planters to the Cameroons Province, the plantations were in full production. Further acreage was brought into cultivation and employment rose from 11 000 in 1924 to 13 500 in 1928, 15 500 in 1935, and 25 000 in 1938. The number of German planters in the Province in the 1930s was between 200 and 250, and they were almost virtually in control of the economic life of the territory.

The expansion of the plantations brought many economic changes to the Cameroons

Province. The port facilities at Tiko and Victoria were expanded by the plantation owners, and a new wharf for loading bananas directly on to ocean-going steamers was constructed. The Germans also constructed a number of relatively clean and comfortable workers' camps, numerous shops, warehouses, and office buildings. By virtue of German control of the plantations, the overseas trade of the Cameroons Province was mainly with Germany, not with the United Kingdom. As the Cameroon Report for the year 1929 shows, Germany bought all the territory's bananas and most of its cocoa, palm products and rubber, and shipped almost all produce in German bottoms. At the same time Germany supplied the majority of the imports, mostly equipment for the plantations and consumer goods sold to the Africans from the planters' own stores.

The British administration's economic policy ruled out most types of government action and only attempted to influence private concerns, mostly the German planters. Most investment in the Cameroons Province during the mandate period was undertaken by German nationals. The Nigerian government, which was fully aware of the economic potential of the province, feared investing in it because the territory's political future had been made uncertain by the mandate system.

An aspect of the economy that was neglected by the British administration in Cameroon was the development of roads. Throughout the mandate period there was only one road in the Cameroons Province, from Tiko and Victoria through Mutengene, Muyuka, Kumba and Mamfe. By the time of the outbreak of the Second World War, 67 km of this lone road remained to be completed between Mamfe and Bamenda, through some difficult country. There was only one dry-season road through Mamfe, linking the province with Nigeria, and two dry-season roads from Kumba to Loum and Bamenda to Mbouda linking the territory with French Cameroon. The most efficient surface communication with both Nigeria and French Cameroon was by sea. A motor ring road built during the period circled the Bamenda grassfields, joining the Bamenda township of Abakwa, the Ndop Plain, Nso, Nkambe and Wum.

To encourage the building of roads in the Province, the British maintained compulsory labour for public works in the labourers' own districts. The administration however maintained that such compulsory labour must be sanctioned by the government, and the labourer must be paid the current wage.

Another aspect of the economy worth mentioning was the development of traditional long-distance trade. At the end of hostilities in 1916, traditional trade in the Cameroons Province resumed and became widespread in all directions. Trade in salt from Mamfe flowed north, east and west to the grassfields, Dschang and Bamileke highlands and Nigeria. The old time kola-nut trade from Nso and other areas flowed north to the markets in French Cameroon and Northern Nigeria where the nuts were absorbed by Hausa and Fulbe traders. There was also trade in farm and hunting utensils like the iron hoe, the cutlass, the axe and the spear. The chief local source of these farm and hunting implements was the Ndop Plain, although some implements also came from Nso and Oku areas. Traditional trade to markets within the Cameroons Province and outside to Nigeria and French Cameroon was considerable. Traditional trade became an essential economic activity because of the geographical distribution of the important consumers' commodities. The only major hindrance to traditional trade during the mandate era was the blockade on the boundary with French Cameroon through the strict enforcement of customs formalities and the international laws against Africans crossing it.

The attempt by the colonial administrations in British and French Cameroon to control the trade across the boundary transformed the once-legitimate commerce between the two territories into smuggling. Contraband trade from British to French Cameroon and vice versa began to be conducted in every item of trade. In the grassfields areas, large-scale smuggling was carried on in cattle and currency. Cattle-dealers easily grazed their herds across the boundary to whichever side the cattle-market was better, almost always avoiding the payment of duty on them. Cattle-dealers also made much profit through smuggling currency and exchanging it on the black market. The Bakossi cash-crop planters and others in the south usually hid the bulk of their cocoa and coffee harvests and sold it in French Cameroon. There was large contraband trade in tobacco, salt, gunpowder, textiles, beer, soap, kerosene and matches. In the 1920s and 1930s, both British and French authorities were reported to find it difficult to cope with the problem of detecting and arresting the large number of smugglers across the Anglo-French boundary. The increase in smuggling probably resulted from the fact that although it was considered illegal by the colonial administrations, traditional opinion approved of it and considered it a legitimate trading activity. There was no way of putting an end to it so long as the international boundary between the British and French Cameroon continued to be strictly patrolled.

In general, the British did very little to develop their own sphere of Cameroon during the mandate period. The territory was considered and treated as unimportant in the development of the Nigerian economy. Very little government revenue was used for development, although every opportunity was used to exploit the territory's resources. There was never at any time during the mandate period a separate budget for British Cameroon. The British saw Cameroon as a territory which Germany might later re-acquire and so did not treat it as a significant part of their colony.

Education

As soon as the British occupied the Southern Cameroons in 1916, efforts began to be made to turn the former German schools into English schools under the corresponding denominational agencies. From the onset, regulations laid down in the Educational Ordinance of Nigeria were applied in British Cameroon, taking into consideration the prevailing circumstances. But the major problem facing the re-establishment of schools continued to be a lack of teachers. The population as a whole was eager for education and the money for this was available, but qualified teachers, or even unqualified teachers of suitable character, were not forthcoming in numbers commensurate with the demand. Another problem was that of language. Because Cameroon education was originally in German, English was a foreign language which Cameroon youths who had received some education had to learn from scratch. Besides, the absence of resident missionaries of the various denominations from the territory until the 1920s also meant that mission schools could not open. These three major factors delayed the re-establishment of schools and the full application of the Nigerian Educational Ordinance in the Cameroons Province.

Schools began to operate in the Cameroons Province only after the mandate system had come into force and missionaries of the various denominations had started returning to the territory. The administration planned to have one government school fully staffed with certificated teachers and fully equipped to stand as a model school in each of the four divisions of the province. Efforts were made to recruit teachers from Nigeria, and from 1923 Cameroon students began to be sent to Nigeria to train as teachers. By 1924, there were already operating 6 Government Schools, 5 Roman Catholic Schools, 33 Protestant Schools nominally cared for by the French missionaries from Douala, and a number of Native Administration Schools. By 1926 when the Basel missionaries returned to the territory, there were 12 Native Administration Schools, 6 Government Schools and a total of 120 mission schools.

It was in 1926 that the administration fully applied the Nigerian Educational regulations in the Cameroons Province. It laid stress on the Three Rs, the teaching of English and practical training as well as a syllabus that was more closely adapted to the African cultural background. Efforts were made to introduce vernacular teaching in schools, and the Government, Native Administration and Catholic Schools were already following the official syllabus. A simple knowledge of the Three Rs and doctrine were the only subjects taught in the 130 Basel Mission Schools. The language difficulty continued to be a problem, for the only *lingua franca* in Government Schools was Pidgin English. In the Native Administration Schools where the vernacular could have been used, most suitable teachers were Nigerians. The Basel Mission Schools in the south often taught the Douala language while many of those in the grassfields taught *mungaka*. In spite of this, it was reported in 1928 that although English had to be taught in schools from the beginning, the standard of efficiency had not been impaired.

On 1 October 1925, a Normal Class for the training of teachers was opened in the Victoria Government School. Those who qualified for admission had to have served as contact pupil teachers for two years, or to have passed examination under schedule D or E, or to have passed out of Class Two of the secondary department. The course lasted two years for qualified candidates, with an extra year of intensive practical training for unqualified candidates. In 1926 the Normal Class was transferred to Buea and in 1932 to a newly-acquired site at Kake as an Elementary Teacher Training College. At Kake it became a full three-year course.

The first graduates of the Normal Class came out in 1927 as the first locally-trained teachers. The Normal Class was opened for the training of Government, Native Administration and Mission teachers, while scholarships continued to be offered to other graduates of Government and Native Administration schools to study in Nigerian higher institutions. Until Cameroonian graduates of the Normal Class and Nigerian institutions began to be available, Government Schools were mostly staffed with teachers drawn from Britain, the West Indies and Nigeria. Catholic missionaries in Nigeria sent Nigerian teachers to man the few Catholic Schools that existed before Cameroon Catholics began to qualify from Nigerian Teacher Training institutions and from the Normal School or the Kake Teacher Training College. The Catholic and Basel Missions opened their own teacher training colleges at Njinikom and Nyassoso respectively in 1944, and the government opened another for training senior elementary teachers at Kumba in 1945.

The first secondary school in the Cameroons Province was opened by the Catholic Mission at Sasse, near Buea, in 1939. Before then, Cameroonian parents sent their children to secondary schools in Nigeria. Even after Sasse College, which was strictly for boys, had been opened, many children continued to trek to and enroll in Nigerian secondary schools. They even went there first to write the entrance examination, which they might not even pass, before going back to enroll if they were selected. Only very limited places were open to Cameroon pupils in Nigerian secondary schools and colleges.

The missions

The First World War in Cameroon ended with the expulsion of all German missionaries together with other German nationals from the territory. While French missionaries were immediately available to take over the missions and missionary establishments in the French sphere after the partition of the territory in 1916, missions in British Cameroon were left untended for many years. During the period before the arrival of resident missionaries in the Cameroons Province in the 1920s, the Christian churches in the British territory were cared for by the local catechists who relied very much on visiting Protestant pastors and Catholic priests from the French Cameroon and British Nigeria. It was hoped that the end of the global war and the signing of peace might lead to the return of German missionaries to their former stations in the colonies, but the peace arrangement in Versailles did not allow German nationals to resume their work in Africa. The Versailles proclamation stated that German mission property should be taken over by trustees composed of persons holding the faith of the mission whose property was involved.

During the long period of the absence of resident missionaries from British Cameroon, the faith of the various Churches was kept alive by the local catechists. Before the last Basel missionary, the Rev. Reinhold Rohde, left the Cameroons Province, he ordained the local catechist, Johannes Litumbe Ekesse, to whom he commended the Basel Mission Church in the whole territory. Pastor Ekesse was assisted in the running of the Basel Church by many catechists and evangelists in the interior stations. Among those Basel Mission catechists frequently mentioned in the grassfields hinterland were Johannes Nkosu, Johannes Mossi, Johannes Asili and Jacob Shu. These catechists received a great deal of encouragement from visiting ordained ministers from French Cameroon. In the early 1920s, for example, the Rev. Pastor Baertschi visited Nyasoso from Ndunge and helped the catechists there to solve their problems. In 1922 Rev. Pastor Frey from Foumban began visiting the Basel Churches in the grassfields. Rev. Pastor Allegret, a regular visitor to the Presbytery in the British territory, was able to persuade the reluctant British Resident in Buea to allow ordained Protestant missionaries to continue to visit the Basel stations more regularly. Thus in 1921 it was reported that the Protestant Churches in British Cameroon were much indebted to the French Protestant missionaries in Douala who visited them occasionally and sent a native pastor to itinerate and supervise.

The Basel Mission continued to depend on local catechists and visiting missionaries until 1925 when the British authorities allowed the German missionaries to return to their stations in British Cameroon. When German missionaries arrived, they were amazed that the injury done to the church in the Cameroons Province by the absence of resident missionaries had been repaired by the local catechists and the visiting pastors. Between 1925 and 1940, the German Basel missionaries increased both their mission stations and the number of converts. Shortly before the outbreak of the Second World War, they had mission stations with resident pastors at Victoria, Bombe, Nyasoso, Esosong, Dikume, Besongabang, Fotabe, Bali-Nyonga, Mbengwi, Kishong, Wee and Bafut. They also had 53 European missionaries, 25 of whom were ordained, 504 African assistants and 31 981 mission adherents. Because of their long absence the Catholic Mission had overtaken them in the number of converts. In 1940 the German missionaries were again removed from the territory and interned in Jamaica. Further damage was again done to the Basel Mission in the Cameroons Province.

The second Church to suffer great inconvenience as a result of the war and the long absence of resident ordained missionaries from British Cameroon was the Catholic Church. Although the Catholic Mission did not have even a single native ordained priest in the Cameroons Province during the interim, before the arrival of permanent missionaries, it was much more fortunate than the Protestant Churches. There were many reasons for this. First, while in their internment camps in Rio Muni and Fernando Po, the expelled German missionaries continued to teach doctrine and to baptise hundreds of Cameroonians (conscript soldiers and their wives and carriers) who had accompanied the German military command into detention. In 1919 all the Cameroonians returned to their country, most of them already Catholic Christians or deeply indoctrinated catechumens. Those repatriated to the Cameroons Province swelled the number of converts in their groups of origin and also brought courage and hope to the few converts who were being persecuted by the traditional authorities. Second, the major Catholic stations in the Cameroons Province were visited more regularly by priests from Nigeria and French Cameroon than were Protestant stations. We can list among the priests who visited regularly Fathers Joseph Shanahan and James Mallet from Nigeria, and Fathers Douvry, Retter and William Bintner from French Cameroon.

Third, the local Catholic Church stations had a much more committed and determined group of catechists and early Christians than did other Churches. Amongst other leading catechists were Mathias Effiem, who for a long time was in charge of the Church in Victoria Division; Gabriel Lifaka of Bojongo; Pius Epie of Baseng in Kumba Division; Michael Tim of Njinikom; and Paul Mbiybe Tangwa and Andreas Ngah of Nso. What has been said of early white missionaries applies to these pioneer catechists. They dedicated their entire lives in single-minded devotion to the Church, usually in the face of heavy odds including the risk of death. Fourth, from 1920 to 1922 when the Mill Hill Fathers arrived to take charge in the Cameroons Province, some of the Catholic priests in Dschang, Nkongsamba, Douala and Foumban extended their parishes, as it were, to include neighbouring mission stations in the British territory. The last reason is that the period of 'orphanage' was shorter for the Catholic Mission than for the Protestants. For these reasons, the Catholic Mission increased its converts manyfold and overtook all the Protestant Missions put together in the Cameroons Province.

The period of 'orphanage' for the Catholic Church came to an end on 26 March 1922. On that Sunday morning four pioneer Fathers of the Mill Hill Missionary Society landed in Victoria. They were: Joseph William Campling, Benedict Robinson, Michael Moran and William O'Kelly. They were posted by Father Campling, their leader, to Bojongo, Sasse and Kumbo in the grassfields. Father Campling himself took charge in Soppo, Buea. On 16 August 1923 the Apostolic Prefecture of Buea was created with Fr Campling as its first Prefect and Suffragan Bishop to the See of Onitsha in Nigeria. Many more Mill Hill Fathers continued to arrive in the Cameroons Province from 1923 onwards. By the time of the outbreak of the Second World War the Roman Catholic Mission had resident priests, often a parish priest and an assistant, at Tiko, Bota, Bojongo, Sasse, Soppo, Kumba, Ikassa, Baseng, Okoyong, Mbo, Mankon, Njinikom and Shisong. In 1936 the Mission had a total of 34 ordained priests, 12 European Reverend Sisters, 269 catechists and 36 084 mission adherents. It was the largest Christian Church in the Cameroons Province.

The third and last Mission which suffered hardship as a result of the removal of German missionaries from British Cameroon was the Baptist Mission. It was not until 1927 that the German Baptist missionaries resumed work in the Cameroons Province. It was in that year that the Baptist Mission had a European missionary in charge for the first time since the war. The English Baptist Mission at Victoria continued its autonomous existence under the leadership of African pastors, although it eventually accepted supervision by the American Baptists.

Medical and health services

During the period of German rule Cameroon made great progress in the development of modern medical and health services. Hospitals and other medical centres were established in different parts of the territory. But during the hostilities of the First World War, the retreating German medical staff destroyed some of the hospitals and removed or destroyed medical equipment in all the centres. The Allied Forces medical staff succeeded in repairing and using some of the medical centres and hospitals for the treatment of the sick and wounded troops. At the end of the Cameroon campaign the British military administration received no formal instructions on the establishment of medical posts in British Cameroon, and almost the entire personnel of the Royal Army Medical Corps left the Cameroons Province shortly after the partition of the territory. Before long, however, medical posts which later became hospitals were established in the four divisions of the Province and a handful of doctors and junior medical officers who had served with the expeditionary force were appointed to them.

There were three bodies directly concerned with the organisation of medical and health services in British Southern Cameroons during the period between the wars. These were the government, the missions and the Native Authorities. At the head of the entire medical establishment in the territory was the Director of Medical and Sanitary Services who was resident in Lagos, and much later in Enugu. Towards the end of the mandate period, the Medical and Sanitary Services were separated and each placed under a director. The government, the missions and Native Authorities were all subject to regulations issued by the Director of Medical Services.

The British mandatory administration did not do much to improve upon the medical and health services in Cameroon. As far as the establishment and equipment of hospitals and other medical centres were concerned, the territory was almost a backwater compared with developments in Nigeria. Up until 1927 when some construction work was begun on hospitals, the administration depended entirely on the old German buildings in the divisional headquarters for medical services. Most of these buildings were no longer adequate for medical services. For example, nothing was done about the single-house government hospital in Victoria, which was always over-crowded with patients, until 1929 when the administration allocated £350 for the construction of two semi-permanent buildings to serve as wards. In Buea the old German bungalow continued to serve as a hospital until 1933 when the only resident doctor was withdrawn and attached to the tsetse-fly investigation team at Tiko. In Kumba where no resident doctor was available until 1925, the problem of hospital buildings could only be solved when the sum of £2500 was allocated for the construction of hospitals in Kumba, Mamfe and Bamenda. The Kumba hospital was completed in 1928. In 1933 an additional ward was built to make a total of three regular and one isolation wards.

In Mamfe where a resident doctor was available as early as 1917, medical services were hindered by the isolation of villages and difficult communication. To solve the problem of attending to distant patients, the doctor in Mamfe decided to establish wayside clinics along the Mamfe – Kembong, Mamfe – Tali and Mamfe – Widekum roads. In all there were eleven wayside clinics which the doctor visited regularly on specific days of the month. In Bamenda Division the two hospitals in Bamenda town and Kumbo in Nso continued to attend to patients in temporary buildings for many years. In 1928 the common-plan hospital in Bamenda was completed before being expanded in 1932 with funds provided by the Native Authority. In Nso where a medical district was created in 1923, a hospital was not established until 1925. The temporary buildings were soon improved and a medical ward, consultation rooms, an office block, a dispensary, doctor's and nurses' houses were provided with funds supplied by both the government and the Nso Native Authority. In 1929, however, the resident doctor in Nso left and was not immediately replaced.

In all, there were only six government hospitals in the Southern Cameroons between the wars providing medical services for an estimated 500 000 inhabitants. Statistics show that in 1938 the government medical and health services in the Cameroons Province were run by six medical doctors, one nursing sister, thirty-one nurses, six dispensers, one sanitary superintendent, five sanitary inspectors, and twenty-six other medical personnel. All the hospitals and dispensaries lacked the necessary personnel, equipment and drugs for effective work. The sanitary department which functioned as a preventive service was responsible for vaccinations. Sanitary inspectors made regular visits to villages and houses to insist on personal hygiene and the destruction of such disease-carrying insects as bed-bugs, lice, mosquitoes and tsetse-flies.

Missionary medical and health services in British Cameroon were insignificant before 1928. What existed until then were dispensaries for the converts of the particular denomination. Some or all of these dispensaries were either unknown to the government or known but unrecognised as adequate for medical services. After 1928 missionary medical activities were accelerated and health centres began to be established according to the conditions laid down by the government. Those mission medical institutions which met government requirements were to qualify for health subsidies. The major requirements concerned the training of medical personnel and the provision of medical services to the general public rather than solely to the converts of the denomination.

But it was not until 1934 that the government really began to give subsidies to the missions for medical purposes. Although these subsidies were meagre and irregular, they nevertheless stimulated missionary medical activities in all the divisions of the Cameroons Province. Thus the Basel Mission was able to improve upon the services in their best-run dispensary in Victoria from 1936, and also established medical centres at Nyasoso, Bali and Bafut. The German Baptist Mission operated a popular dispensary at Soppo, and others at Ndu and Mbirnkan in the grassfields. The Catholic Mission ran a small dispensary at Sasse and orphanages and welfare clinics at Okoyong and Shisong. The Catholic orphanages and welfare clinics were run by religious sisters with superior nursing qualifications. In 1939 the maternity and natal clinic services, which had been greatly neglected by the government, were introduced in Shisong. These two services became so popular that Shisong had 240 children in their orphanage in 1939 and also registered 220 deliveries in the same year.

Native Authorities took charge of medical and health services in the remote areas of the division which were inaccessible because of bad roads or were affected by epidemics. They established and ran dispensaries, and often provided additional funds for construction work or purchase of equipment and drugs in government hospitals. When the problem of providing maternity and child welfare clinics continued to be neglected by the government, Native Authorities attempted to solve it by training their own midwives and welfare officers in Nigerian institutions to run those services in their districts. Native Authorities also provided sanitary services in their localities.

Their dressers, dispensers and vaccinators frequently toured the villages attending to patients, vaccinating against epidemics, and insisting on personal and public hygiene. Native Authorities medical staff, few of them holders of the primary school certificate, were trained in the divisional hospitals in the province. Refresher courses were frequently organised for the mobile staff.

The British Northern Cameroons 1916-45

As already mentioned, Britain administered Cameroon as an integral part of the Colony and Protectorate of Nigeria which was divided, for administrative purposes, into the Northern Group of Provinces and the Southern Group of Provinces, or Northern and Southern Nigeria respectively. Thus the territory of British Cameroon which lay along the eastern frontier of Northern and Southern Nigeria was naturally divided into Northern and Southern Cameroons, each of which was added to the Nigerian group of provinces to which it geographically belonged. Northern Cameroons with an area of 44 928 square kilometres was therefore administratively tied to Northern Nigeria; it was also entirely separated from the administration in the Southern Cameroons. The territory, unlike Southern Cameroons, did not constitute a single administrative entity. On the contrary, it was fragmented into three parts and attached to the three Northern Nigeria provinces of Bornu, Adamawa and Benue. Northern Cameroons was not even a whole territory by itself due to a gap of 72 kilometres between northern and southern Adamawa, in the River Benue Basin.

British administration of Northern Cameroons was based on the system of indirect rule already very successfully applied in Northern Nigeria. In extending the system to Northern Cameroons, the British found the peoples of the northern part of the territory much more suitable for it than those of the south. The reason for this is that the northern part was occupied by groups with centralised traditional administrations under the emirates of Bornu, Mandara, Dikwa and Yola. The southern peoples, on the contrary, were largely non-Islamised, widely dispersed, had weaker traditions of centralised rule, and shunned Fulbe overlordship. These peoples proved less receptive to indirect rule than those of the north. In any event, local administration was conducted by district heads whose responsibilities included the collection of taxes, the maintenance of peace, the enforcement of laws, the supply of information on the district, and conducting censuses.

Compared with the Southern Cameroons, which constituted an administrative province in Southern Nigeria, Northern Cameroons was a developmental backwater of British rule in Northern Nigeria. Little or no efforts were made to develop the territory economically or in any other way. Neither agriculture nor animal husbandry was stimulated, and investment was neither encouraged nor obtained. Education, which was largely in the hands of Christian denominations, was retarded by the resistance of Moslems to Christian activity in the territory. Throughout the mandate period, Northern Cameroons was totally neglected, remained poor, isolated, and dominated by the emirates.

Further reading

Prosser Gifford and W.R. Louis (eds), *Britain and Germany in Africa: Imperial Rivalry and Colonial Rule* (Yale University Press, New Haven, 1967).

Austin Langmia Forkusam, *The Evolution of Health Services in the Southern Cameroons Under British Administration 1916 – 45* (DES Dissertation, Yaounde, 1978).

Victor T. LeVine, *The Cameroons From Mandate to Independence* (University of California Press, Berkeley and Los Angeles, 1964).

Sir F.D. Lugard, *The Dual Mandate in Tropical Africa* (William Blackwood, London, 1923).

Kenneth Robinson and Frederick Madden (eds), *Essays in Imperial Government* (Basil Blackwell, Oxford, 1963).

Ralph Shram, *A History of Nigerian Health Services* (Ibadan University Press, Ibadan, 1971).

Questions

1. What is 'indirect rule'? How was 'indirect rule' organised in the British Southern Cameroons during the mandate period?
2. Why did British nationals refuse to buy the captured German estates in Cameroon when they were put up for auction in London in 1923 and 1924?
3. How was education organised in the British Southern Cameroons during the mandate period?
4. Discuss the problems of the different Christian Missions in the Southern Cameroons from 1916 onward and how they were solved.

Chapter eight

The Second World War and the trusteeship system

The Second World War began in Europe on 1 September 1939 when the German Chancellor, Adolf Hitler, invaded Poland. On 3 September, both the British and French Governments separately demanded German withdrawal from Poland by 11 a.m. and 5 p.m. respectively. Hitler rejected both ultimatums and the two governments declared war on Germany the same day.

The Second World War, though a European conflict, touched Cameroon very closely. Long before the invasion of Poland, Germany had denounced the Treaty of Versailles and laid claim on her former colonies, including Cameroon. This chapter will study Cameroon during the long war, from the German claims to the international trusteeship system.

Germany's claims on Cameroon

The Versailles Treaty of 1919 had attempted to prevent German nationals from returning to their former colonies by empowering Allied and mandatory powers to retain or liquidate all German property within their colonial territories. The French Government followed the terms of the Treaty to the letter and by 1925 had disposed of all former German property in French Cameroon. None of the property disposed of was sold to the Germans. This achievement almost entirely precluded the return of the Germans to the French mandated territory. Eventually, after September 1926

when Germany was admitted to the League of Nations, Germans were allowed to return to French Cameroon to work with the various French, British and German trading companies that had dealings in Douala and Kribi. In any event, by 1938, the number of German nationals in French Cameroon was hardly more than sixty.

The situation was different in British Cameroon where large German estates and enterprises had been established. Although two auctions were organised in London in 1922 and 1924 to dispose of these estates and enterprises, neither the British government nor British business companies were anxious to acquire and own ex-enemy property. Perhaps the major reason for this was the uncertainty over the security of tenure. During the second auction His Majesty's Government decided to remove the restrictions earlier placed on German nationals. As a result, almost all the estates and enterprises were bought by their original owners. This outcome led to the massive return of German nationals to British Cameroon. In 1938 there were 285 German nationals, including 56 female adults and 29 children resident in British Southern Cameroons (compared with only 86 British including 16 female adults and 4 children). This number does not include frequent visitors who came and went during the year.

The massive return of Germans to British Cameroon and their popularity with their employees and former workers, who favoured a return of the German administration, probably encouraged Germany's claims to her former protectorate. It will be recalled that by Article 119 of the Versailles Treaty Germany had renounced her rights and titles over her overseas possessions in favour of principal Allied and Associated Powers. But that renunciation was imposed rather than negotiated. The Germans had petitioned the peacemakers without success that colonial questions be handed over to a Commission of Inquiry and that Germany be allowed to administer her former colonies as mandates of the League. In 1923 Adolf Hitler who was serving a prison term after an abortive Nazi *putsch* in Munich denounced the Versailles Treaty, saying that for as long as it stood, Germany would never recover its former strength. He demanded that the Treaty be abrogated and that land and soil (including the colonies) be made available to feed the United German nation. Hitler's denunciation of Versailles and demand for land and soil to feed the nation began Germany's campaign to regain her overseas territories.

In October 1925, the German Minister of Foreign Affairs, Dr Gustav Stresemann, officially raised the issue of Germany's former colonies at the Locarno Conference. The following year, on 8 September, Germany was admitted to the League of Nations where, again, she raised the issue of her former colonies. From that year onward, attention began to be focused on these territories, as important figures in the German Government began to feature prominently in the activities of organisations demanding their repossession. After Adolf Hitler became Chancellor on 30 January 1933, the German Government openly made the return of colonies an official policy aim. Hitler personally made sure that colonial claims formed a key part in his speeches.

The German campaign for the recovery of Cameroon and her other lost colonies was centred on some five major arguments. The first argument was that as an imperial power, Germany deserved colonial rights and aspirations. The Germans claimed that the restoration of equality between Germany and the other European imperial powers could only come through Germany re-acquiring her colonies. The second argument advanced by the Germans was that their nation needed colonies to receive surplus population from overpopulated Germany. Thirdly, Germany needed colonies for basic resources to feed her people and supply her industries: in other words, Germany needed colonies for food and raw materials. The fourth argument was that Germany needed colonies to enhance her prestige which had shamefully been lowered by the terms of the Versailles Settlement in favour of her arch-rivals Britain and France. Finally, the Germans argued that Germany merited colonies because she was perfectly able to govern them. They directed the attention of the civilised nations to the values of German civilisation and to ways in which these would be beneficial to the uncivilised communities of Africa.

The German campaigners brought pressure to bear on Britain and France over their claims in Cameroon. This pressure, which made the French in particular feel insecure in Cameroon, led to the realisation that it would serve French purposes to allow Cameroonians to organise freely and to speak out against the return of their country to Germany. This resulted in the formation of an organisation known as *Union Camerounaise* in Paris in 1937. The programme of this organisation, which we shall come to later, included two major demands: namely that Cameroon should not be returned to Germany, and that Cameroon should be transferred from the B to the A mandate. Another organisation known as *Jeunesse Camerounaise Française* was established in Cameroon in 1938 to lead and voice Cameroonian 'public opinion' against German propaganda. The French saw this latter organisation as an effective instrument of anti-German propaganda which would demonstrate that the people of Cameroon did not approve the idea of joining the Nazi Republic. The British were lukewarm about Germany's campaign for the recovery of her lost colonies. It can be said in conclusion that although it appeared at certain times that

Britain and France were willing to relinquish Cameroon and other mandated territories in an attempt to satisfy Hitler's insatiable territorial demands, the two powers had not come to terms with the German Chancellor on the question by the outbreak of the Second World War in 1939.

The immersion of Britain and France in the war

The rise of Adolf Hitler to power and his determination to bring German minorities outside the German state into the Reich precipitated the outbreak of the Second World War. It all began in February 1938 when Chancellor Hitler lamented that because of the 'mad act of Versailles' over ten million Germans lived in two of the states adjoining Germany's frontiers. The following month Germany annexed Austria and encouraged the German minority in Czechoslovakia to demand the delimitation of German areas with full autonomy and to order reparations for all damages suffered by them since 1918. In August Hitler claimed that the misery of the Sudeten Germans in Czechoslovakia was indescribable and that the Czech Government was seeking to annihilate them. In mid-March 1939 Hitler employed alleged new anti-German activities as an excuse for invading Czechoslovakia. This was followed by the annexation of Memel and demands upon Poland regarding Danzig and the Province of Permoze. On August 29 the German Government announced that 'only a few hours remained' for the right solution to be found to the Polish problem. At 7.15 p.m. on the same day Germany demanded that a fully-empowered Polish emissary should humbly present itself in Berlin the following day and sign proposals for a solution to the Polish – German problem. No authorised Polish representative appeared in Berlin. Germany now had reason to invade Poland.

Meanwhile, during the summer of 1939, more likely as a result of Hitler's preposterous demands and invasion of weak states, new international alliances began to form. Britain and France negotiated mutual assistance pacts with Turkey, Rumania and Greece and formalised their commitment to lend Poland effective support in the event of any action which clearly threatened her independence. Germany, on her part, agreed with Italy to enlarge the Berlin – Rome Axis into a full political and military alliance and to negotiate non-aggression agreements with Denmark, Estonia, Latvia and Russia.

The Second World War broke out in Europe on 1 September 1939, when at 5.45 a.m. Germany began an invasion of Poland. Cameroon was hardly affected by that invasion which, with the assistance of the Soviet Union, led to the collapse of Poland in less than one month. But Britain and France, the two mandatory powers in Cameroon, were worried about the invasion of Poland and declared war on Germany shortly after the invasion began. After successfully occupying Poland, the German Chancellor offered peace to Britain and France. The offer was rejected. On 9 April 1940, Germany followed her successes in Poland with an invasion of Denmark and Norway which quickly capitulated. On 10 May Germany began a blitz attack upon France via the Low Countries. The Netherlands capitulated on 15 May and Belgium on 28 May. On 10 June Italy entered the war on the side of Germany, with whom she combined to invade France. On 21 June 1940, France shocked the world by her humiliating capitulation.

The fall of France brought Germany very close to recovering Cameroon and other lost colonies. Hitler had become master of the mainland of Western Europe. France, which might have been counted upon as a power which could meet Hitler's forces on equal terms, lay defeated. The only hope for her recovery lay in the 'Free French' forces of General Charles A.J.M. de Gaulle who had fled to England and established his base in London. France itself was divided between the German-occupied portion and an unoccupied zone under Marshal Henri Phillippe Pétain. General de Gaulle, however, continued to refuse to accept the defeat of France and to declare that France had lost a battle, not the war.

Great Britain, the other mandatory power in Cameroon, stood alone in Western Europe against Hitler. Several weeks before the fall of France the British Prime Minister, Winston Churchill, had sounded a clarion call for total war against what he described as 'a monstrous tyranny'. Churchill told his people and all the peoples of the British Empire and of other democracies that his government's policy was to wage war by sea, land and air with all the might and the strength that God could give until victory was achieved.

In August 1940 the 'Battle of Britain' began with fierce German attacks on British shipping and cities. Hitler hoped to terrorise Britain to surrender or, failing that, to weaken Britain's defences so as to make it possible for German ground forces to land and occupy the country. He failed to achieve either of these objectives. That failure marked the first important setback for Germany, which was ultimately to lose the war. The failure also raised the hopes of General de Gaulle's 'Free French' forces everywhere that all was not lost, and encouraged Britain and France to believe that Cameroon and other mandated territories might not revert to Germany.

The collapse of France and developments in Cameroon

The humiliating surrender of France to Hitler's invading forces in June 1940 led to a number of developments in the mandated territories of Cameroon. The pro-German puppet government of Marshal Pétain failed to gain the loyalty of Cameroonians. This was in spite of the fact that by the end of 1940 all the territories of French Equatorial Africa excepting Chad had sworn allegiance to Pétain. For a while, French Cameroon, like Chad and some other French overseas possessions, was stranded and without direction before General de Gaulle's resistance French Committee of National Liberation (the 'Free French') was organised

in London. The indigenous elite and the majority of French settlers in Cameroon found it easier to resist than to accept the pro-German Vichy regime. Cameroonians were convinced that capitulation would mean the eventual incorporation of their country into Hitler's empire. Marshal Pétain even sent two envoys to Cameroon: the first, Rear-Admiral Planton, to enforce obedience to Vichy and the second, Inspector of Colonies Huet, to set up a pro-Vichy regime. The one was snubbed and the other's plans were upset.

The Commissioner of the French Republic in Cameroon, Richard Brunot, began to seek ways of safeguarding Cameroon from the hands of both Marshal Pétain and Hitler. First, Commissioner Brunot tried to form an African bloc of loyal or anti-German French African possessions to repudiate the armistice in France and continue the war in Africa. Second, he held meetings with British representatives in French Cameroon and organised public meetings at which the determination of the people to continue the struggle was reaffirmed. Third, Commissioner Brunot took steps to institute an independent Council of Government, and to form a military and economic alliance with British Nigeria. Finally he supported the possibility, which the British Government was contemplating seriously, of occupying and protecting French Cameroon from both Vichy France and the Nazis. In fact, in July 1940, he intimated to the Governor-General of Nigeria, Sir Bernard Bourdillon, that there should be a token assumption of the mandate by the British.

For some time in July and August 1940, the British authorities in London were ready to cooperate with Commissioner Brunot and take over the administration of French Cameroon through the government of Nigeria. Their justification was that the French government was no longer in a position to carry out its mandatory obligations, that assumption of control by His Majesty's Government was the only means of preserving the status of the territory, and that the inhabitants of French Cameroon also desired such a takeover.

9 *Colonel Philippe Leclerc*

The British plans for French Cameroon were still at the planning stage when new developments overtook them. In August envoys of General de Gaulle arrived in Cameroon and upset the plans of the Vichy administration. On the night of 26 August 1940, the British authorities in Nigeria and British Southern Cameroons helped Colonel (later General) Philippe Leclerc and twenty-four companions to sail from Tiko to Douala. Assisted in Douala by the British local representative and by a group of partisans, Leclerc successfully took over the administration of the town and rallied the population to General de Gaulle. Leclerc at once dispatched two companies of riflemen to Yaounde where the Vichy emissaries were still creating a state of uncertainty. Leclerc's riflemen captured the town without a fight. Colonel Leclerc then notified General de Gaulle in England that Cameroon had fallen to him. On

8 October 1940, General de Gaulle himself landed in Douala to symbolise Free French victory in Black Africa. Leclerc left Yaounde after several months, turning the administration over to Free French civilian officials.

With French Cameroon securely in General de Gaulle's camp, the peoples of British and French Cameroon began to contribute enthusiastically to the Allied war effort. Some made cash contributions to the British or Free French War Funds. In 1941, for example, the people of Bamenda Division contributed £181.15.0d. to the British War Fund. In the various parts of the Cameroons Province and French Cameroon many people were spontaneously volunteering for active service in the British Royal West African Frontier Force (RWAFF), or the Free French forces. Thousands of these volunteers trekked from British Cameroon to recruitment centres in parts of Eastern and Northern Nigeria and many more were recruited within the territory. In French Cameroon thousands volunteered to join Colonel Leclerc's forces against the Italians in Libya. Many from British Cameroon saw active service in Palestine and in Burma. The great enthusiasm to enlist in the Allied forces was irrespective of the fact that Cameroonians were not required by the terms of the mandate to undertake military service. Recruitment was voluntary and no pressure was exerted on any Cameroonian to enlist. In 1942 General de Gaulle returned to Cameroon to thank Cameroonians for their sacrifice on behalf of France. He assured the people of French Cameroon that the future of their territory in the new French Empire appeared extremely promising.

Although there was much enthusiasm for the British and French war efforts, many anti-French Cameroonians suspected of pro-German sympathies suffered great repression. Throughout the period before the outbreak of the war, many inhabitants of French Cameroon had demonstrated in various ways their dislike of French rule. Some had petitioned the League of Nations and others, like the members of the Native Church in Douala, had staged public demonstrations against the administration. Those who had served under the Germans recalled nostalgically these earlier days. Some of these latter who could speak, read and write German had formed German-speaking clubs where they met frequently to sing and socialise. Besides, the return of the Germans to their businesses in Cameroon from 1925 onward had created a favourable climate for the revival of the German language and increasing admiration for German ways. It was even believed in the 1930s that the Germans were more popular in their former protectorate than they had ever been during their period of rule. With the outbreak of the war, the fear felt by the French on the German question led to the persecution of anyone who identified with anything German.

The French employed severe measures, including imprisonment and even execution, to put an end to pro-German sympathies in Cameroon during the Second World War. Those who had formed societies of German-speakers or demonstrated their ability to speak German were arrested and imprisoned. The mere fact of speaking German rather than French, and thus being able to communicate or correspond with the enemy, was held to be dangerous to the security of the territory. In 1940 an organisation which sent intelligence reports to the German authorities at Fernando Po was discovered, and Cameroonians connected with this in both the British and French territories were arrested, interrogated, molested and detained in Douala. In 1941, seventy-one Cameroonians were brought to trial in Douala on charges of collaborating with the Germans and conducting anti-French propaganda. Those convicted were given severe sentences, often up to ten years with hard labour. On 19 March 1941, Dikongue Theordore Meeton was sentenced to death and executed by the French for allegedly communicating and conniving with the Germans in Fernando Po.

The Second World War became genuinely global when Japan joined the Berlin – Rome Axis, attacked Pearl Harbor on the Hawaiian island of Oahu, and declared war on the United States and the British Empire on 7 December 1941. Italy and Germany and their puppet-states also declared war on the United States during the winter of 1941 – 42. The United States in return declared war on Japan on 8 December 1941, and reciprocally against the other Axis Powers. On 1 January 1942, twenty-six nations representing Europe, Asia and both Americas signed an agreement in Washington pledging to use all their resources to defeat the Axis Powers. But the war dragged on until 1945. On 6 June 1944, Allied troops began landing in France and by October had succeeded in driving the bulk of the German forces out of that country. On 23 October, the Allied Governments recognised the provisional government of General de Gaulle in France. On 4 May 1945, the German resistance collapsed and on 8 May, a representative of the German High Command signed an Act of Military Surrender. The war ended on 2 September 1945, when Japan signed the surrender accepting unconditionally the Potsdam Declaration.

The Brazzaville Conference of 1944

The French African Conference at Brazzaville, better known as the Brazzaville Conference, was convened from 30 January to 8 February 1944 at the instance of General de Gaulle. Its aim was to discuss French colonial policy, and particularly French policy in sub-Saharan Africa, even though at the time mainland France was still occupied by enemy forces. The Conference was presided over by General de Gaulle himself.

For many good reasons, de Gaulle and his Free French Committee of National Liberation attached a great deal of importance to the Brazzaville Conference. In the first place, the Conference was meant to be a tribute to sub-Saharan French African territories which served as Free French soil, untouched by German forces, after the fall of France in 1940. Secondly, Cameroon and many other French African territories did not hesitate to accept

General de Gaulle's declaration that France had only lost a battle and not the war, and rallied to his support by the end of August 1940. In fact Chad and Cameroon were the first territories in Africa to respond officially to de Gaulle's appeal for support. Thirdly, Cameroon and the countries of French Equatorial Africa were the first to begin supporting the Free French war effort by supplying men and material for General Leclerc's campaigns in North Africa. Finally, Africa's confidence in France and in de Gaulle's leadership, and the readiness of Africans to regard themselves as Frenchmen and fight for France's liberation after 1940 salvaged French self-respect and restored France's confidence in herself. For all these reasons, the importance of Africa to France had increased, and its inhabitants deserved to be treated better than ever before. The Brazzaville Conference was therefore a forum for discussing new French colonial policies to be adopted in Africa after the war. It was of course clear that the conclusions reached at Brazzaville would influence French colonial policy everywhere. Cameroon was to benefit immensely from the resulting recommendations.

Official representation at the Conference was restricted to Black Africa. Participants included a delegation of the Free French Committee led by General de Gaulle, French colonial governors and officials, parliamentarians, a few trade unionists, and a bishop. There were observers representing the French colonial governors of Algeria, Morocco and Tunisia. No African was invited and the only official black person attending was the Governor-General of French Equatorial Africa, Felix Eboue, a native of French Guiana. Brazzaville was therefore a meeting of Frenchmen to discuss new colonial policies for Africa.

The recommendations made at Brazzaville ranged over a wide field and fell into three groups: social, economic and political. The social reforms proposed were to affect immediately the great majority of Africans. Respect for, and the progress of, African life was to be the foundation of France's entire colonial policy. The indigenous African would no more be subject to eviction and drudgery. On the question of citizenship the advanced notable, *notable évolué*, status already in practice in Equatorial Africa, would be a model for all African territories. The hated *indigénat* or summary punishment for Africans would be abolished at the end of the war and a new uniform penal code introduced. A pension scheme and a six-day 48-hour working week would be established. Trade unionism would be given offical encouragement. The absolute superiority of the freedom of labour to come into practice after five years was unanimously affirmed. Labour Inspection Services would be established with a view to regulate work for Africans, and medical and health services would be greatly expanded and improved. The educational system would remain basically French in character. Educated Africans would be given a certain measure of administrative and economic freedom, and their responsibility would be gradually increased so that they could participate in the management of public affairs in their own territory.

In the economic domain the Conference recommended that measures such as state aid to the industries and the rapid extension of education which would involve the expenditure in Africa of considerable sums of French public money should be encouraged. A definite plan of development of the colonies should also be drawn up. During the fifteen years between the end of the war and the independence of most states the economic and social recommendations transformed the French African colonial slums into an area with the basic infrastructure of a modern developing economy.

In the political sphere Brazzaville made far-reaching, though seemingly timid, recommendations. The Conference made it clear that the French African territories were indissolubly linked to metropolitan France and that Africa would be represented in a new Federal Assembly for France and its Empire. In addition Africans would be represented in the French Constituent Assembly to draw up a constitution for the Fourth Republic. There would also be representative assemblies in each colony elected by universal suffrage under two electoral colleges, one for Africans and another for Europeans. Africans would be given the citizenship of the Empire rather than of France. The idea of self-government in the colonies, even in the distant future, and the possibility of evolution outside the French imperial bloc would not be entertained. The future of the colonies, it was affirmed, lay with France, and France alone. The political power of France would be exercised with precision and rigour in all the imperial lands.

The Brazzaville recommendations were all realised in substance within five years of the Conference. In Cameroon, a decree of 7 January 1944, anticipated those on labour reform. It required that a number of administrative officials and medical doctors be enrolled as labour inspectors; it applied French regulations to local working hours, established a social security scheme, and forbade the practice of paying workers in kind. After the Conference, a new system of recruitment and training for colonial administrators was introduced. A new and uniform native penal code for Africa was published, and the various systems of native customary jurisdiction were soon drastically reorganised. Taxation in kind and forced labour were abolished. Authorisation was given for the formation of trade unions. The *indigénat, prestation*, and distinction between *citoyens* and *sujets* were abolished. The inhabitants of Cameroon were placed on the same footing as French citizens, at least in the enjoyment of civil liberties. From 1946 France under the Fourth Republic created new political institutions and allowed Africans to participate in them.

From the mandates to the trusteeship system

It can reasonably be argued that the League of Nations and the mandates system which it set up and under which Cameroon was administered during the period between the wars, came

to an abrupt end with the outbreak of the Second World War in 1939. But the League and the mandates system were not officially and effectively replaced until the end of the war and the establishment of the United Nations Organisation (UNO) and its Trusteeship System in 1945. Between the two events, that is from the collapse of the League to the formation of the UNO, Cameroon and other territories which were administered under the mandates system reverted to the actual, if not legal, possession of the mandatories. With the fall of France in June 1940 Cameroon and other French-administered territories overseas were stranded for some time without a colonial administering authority. Thus when the emissaries of General de Gaulle established control and loyalty to Free France in August 1940, and French authority in Cameroon was re-established, that authority was no longer controlled by the Permanent Mandates Commission of the League of Nations, but fell under the French themselves.

Indications that the League of Nations and its auxiliary organisations had come or were really coming to an end were first given on 14 August 1941 and 1 January 1942. On the first date President Franklin Delano Roosevelt of the United States and Prime Minister Winston Churchill of the United Kingdom met aboard warships in the North Atlantic and produced the 'Atlantic Charter' which called for the establishment of a wider and permanent system of general security in the world. Their apparent intention was to internationalise and inspire the ideological drive of the democratic front. On the second date twenty-six states representing Europe, Asia and the Americas met in Washington and signed a 'United Nations' agreement accepting the provisions of the Atlantic Charter and pledging to use all their resources to defeat the Axis Powers of Germany, Italy and Japan and their satellite states. The signatory governments agreed that other nations rendering material assistance and contributions to the struggle for victory over Hitlerism might adhere to the Washington accord. With the 'Atlantic Charter' and the

'United Nations' declarations, the way was opened for the formation of the UNO.

On 30 October 1943, the United Kingdom, the United States and the Soviet Union (the 'Big Three') together with China met in Moscow and recognised, in accordance with the 'United Nations' declaration of 1 January 1942, the necessity of establishing at the earliest practicable date a general international organisation based on the principle of the sovereign equality of all peace-loving states, for the maintenance of international peace and security. By the end of the war in 1945, the number of states that had accepted and joined the Washington 'United Nations' declaration had risen from twenty-six to fifty-one. These nations created a number of organisations for maintaining peace and binding up the wounds of war. Among these was the world security organisation, the UNO under a newly-drawn Charter, to prevent the recurrence of war, strengthen the will of peace, and promote social justice.

The conference which resulted in the formation of UNO met at San Francisco, United States, from 25 April to 26 June 1945, with delegates representing 50 nations. The French delegation to the Conference included a Cameroonian, Prince Alexander Douala Manga Bell. The San Francisco delegates debated and agreed on a Charter to establish a United Nations Organisation. The Charter was then submitted to member states for approval. By 24 October 1945, the requisite number of nations had ratified the Charter and the United Nations Organisation came into existence. On that date the League of Nations was juridically replaced, although other meetings of the Conference continued until 18 April 1946.

The UNO Charter provided among its six instruments the creation of the Trusteeship Council to supervise the international trusteeship for dependent states. Such dependent states, to be referred to as trust territories, would include territories which might be detached from enemy states as a result of the Second World War, and territories voluntarily placed under the system by states responsible for their administration.

Among the basic objectives of the trusteeship system spelt out in the UN Charter was the promotion of the political, economic, social and educational advancement of the peoples of the trust territories, and their progressive development towards self-government or independence.

Cameroon, which was held under mandate, was to become a trust territory. The terms of the trusteeship for territories held under mandate were to be agreed upon by the directly concerned mandatory power. In fulfilment of this clause, the United Kingdom and France, which were now the UN Administering Authorities in Cameroon, were invited in January 1946 to submit their Trusteeship Agreements to the Organisation for approval. The two Authorities submitted agreements which were similar but not identical in content. On 13 December 1946, the General Assembly of the UN approved the Trusteeship Agreement for France. France had sent Prince Alexander Douala Manga Bell and Dr Louis-Paul Aujoulat from Cameroon among their delegation to defend France's Trusteeship Agreement for Cameroon.

Trusteeship agreements for French and British Cameroon

The Second World War brought into existence the United Nations and the trusteeship system as replacements for the defunct League of Nations and the mandates system. Both the UN Charter and the Trusteeship Agreements laid down basic guidelines for the postwar administrative, political, economic and social developments in the trust territories. Knowledge of the essential Articles of the UN Charter relating to trust territories and the French and British Trusteeship Agreements for Cameroon, together with their contradictions and ambiguities, is necessary for an appreciation of postwar developments in the two trust territories.

Of the 110 Articles of the UN Charter, fifteen concerned the establishment of the international trusteeship system. Of those fifteen, seven are particularly worthy of examination. Article 75 lists among the four basic political objectives of the trusteeship system the promotion of the progressive development of the inhabitants of the trust territory towards self-government or independence as may be appropriate to the particular circumstances of each territory and its peoples and the freely expressed wishes of the peoples concerned. Articles 79 and 81 state that the terms of the trusteeship for each territory shall be agreed upon by the states directly concerned and shall in each case include the terms under which the trust territory will be administered. Article 85 states that the functions of the UN with regard to trusteeship agreements shall be exercised by the General Assembly and that the Trusteeship Council, operating under the authority of the General Assembly, shall assist the General Assembly in carrying out these functions. Article 86 lists the UN members of the Trusteeship Council, stating that the total number of members must be equally divided between those who administer trust territories and those who do not. Article 87 states that the functions and powers of the Trusteeship Council include consideration of reports submitted by the Administering Authority, acceptance and examination of petitions, provision of periodic visits to the respective trust territories, and formulation of a questionnaire which would be the basis of an annual report by the Administering Authority to the General Assembly.

It is clear from the articles of the UN Charter in general and those listed above in particular that the Organisation was dedicated to the principle that colonial rule must eventually come to an end everywhere. It did this by enunciating the goal of self-government for all colonial territories and the possibility of independence for the former mandates for whom a trusteeship system had been established. The UN trusteeship system, unlike the League of Nations mandates system, had stronger supervisory powers over the Administering Authorities. The acceptance of the Charter of the UN by colonial and Administer-ing Authorities in the trust territories implied acceptance of the principle of self-government or independence for all the colonial territories.

But the trusteeship system set up in the Articles of the Charter contained major ambiguous and contradictory provisions which plagued the smooth functioning of the supervisory machinery. The UN Charter established no criteria for determining which of the political objectives – self-government or independence – would be most appropriate for a colonial or trust territory. Nor did it specify whether the particular circumstances of the territory or the expressed wishes of the people concerned would take precedence in determining the political future of the particular territory. Instead of the UN leaving the day-to-day supervision of the administration of the trust territories in the hands of specialists in colonial affairs who were not representatives of their respective nations, the Organisation established as the organ of routine supervision a Trusteeship Council of national representatives in which the Administering Authorities and non-administering members had an equal number of seats. This situation provided the opportunity for colonial powers and Administering Authorities of the trust territories to prevent the Council from acting against their wishes.

The Trusteeship Council, although carrying out most of its functions under the authority of the General Assembly, in which final responsibility was placed, was, like the General Assembly, a principal organ of the UN possessing an authority of its own. The Charter provided no means for settling possible deadlocks between the General Assembly and the Trusteeship Council. The trusteeship system left the obligations of the former mandatory powers unclearly defined. The Charter did not state explicitly whether a mandatory power had obligations to place a mandate under trusteeship and/or whether it was obliged to accept any amendments which the General Assembly might propose to the terms of the trusteeship agreement. Finally, the official French version of Article 76 of the Charter listing the political objectives of colonial and trusteeship territories did not say exactly the same thing as the official English text, although both texts had equal validity. Thus potential existed for disputes to develop over interpretation of the texts.

Concerning the Trusteeship Agreements, France had very reluctantly accepted the placing of Cameroon under the trusteeship system. Having done so, she proposed a Trusteeship Agreement which was approved without amendment by the UN General Assembly on 13 December 1946. In it, the French government as Administering Authority undertook to promote the basic objectives of the trusteeship system and to collaborate fully with the General Assembly and the Trusteeship Council in the discharge of their functions. The Agreement permitted France full legislative, administrative, and jurisdictional powers in Cameroon in accordance with French law as an integral part of French territory, subject to the provisions of the Charter and the Agreement. France agreed to take measures to ensure for the local inhabitants a share in the administration of their territory and, in due course, to arrange appropriate representative democratic bodies to enable the inhabitants freely to express an opinion on their political regime. France was to take into consideration local laws and customs in framing laws relating to the holding or transfer of land; no land belonging to any native or group might be transferred except between natives. Finally, France agreed to submit an annual report to the General Assembly and to appoint a representative or qualified experts to participate in the examination of petitions received by those bodies on French administration in Cameroon.

France's Trusteeship Agreement for Cameroon appeared to take her a long way away from her original goal in the territory. But in order to pursue that original goal she insisted in the Agreement that Cameroon should be administered as an integral part of France. The French laid great emphasis on self-administration rather than self-government or independence towards which she was to direct the territories she was administering in Black Africa. She interpreted her obligations in Cameroon in such a way as to allow her to pursue the goals of trusteeship through the policy of assimilation.

The British, unlike the French, did not hesitate to accept all the provisions in the UN Charter and they willingly agreed to the formation of trusteeship over their Cameroon mandate. Their Trusteeship Agreement for Cameroon adopted all the objectives and requirements of the trust territory of Cameroon. But in doing so, the British hoped that the trusteeship would not alter their existing policy of the eventual integration of Cameroon with Nigeria. In fact, the stipulation in the Agreement that the Administering Authority was entitled to constitute Cameroon into an administrative union or federation with adjacent territories under British sovereignty or control permitted Britain to feel that little or nothing would change under the new international arrangement.

In all, the shift from the mandate to the trusteeship system marked a milestone in the political and administrative development of Cameroon. Several new elements were introduced into the process of international supervision of the administration of the trust territories. On-the-spot investigation by visiting missions elected by the UN promised to be effective in bringing pressure to bear on the Administering Authorities in Cameroon and elsewhere. The system was geared to a more extensive and somewhat more explicit set of goals, which included political advancement towards self-government or independence.

Further reading

A. Bullock (ed.), *Germany's Colonial Demands* (OUP, London, 1939).

David E. Gardiner, *Cameroon: United Nations Challenge to French Policy* (OUP, London, 1963).

F.S. Joelson, *Germany's Claims to Colonies* (Hurst and Blackett, London, 1939).

Richard Joseph, *Radical Nationalism in Cameroon* (OUP, Oxford, 1977).

Victor T. LeVine, *The Cameroons: From Mandate to Independence* (University of California Press, Berkeley and Los Angeles, 1964).

Edward Mortimer, *France and the Africans 1944–1960* (Faber and Faber, London, 1969).

Neville Rubin, *Cameroon: An African Federation* (Praeger, New York, 1971).

Raymond Phineas Stearns, *Pageant of Europe* (Harcourt, Brace & World, Inc., New York and Burlingame, 1961 Revised Edition).

Jean Suret-Canale, *French Colonialism in Tropical Africa 1900–1945* (C. Hurst & Company, London, 1964).

Questions

1. Why did Germany lay claims to and campaign to regain Cameroon and other lost colonies during the 1930s?
2. What were the consequences of the fall of France to German forces in June 1940 on Cameroon and other French colonies?
3. What efforts were made by the administration of Richard Brunot in French Cameroon, General de Gaulle's envoys and the British officials in Nigeria to prevent both the pro-German Vichy regime in France and Germany from recovering Cameroon in June 1940?
4. Discuss the achievements of the Brazzaville Conference of 1944 and their importance for Cameroon.
5. How was the trusteeship system different from the mandates system which preceded it?
6. What were the terms of the Trusteeship Agreements for French and British Cameroon?

Chapter nine

Cameroon under French rule: 1946-59

The period from 1946 to 1959 can be termed the period of decolonisation in French Cameroon. It was the period of the reluctant but gradual dissolution of French rule in the territory. The colonial reforms included in the 1946 French Constitution and the placing of Cameroon under the UN Trusteeship system were two significant events which made the dissolution of French rule possible and opened the way for the triumph of nationalism and the winning of independence in 1960. This chapter will be devoted to the study of the French in Cameroon and the administrative, political, economic and social changes that the territory underwent during this very important period in the history of Cameroon.

Cameroon and the French Constitution of 1946

One of the recommendations which emerged from the Brazzaville Conference of 1944 was that French dependencies overseas should be represented in the forthcoming French Constituent Assembly which would debate and draft a constitution that would govern relations between France and the French world. In applying that recommendation, elections to the Constituent Assembly were fixed for 21 October 1945. The thirteen territories of French Equatorial and French West Africa were grouped into eight constituencies with Cameroon, Guinea and the Ivory Coast each forming a single constituency. Each African constituency was allotted two seats, one reserved for the first college to represent the tiny European population and one for the

second college to represent the majority indigenous population. The two deputies from Cameroon to the Assembly were Dr Louis-Paul Aujoulat representing the first-college electorate and Prince Alexander Douala Manga Bell representing the African electorate. Elections to the French Constituent Assembly were the first-ever representative political elections to be held in Cameroon.

Dr Louis-Paul Aujoulat was a French physician and Catholic lay missionary who had worked mainly in the interior of Cameroon. Born in 1910 in Saida, Algeria, he studied medicine and came to Cameroon in 1936. In his capacity as lay missionary he was co-founder, and later president of the Catholic Mission society Ad Lucem. Between 1945 and 1955 he represented Cameroon in the French National Assembly. He was one of the two members from Cameroon in the French delegation to defend the French Trusteeship Agreement for Cameroon at the UN. He was Under-Secretary of State in George Bidault's cabinet and between 1949 and 1955 served as Secretary of State for Overseas Territories in the Cabinet of French Prime Minister Pierre Mendès-France. He was mainly responsible for the passage in 1952 of a new reformed Overseas Labour Code. Dr Aujoulat also served in the Cameroon Territorial Assembly between 1952 and 1956 and was the founder and chairman of the *Bloc Démocratique Camerounais*, a political party to which both the Cameroon's first Prime Minister, André-Marie Mbida, and the future first President of independent Cameroon, Ahmadou Ahidjo, belonged. Throughout his political career he was anxious to halt the spread of Marxism and 'separatism' in Cameroon and French Africa by encouraging the introduction of a genuine policy of colonial reform. He died in France in 1985 at the age of seventy-five.

Prince Alexander Douala Manga Bell (1897 – 1966), a man of considerable European culture, was a paramount chief of the Duala and a leading Cameroon politician. He was the son of King Rudolph Douala Manga Bell whom the Germans had hanged in 1914 on charges of treason. After primary education in Douala and some secondary education at the court of Wilhelm II, Prince Douala Manga Bell entered the University of Heidelberg from which he graduated *magna cum laude*. He later served as a cavalry officer in the German army. During the First World War he deserted and escaped to France where he lived until the Paris Peace Conference of 1919. He returned to Cameroon after the Conference and attempted to organise a nationalist opposition to the Anglo-French partition of the territory. He also became a major critic of the French mandatory administration. Notwithstanding that, he was highly regarded by the French, who restored to him a measure of authority and after the Second World War named him a member of their delegation to the 1945 UN Conference in San Francisco. Douala Manga Bell was elected both in 1945 and 1946 by the second-college electors to represent Cameroon in the French Constituent Assembly. He went on to win elections in 1946, 1951 and 1956 to the French National Assembly. When Cameroon became independent in 1960, he was elected a deputy to the country's first National Assembly.

The first meetings of the French Constituent Assembly to include Dr Aujoulat and Prince Douala Manga Bell began in Paris on 6 November 1945 After many months of deliberation, the draft Constitution produced by this Assembly was rejected by the French in a referendum on 5 May 1946. The following month, a second Constituent Assembly was elected, with exactly the same franchise as the previous Assembly. Dr Aujoulat and Douala Manga Bell retained their seats, the latter with an overwhelming majority. The Constitution produced by the next Constituent Assembly was unenthusiastically accepted in a second referendum on 13 October 1946. Under this Constitution France and her African dependencies were to live for the next twelve years. It served both the French Republic and the French Union.

The October Constitution of the Fourth French Republic contained many constitutional changes concerning the French administration in Africa. As far as Cameroon was concerned, the Constitution stated that unlike other dependencies which were formally included in the French Union, she would be an 'Associated Territory' of the Union because of her special position in international law as a Trust Territory of the UN. This specification, however, was merely on paper because, in practice, France continued to treat Cameroon in exactly the same way as her other overseas dependencies, that is, as an integral part of the French Union. Another provision in the Constitution was that, like other overseas territories, Cameroon would elect representatives to both houses of the French Parliament and to the Assembly of the French Union. While the deputies to the National Assembly were to be elected directly by the Cameroon electorate, those to the Council of the Republic and the Assembly of the French Union would be elected indirectly by the local representative assembly.

The greatest and most important innovation among the changes introduced by the 1946 French Constitution was the creation of a local representative assembly of Cameroon. On the basis of this constitutional provision, a law was passed on 7 October followed by a decree on 25 October 1946 provisionally establishing the *Assemblée Representative Camerounaise* (ARCAM) to which representatives would be elected on a double-college system. Although ARCAM was not given legislative powers and could not deliberate on political questions, it possessed powers to deliberate on the local budget submitted to it by the administration, and had to be consulted by the administration in a number of areas such as labour conditions, the disposition of public lands, education, and the execution of social and labour programmes.

The Constitution made all Cameroonians, as it did all the inhabitants of French overseas territories, citizens of the French Union. In doing so, however, it distinguished between citizens who were subject to French 'civil law', *citoyens de droit commun*, and citizens who preserved their 'personal status', *citoyens de statut personnel*. All the French nationals and a handful of Cameroonians who had acquired 'civil law status' were citizens in the first category; the vast majority of the indigenous inhabitants were 'personal status citizens'. The Constitution made it clear that all citizens with 'civil law status' possessed the unrestricted franchise as first-college voters, while only citizens with 'personal status' who satisfied specially enumerated conditions might qualify to vote in the second-college.

In 1946, second-college electors included persons who had at any time held posts of responsibility in private or public enterprises, veterans, owners of property whose title had been legally registered, and holders of hunting and driving licenses. This basic list was supplemented in 1947 to include those who were literate in French or Arabic. In 1951 tax-paying heads of families, mothers of two children 'living or dead for France', and civil or military pensioners were included, and, in 1952, all heads of families without reservation joined the list. As the list of second-college eligibles increased so also did electoral lists. The first enumeration in 1946 produced 2611 first-college registered voters out of 4000 French citizens and 38 976 second-college voters out of more than 3 000 000 indigenous Cameroonians. By 1953 the second college had grown to 592 331. The rate of increase was much greater after 1953.

The era of elections and representative institutions

The first elections to a representative institution stipulated in the October Constitution were to the French National Assembly. They were held on 10 November 1946, less than one month after the approval of the Constitution. Three out of a total of 618 deputies were to be elected from French Cameroon, one by the first-college electorate and two by the second college. Cameroon was the only territory in Black Africa to have two separate second-college constituencies: the northern and southern constituencies. Dr Louis-Paul Aujoulat was elected in the European first-college national constituency, while Prince Alexander Douala Manga Bell and Jules Ninine, a black administrator of West Indian origin, were elected in the second-college southern and northern constituencies respectively.

Other elections to the French National Assembly in which Cameroon participated were held in 1951 and 1956. The elections of June 1951 gave the vote for the first time to a significant number of Cameroon women and also greatly shifted the balance of the African electorates from the towns to the countryside. While maintaining the lone first-college constituency for French citizens, a third second-college constituency was created in the centre of Cameroon – the area around Yaounde. Dr Aujoulat who was against the double-college system of elections in the overseas territories transferred from the first to the second college and won the new constituency in the centre. His former first-college seat was won by the Gaullist Molinatti. Prince Douala Manga Bell and Jules Ninine retained their seats in the south and the north. In the elections of January 1956, Prince Douala Manga Bell and Jules Ninine retained their seats. Dr Aujoulat lost his seat in the centre to André-Marie Mbida, whom we are going to talk about later. Molinatti was defeated by Plantier in the first-college constituency.

The elections which aroused a great deal of enthusiasm in the politically conscious Cameroon elite were those to ARCAM in Yaounde. The number of representatives to the ARCAM was fixed by the decree of 25 October at 40 : 16 for the first college, 18 for the second college who were to be nominated by the High Commissioner of the Republic. The elections were held on 22 December 1946 for the second college and on 19 January 1947 for the first college. Among the indigenous Cameroonians who won seats to the first-ever session of ARCAM were such men as Ahmadou Ahidjo, Prince Douala Manga Bell, Joseph Kamga, Charles Okala and the Fon of Bamum, Seido Njimoluh Njoya who were to play prominent roles in the political future of their country.

The importance of the elections to the representative assembly, and the coming into existence of ARCAM itself, was the fact that, for the first time in the history of Cameroon, new political and administrative notions were introduced and entrusted to people whose political consciousness did not benefit from an education which, in metropolitan France, was based on a long tradition of participation in public life. Service in the assembly and its various committees gave the indigenous representatives the opportunity to learn the working of the French political and administrative systems. Besides, the presence of Frenchmen on the first-college seats in the assembly accelerated the political education of the indigenous representatives. Most of these Frenchmen, among them people holding important positions in the administration, economic enterprises, missions and schools, held the posts of committee chairmen and reporters in the early years of ARCAM, but gradually ceded the majority of these positions to Cameroonians.

During the first decade of ARCAM, representatives sought to make the widest possible use of the powers that the assembly possessed. Members were not yet divided by political parties, and deliberations were carried on in the kind of non-political body the French wanted it to be. In fact, candidates presented themselves in the December – January elections as individuals rather than as members of political parties. ARCAM gave advice on several issues which the administration heeded, including those on matters on which it was not bound to do so. The electoral law of 6 February 1952 changed the name of the assembly from ARCAM to ATCAM, *Assemblée Territoriale Camerounaise*, prior to the elections of 30 March. By the decree of 16 April 1957 ATCAM became the state legislative assembly, *Assemblée Legislative de l'Etat*.

The emergence of political parties

Developments in the French Trust Territory of Cameroon after the 1946 French Constitution encouraged the formation of real political parties in the territory. But the germ of political parties in French Cameroon must be traced back to the interwar period.

Before the Second World War, the first protest groups to express opinions on issues concerning French Cameroon and the Cameroonians began to be organised. The very earliest of such groups worth mentioning were the France – Cameroun Association and the *Comité de Défense des Intérêts du Cameroun* led mostly by the Paris-based Duala elite. These groups were formed principally to campaign for the rights of the Cameroonians and against the French mandate. The *Comité de Défense des Intérêts du Cameroun* fought particularly to compensate for and combat the restriction on the organisation of political activity in Cameroon.

In 1937 a quasi-political organisation, *L'Union Camerounaise*, was formed and led by Jean Mandessi Bell and Leopold Moume-Etia. This shortlived organisation petitioned the League of Nations, urging it to convert Cameroon into an 'A' mandate. When German propaganda for the return of her former colonies forced some British and French leaders to begin to talk about colonial concessions to Germany, *L'Union Camerounaise* petitioned the leaders of the Governments of the United States, Great Britain and France against any possible return of Cameroon to Germany. The organisation also showed concern about the economic restrictions placed on Cameroonians in their country and their illegal expulsion from France. The French regarded members of *L'Union Camerounaise* as possible supporters of Germany despite all their protestations to the contrary. In any event, these earlier organisations, though formed by Cameroonians, operated in metropolitan France rather than in Cameroon.

The first Cameroon-based quasi-political organisation was *Jeunesse Camerounaise Française* or Jeucafra in 1938. It originated as a rival group to *L'Union Camerounaise*, with the blessing of the French. Its three principal aims were: to keep Cameroon out of the hands of the Germans; to rid Cameroon of its international status, tighten the French hold on the territory, and bring it into line with the other French African dependencies; and to make the organisation a real political group in the territory, able to express the genuine political aspirations of all Cameroonians. It had as its President Paul Soppo Priso of the Duala, as Vice-President André-Fouda of the Ewondo, and as Secretary-General Louis-Marie Pouka of the Bassa group. Soppo Priso, who eventually became a very wealthy Cameroon businessman, served three terms as a member of the Cameroon Assembly from 1947 to 1960 and was its President from 1954 to 1956.

The importance of Jeucafra in the political history of Cameroon should not be minimised. Although the organisation doubtless collaborated with the forces of French colonialism, it also succeeded in the promotion of a Cameroon sense of national identity. It made it possible for Cameroonians to travel freely about, meet the aspiring leaders of the different regions, exchange information about local problems, discuss political questions concerning the future of Cameroon, and put forward political demands which represented some of the fundamental grievances of a cross-section of the population. Among the numerous demands made by Jeucafra were the following: that the indigenous people be allowed greater participation in the running of public affairs; that institutions of higher education be introduced and Cameroon students be awarded scholarships for advanced study in France; that political rights, including the extension of the same rights enjoyed by the Frenchmen in Cameroon, and the freedom of speech and of the press, be guaranteed; that a territorial

assembly with legislative powers be introduced; and that Cameroon be represented in the French parliament.

Jeucafra also made demands concerning the colonial economy of Cameroon. It demanded the suppression of the *indigénat* and an end to forced labour. It called for the establishment of codified labour regulations and increases in wages and salaries. Jeucafra called for the restructuring of Cameroon's economy, which was an impediment to the development of the territory and disadvantageous to Cameroonians. The organisation also called for the nationalisation of major industries in Cameroon and the introduction of industrialised methods which would boost the production of sugar, rice, tobacco, livestock, canned foods and fish. Finally, it called for the exclusion of white traders from both the rural and periodic local markets.

Following the Douala labour strikes which degenerated into riots from 21 to 30 September 1945, Jeucafra summoned a congress at which a series of demands parallel in many respects with those outlined above were made. It then sent a delegation to present these demands to the territorial administration in Yaounde and the French Government in Paris.

To conclude this discussion of Jeucafra, mentioned must be made of its importance in the education of French Cameroon politicians. The organisation served as a major school in which nearly all significant politicians during the postwar period received their training. Unlike *L'Union Camerounaise* which it rivalled and surpassed, Jeucafra survived the Second World War, which served to amplify its demands. The organisation also served as a bridge between the interwar protest groups led mostly by the Duala and the new era of a much broader-based political arena ushered in by the Second World War, the Brazzaville Conference, the new French Constitution, and the Trusteeship system. At the end of the late-1945 congress after the Douala riots, Jeucafra transformed itself into the *Union Camerounaise Française* or Unicafra.

Unicafra was led by André Fouda and other

cautious moderates until it was dissolved in 1947. During its short life, Unicafra voiced both the aspirations of Cameroonians and loyalty to France. It was succeeded in April 1947 by the *Rassemblement Camerounaise*, or RACAM, founded and led by Reuben Um Nyobe (whom we are going to talk about in a moment) and other left-wing trade unionists. RACAM attacked France's assimilationist policies and demanded independence for Cameroon. It was immediately banned by the French administration. Earlier, in 1946, another attempt at forming a political party had resulted in the formation of the *Rassemblement du Peuple Camerounais*. This organisation lasted only a few months, although its name was revived many years later, in 1955, by members of a local anti-UPC group in the Bamileke region. Lastly, there was the *Front Intercolonial*, composed of ex-servicemen led by those of their members who had returned to Cameroon from France in 1945. This organisation voiced the demands of ex-servicemen, and its members were very active in the trade union movement. None of these or any other political organisation formed before the end of 1947 participated in any of the elections into the metropolitan or territorial institutions. In fact, candidates in these elections presented themselves to the electorate as individuals rather than as members of this or that party.

By the beginning of 1948 French Cameroon was still without a real political organisation that would enable Cameroonians to vigorously pursue their collective interests. It was not until 10 April 1948 that a small group of Cameroonians met in the city of Douala to found what was soon to become Cameroon's first coherent political organisation, the *Union des Populations du Cameroun* or UPC. The new party's ultimate goals were: to group and unite the inhabitants of the territory in order to permit the most rapid development of the peoples and the raising of their standard of living; to consolidate the peoples of Cameroon into a federation; to implement a policy of rapid democratisation; and to emancipate the people exploited by colonial firms. These immediately-declared

statutes of the party were communicated to the administration for approval. Finding nothing in them likely to provoke the disturbance of public order, or threaten the trusteeship authority, or to endanger individual lives, the administration officially recognised the UPC on 9 June 1948. In doing so, the administration had no doubt that the new party would soon acquire considerable importance in the territory. But subsequently the UPC set out details of a programme which would not have been accepted by the French administration if it had formed part of the party's statutes. The most important items on the programme included three key political goals: national independence within a fixed time-limit; the abandonment by France of its policy of assimilation; the suppression of the Anglo-French boundary of 1916 and the reunification of the British and French Cameroon.

The architect of the UPC and its Secretary-General was the talented and courageous man, Reuben Um Nyobe. Born in 1913 of Bassa parents, this man of modest origins attended the Protestant schools in the villages near his home in the Sanaga-Maritime area. He later won a place in the teacher-training school, *Ecole Normale de Foulassi* at Sangmalima, where he spent only a year and was expelled in 1932 because of a conflict with his teachers. Um Nyobe continued his education independently, successfully passed a civil service examination, and was employed in the government finance office in Douala. Even then, he continued to seek to acquire a higher education on his own. In 1939 he became a clerk in the civil court in Yaounde, later moving to Edea. In 1944 he became an active participant of the discussion group of the French trade union, the *Confédération Générale du Travail* which was attempting to establish a local branch and initiate Cameroon's public employees. In 1946 he attended the Bamako Congress (in Mali) which resulted in the formation of the *Rassemblement Démocratique Africaine* or RDA, the largest group of African parties in metropolitan French politics. Back in Cameroon from Bamako, Um Nyobe set to work to found and lead a local section of the RDA, the RACAM. In 1946 and 1947, he devoted all his efforts to the formation of numerous trade unions which were linked together in a Regional Union, the *Union des Syndicats Confédérés du Cameroun*, of which he was the Secretary-General. In 1948 he and several trade union colleagues founded the UPC party which remained legal until 1955 when it instigated a territory-wide insurrection and was outlawed. Um Nyobe and other UPC leaders took refuge for a while in British Cameroon. He soon returned to the French territory to organise a guerrilla resistance to the administration. He was killed in a skirmish with government troops on 13 September 1958. During the last decade of his life, Um Nyobe worked unceasingly for his country's independence. His two close party collaborators were Felix Moumie and Ernest Ouandie.

Following the formation and popularity of the UPC, more political parties emerged in French Cameroon. Between 1948 and 1 January 1960 when independence was achieved, scores of political parties were formed, most of them shortlived. Among those that exerted some influence in the territory was the *Evolution Sociale Camerounaise* or Esocam, organised in 1949 by a number of Bassa to oppose independence and reunification in the immediate future. Another party was Dr Aujoulat's *Bloc Démocratique Camerounaise* or BDC, formed in 1951 to counteract the increasing influence of the UPC, to influence the adoption of the single electoral college, to fight for the enlargement of the powers of the Territorial Assembly, and to promote the unity of northern and southern Cameroon rather than encourage the unification of the British and French territories. In January 1953, Charles Okala created the *Union Sociale Camerounaise* or USC which claimed to oppose capitalism and imperialism. In 1956 the USC merged with Soppo Priso's shortlived *Mouvement d'Union Nationale* or MUN, formed in June 1956 to tackle the malaise that existed in the territory since the UPC revolt of 1955, and the problems of assimilation and independence.

Between November 1957 and May 1958 Ahmadou Ahidjo (whom we shall talk more about later) organised and led the *Union Camerounaise* or UC, which became the governing party from February 1958 until independence. There was also the *Démocrates Camerounais*, or DC, successor to Aujoulat's BDC, led by André-Marie Mbida, Cameroon's first Prime Minister from 1957 to 1958. None of the political parties lasted a decade in their original state as a legal organisation in the territory.

Trade unionism and labour conditions

A trade or trades union is an organised association of workers in a trade or group of trades or occupations formed to protect their interests and improve their conditions. Until 1944–45, it was illegal for the indigenous workers in French Cameroon to form and to belong to any such organisations. An attempt by the indigenous civil servants in the 1930s to form a civil service union was thwarted by the colonial government, although a similar but more social organisation was allowed to function among the railway workers. The absence of trade unions left the Cameroonian workers at the mercy of their employers, who were French settlers, the *colons*, and who made up most of the colonial administration. These employers, for thir part, took advantage of the situation and exploited the workers to the full. They forced their workers to put in a minimum of 48 hours of hard labour a week, although they paid very low wages and did not provide a day of rest except Sunday. The worker enjoyed neither the benefit of a paid annual leave, family allowance, nor a retirement pension after long service. Besides, forced labour in the rural areas continued to be practised indiscriminately, and women and children were frequently forced to work under the same conditions as men. The absence of organised workers' unions left the indigenous workers of French Cameroon unprotected against abuses by their white employers.

The Brazzaville Conference of 1944 considered the plight of the African worker and recommended labour reforms and the encouragement of trade unions. A few weeks before the Brazzaville recommendations, a Cameroon administrative decree of 7 January set up a special labour department, appointed labour inspectors, applied French regulations to local working conditions, introduced a social security scheme, and put an end to the much-abused practice of paying workers in kind. In September 1944 another decree accorded Cameroonians the first opportunity to form local trade unions and to act in support of their interests. As soon as the formation of workers' unions was legalised, emissaries arrived in Douala from the largest group of French trade unions, the *Confédération Générale du Travail* (CGT), to assist Cameroonians to form their own trade unions. By this time Douala and Yaounde were becoming considerable trade centres, with a large number of African wage-workers working mostly for French firms.

The right to form trade unions was enthusiastically welcomed by the Cameroon workers. Before long, many autonomous trade unions and professional associations began to spring up everywhere in Douala and Yaounde. This situation led between December 1944 and July 1945 to the founding of the 'mother-union' of all the indigenous unions, the *Union des Syndicats Confédérés du Cameroun* (USCC), with a unified leadership and headquarters in Douala. The leading figures of the USCC were Reuben Um Nyobe, Jacques N'Gom, Charles Asale (the first chairman), Moumé-Etia, André Fouda, and Philémon Sekouma. On 18 June 1945 the French published a 'Native Labour Code' as a first step towards the liberal principles enunciated at Brazzaville, as well as improving the terrible plight of the workers in French African colonies. The code abolished forced labour, asserted the freedom of labour, and extended citizen rights to French African subjects. However the Native Labour Code was not implemented in Cameroon or elsewhere, to the indignation of African workers.

Opposition to the Brazzaville recommendations, the labour reforms and the development of trade unions in Cameroon was mounted by the French settlers, the *colons*. The latter feared that the changes which were being quickly introduced would sweep away many of the established benefits which the whites were enjoying in the territory. They therefore decided in April 1945 in Yaounde to form their own union, the *Association des Colons du Cameroun* or Ascocam to protect their interests and to fight against the implementation of any measure in favour of the worker and to oppose the extension of French political rights to the Africans. As soon as Ascocam was formed, branches were established elsewhere in Cameroon, especially in Douala. Members of the organisation were determined to use all the means they had, including force, to destroy the new African trade unions and to maintain the *status quo* regarding forced labour. They were greatly enraged when the Native Labour Code was published in June 1945.

The stand taken by the white settlers and employers against the workers and leaders of their union and the antagonism it aroused made a clash between the two groups inevitable. While the settlers were agitating against labour reforms, workers were expressing opposition to the inadequacies of the Native Labour Code and the obnoxious labour conditions maintained by the whites. On 22 August, a well-attended USCC meeting at which the workers resolved to pursue their rights energetically was held in Douala. After the meeting a delegate of the union, Charles Asalé, left for Paris to attend a CGT conference. The workers were aware of the growing animosity and tension between them and the settlers, who were determined to strike a heavy blow at their union. As tension mounted, a violent outcome was unavoidable.

On Thursday 20 September 1945 railway workers in Douala manifested their discontent and the following day launched a series of wildcat strikes in the city. On Monday 24 September, groups of strikers from all over the city gathered to listen to those exhorting them to stand firm. They were pursued at their public meeting place by members of Ascocam. Soon afterwards the opposing forces of, on the one hand, the workers and the unemployed, and on the other, the *colons* and some members of the police and armed forces confronted each other on the streets. About 200 white rioters, equipped with firearms, were determined to massacre the leaders of the workers' union and overthrow the colonial administration. The armed *colons* had, it would appear, worked themselves up into a frenzy in the belief that they were going to be massacred and that they had been deserted by the administration. The black workers, with weapons of sticks, cudgels and stones, were no match for the whites. By the time the troops from Chad were able to restore peace on 30 September, between 60 and 80 blacks had been killed and many more wounded, although official reports claimed that only 8 people had been killed and 20 others wounded. Only one Frenchman, the secretary-general of the Douala Chamber of Commerce, was killed and another wounded. Leaders of both the CGT and the USCC were kept in jail while investigations into the disturbances were undertaken.

By October 1947, the overseas labour code had still not been passed by the French Parliament, and the African worker remained without legal protection. In the same month the French Government decreed that henceforward, the labour code could only be enacted by a parliamentary law. It was not until two years later, on 30 June 1950 that the French Parliament finally passed legislation providing for equality in pay, recruitment and promotion of all African and European civil servants who had the same qualifications. It took a very long time for the law to be fully applied in Cameroon and elsewhere. The redrafted overseas labour code, a section of which gave Africans practically the same rights as their counterparts in metropolitan France, and completely liberated them from control by the administration, still stood before parliament. Little was being done about it. Exasperated, an all-French-African union in Dakar, Senegal,

began a long struggle in October 1952 to force the passage of the code through Parliament. The following month, on 3 November workers throughout French West Africa supported the Dakar initiative and went on strike. Their action yielded dividends and on 15 December 1952 the overseas labour code was passed and became law. Before the end of January 1953, the code had been promulgated in all the African territories. For the first time, the African worker in French territories was given legal protection.

The legalised African Labour Code instituted a 40-hour working week, down from the minimum 48, and provided a full day of rest and paid annual leave. Colonial administrations in each territory were to fix the minimum hourly wage for workers with a 20 per cent increase over current rates. But it was not until 1956 that the family allowance stipulation was applied. When it finally came into force, each employer was required to pay a monthly allowance for every child aged from one to 14 years whose father worked for him at least 18 days or 120 hours per month, regardless of whether or not the child's father had more than one wife. The allowance had to be paid directly to the child's mother, who also received special grants both before and at the time of birth. In short, the new labour code gave the African worker the same if not better legal protection against exploitation as workers in France.

Political revolts and Cameroon's new statute

Between 22 and 30 May 1955, a series of riotous incidents occurred in more than a dozen towns and on some major roads in southwestern Cameroon which resulted in 26 deaths and about 200 people injured. An armed struggle broke out between the administration and the UPC political party, which the former accused the latter of initiating. In order to understand the origin of these unfortunate revolts, and the events which led both to the banning of the UPC in 1955 and the acquisition of a new statute by Cameroon in 1957, one must be aware of the relationships between the political parties, especially the UPC, and elections to the territorial assembly of Cameroon from 1951 – 52 on.

It has been aptly remarked that the dominant facts of Cameroon politics between 1950 and 1955 'were the growing strength of the UPC in organisation and publicity, and its failure to register this strength in terms of votes.' Although the UPC claimed to be the most popular political party in Cameroon, and international opinion confirmed this claim, the party never ever succeeded in electing a single representative to the Cameroon local assembly. The party attributed this failure to the French administration.

The first parliamentary elections in Cameroon to be contested by local political parties were those of June 1951 for the French National Assembly and of March 1952 for the territorial assembly, ATCAM. The UPC was the only properly organised party to contest the two second-college seats reserved for African representatives in the 1951 elections. It lost both seats; Um Nyobe, the Secretary-General of the party, was defeated by Prince Douala Manga Bell. Following this defeat, the UPC organised and conducted a very intensive campaign for the 24 second-college ATCAM seats. This time another party, the BDC, also entered candidates for the elections and was a major opponent of the UPC. When the votes were counted, electoral successes went mainly to the BDC and to the Muslim chiefs and their protégés. The UPC failed again to win even a single seat.

But the party was convinced that it had performed well in the elections and that Um Nyobe in particular had won his seat but was cheated out of victory by the manipulation of the vote, orchestrated by the administration. Um Nyobe had been defeated by Joseph-Antoine Melone, a priest of the Roman Catholic Church. On 27 May 1952, violence emanating from UPC's defeat flared up shortly after the elections in the Mungo region, and one man was killed and several wounded.

Convinced that the ballot had been rigged by the administration and that the French would never allow it to win an electoral mandate, the UPC began to lose faith in elections as such. Many in the party's leadership began to advocate violence and extreme policies as the only way of achieving victory.

The major themes that continued to divide Cameroon politicians were the issues of independence and the reunification of British and French Cameroon. Moderate politicians who supported the idea of independence wanted it to be preceded by economic development. They were also convinced that unity within French Cameroon divided between the Christian south and the Muslim north was essential before the unification of the two Trust Territories could make sense. Others thought that membership as a state of the Federal French Republic was better than complete independence and separation from France. Still others were of the opinion that any idea of independence for Cameroon was purely a utopian scheme. The UPC alone wanted immediate independence and reunification, and for that reason, sent Um Nyobe every year, beginning in 1952, to put its case before the Trusteeship Council of the UN.

But the UPC could not claim to represent popular opinion in Cameroon, seeing that it had no seat in ATCAM. Moreover, within the territory, the party leadership began to be identified as communist and the organisation was increasingly associated with all sorts of unrest in Cameroon. It was accused of organising strikes and distributing violent propaganda against the administration, the Catholic Church, employers and the *colons*. Yet an attempt by the new High Commissioner, Roland Pré, in 1954 – 55 to gain the confidence of the UPC and establish a working relationship between it and the administration backfired. The UPC responded to this 'friendly' gesture with a new series of strikes and disturbances. The High Commissioner, who had gained a reputation as a progressive administrator and was unswerving in his repression of anti-colonial movements, became convinced that indulgence of the UPC would be a mistake. He decided to take a tough line with the party. On 19 February 1955, he issued an order permitting the use of troops to disperse unruly crowds, and declared it his intention to crush communist activity in the territory.

It became increasingly obvious that a showdown between the administration and the UPC was imminent. During April, further strikes and demonstrations took place in Douala, Yaounde and areas of the Bamileke region. The Catholic bishops, whose church was constantly under UPC attack, issued a joint pastoral letter condemning the party. The UPC responded with further strikes and demonstrations, some of them more violent than ever.

On 15 May an unauthorised UPC meeting at Mbanga in the Mungo region was forcibly dispersed by troops and many people were wounded on both sides. On 22 May another political rally was dispersed by troops; again, many people were seriously wounded and one member of the armed forces died later in hospital. News of the UPC successes against the administration soon spread all over the entire territory of southwestern Cameroon. Between 22 and 30 May, there were riots more or less simultaneously in Douala, Yaounde, Mbanga, Loum, Nkongsamba, Edea, Eseka, Mbombo in the Mungo region, Bafoussam, Bafang, the Sanaga-Maritime region, and along the Douala – Yaounde and the Douala – Nkongsamba highways. By the time the revolts were quelled, 26 people were dead (21 demonstrators, one gendarme, four civilians – two of them Europeans), and about 200 wounded. The administration blamed the riots on the UPC and resolved to suppress it. On 13 July 1955, the party was outlawed and its leaders escaped across the boundary to British Cameroon. From then on the UPC went underground in order to continue its terrorist activity.

In April 1956 Pré, the High Commissioner, was recalled and replaced by Pierre Messmer, who expressed the hope of reaching an agreement with the banned UPC leadership. Messmer soon relaxed the repression against the party and began to think seriously of granting a general amnesty. Soppo Priso's new party, the MUN, strongly supported such a move and also demanded a reversal of the ban on the UPC, although it condemned the use of violence for political ends. The MUN also called on France to accept the principle of complete independence for Cameroon. As a result of Soppo Priso's effort to win back militants of the UPC to legality, followers of the outlawed movement joined the MUN *en masse*, while the BDC and the USC also affiliated with it. But the DC, led by Mbida, was opposed to the amnesty and called for more effective repression against the UPC. Mbida denounced the MUN as a tool of the UPC.

Meanwhile work was continuing on a text of a new Cameroon Statute which the High Commissoner intended to submit to the territorial assembly. Convinced that the ATCAM elected in 1952 no longer had a moral authority to deliberate on the Statute, he ordered new territorial elections to be held on 23 December 1956. But the elections were called when the general amnesty had not been declared and the UPC was still outlawed. Working from underground, the UPC movement called for a boycott of the elections unless the amnesty was granted and the ban on the party lifted. Soppo Priso tried to convince members of the outlawed party in MUN that it was better to fight the elections and then use the new assembly as a platform from which to fight the amnesty and the ban on the UPC. No agreement was reached on this point and the MUN broke up in November. Earlier, moderate and associate members of MUN had withdrawn from the Movement because they were convinced that the organisation's organs had been extensively infiltrated by the UPC.

A few days before the general elections, a terrorist campaign began in the UPC strongholds in the territory. Telephone lines were cut, bridges destroyed, railway lines torn up, houses burnt and the population molested, especially in the region between Yaounde and Douala and the Mungo and Bamileke areas. The administration, which had been taken unawares, reacted brutally. Disturbed regions were filled with troops; a great massacre ensued with hundreds of people being shot on sight.

The general election went on as planned. The results showed that Mbida's DC and Ahidjo's UC were the dominant parties, while Soppo Priso's hurriedly-formed *Groupe d'Action Nationale Camerounaise* (GANC) won only 8 out of 70 seats. The distribution of seats was as follows: the UC and Central and Northern deputies 30, the DC 20, the *Paysans Indépendants* 9, GANC 8, and Independents 3. The new assembly started work on the proposed Statute in the new year of 1957, with Ahmadou Ahidjo as president. The discussion lasted till the end of February when compromises were effected and numerous minor amendments to the draft made. The Assembly then increased the powers of the future Cameroon government and replaced the title 'Territory' with that of 'State under Trusteeship'.

The Cameroon Statute was adopted and became law by decree of the French Government on 16 April 1957. The new state thus acquired a Constitution, a government headed by a Prime Minister, and a citizenship distinct from that of France. The High Commissioner remained responsible for the country's defence, and for its relations with foreign countries and France. Later in the year Cameroon acquired its own flag, a national anthem (announced in October) and a motto. On 9 May, the assembly took the title of *Assemblée Legislative du Cameroun* or ALCAM. The following day André-Marie Mbida became Cameroon's first prime Minister. Mbida then nominated Ahidjo as Deputy Prime Minister and Minister of the Interior. The presidency of the Legislative Assembly passed to Daniel Kemajou. In June the Cameroon Statute was formally inaugurated. Cameroon was now a state under Trusteeship, outside the French Union, although it continued to be represented in the French Parliament.

The Mbida and Ahidjo governments

André-Marie Mbida was appointed as Cameroon's first Prime Minister on 10 May 1957, and was invested five days later by the Legislative Assembly. His government was a coalition of all the parties, except Soppo Priso's GANC which formed the Opposition. Mbida's nomination was made possible by the support he received from Ahmadou Ahidjo and Arouna Njoya who led the largest delegation of 30 members from the North and the Centre.

Although Mbida started well, it was not long after his investiture that he began to face mounting problems. He was caught almost from the beginning with the problem of how to handle the UPC-inspired terrorism which necessitated on the one hand strong measures to deal with it but on the other hand required a peaceful solution. Mbida lacked both the personality and the balanced political judgement to deal with the problem. His impatience with democratic procedure and his intransigence eventually antagonised his political

10 *André-Marie Mbida*

supporters to such an extent that by the time his policies came under attack, few regretted his departure. He adopted an authoritarian and arbitrary style of running the government, and frequently took major decisions without the advice of his cabinet. Moreover, Mbida made the great error of opposing the independence and the reunification of Cameroon which almost all the political groups supported. Finally, Mbida failed to seek a peaceful solution to the problem of terrorism.

In July 1957, Um Nyobe stated the terms on which he and his followers would lay down their arms. These included: the dissolution of ALCAM and the calling of fresh elections; the granting of amnesty for all political prisoners and suspects; and the granting of immediate independence. In September, Um Nyobe reiterated these demands in a proposition addressed to the Prime Minister and the High Commissioner, threatening violence if the demands were not taken into consideration. Mbida rejected the proposals outright and a freak outbreak of violence and terrorism began in the Sanaga-Maritime region. Mbida decided to make his decision clear by visiting Um Nyobe's village of birth, Boumnyebel, and making speeches denouncing the UPC and threatening severe measures against all who did not return to their villages from the bush within ten days. The UPC in turn responded by intensifying violence on an unprecedented scale in the Sanaga-Maritime area and spreading the rebellion to the Mungo and the Bamileke regions. In December, a Bamileke member of ALCAM, Samuel Wanko, and six others were slain near Bafoussam. From then on the terrorists instituted a state of perpetual guerrilla warfare, attacking government offices and destroying documents, burning Church property and murdering missionaries, Europeans, chiefs and supporters of the administration. Before long, the rebellion spread to the big towns of Douala and Yaounde. Mbida responded by acquiring troop reinforcements from France and ordering a systematic search of the forests and villages of the troubled areas for bands of terrorists. This led to the death

of many people. The Prime Minister's political opponents made it clear that his measures were too harsh and renewed their call for a general amnesty.

Mbida's policies were doomed. Opinion in both France and Cameroon was that a peaceful settlement with the UPC should be sought. French authorities believed that a new High Commissioner stood a better chance of helping the Cameroon government to explore the possibility of a peaceful solution. Thus, at the end of 1957, High Commissioner Messmer was replaced by Jean Ramadier, who was instructed to sound out political possibilities and report back to the Minister of Overseas Territories. Ramadier was also expected to ease the replacement of Mbida, if this would lead to positive developments.

Mbida's finishing stroke came on 26 January 1958, when he issued a ten-year programme for an undetermined political future without independence and reunification. The UC rejected the programme and Ahidjo and his followers in the cabinet decided to desert the government. The Prime Minister immediately replaced the ministers with members of his own party, but the High Commissioner, exceeding his authority, refused to endorse the replacements. Mbida immediately complained to Paris, and Ramadier was hastily replaced by Xavier Torre. Mbida resigned for lack of a majority on 17 February 1957, the day the amnesty, passed ten days earlier by the French National Assembly, was promulgated. The following day Ahmadou Ahidjo, a Muslim of Fulani background, was invested Prime Minister. Mbida and his party went into Opposition.

The head of the new government, Ahmadou Ahidjo, had acquired some good administrative experience as Deputy Prime Minister in the Mbida government. Shortly after his investiture, he brought members of Soppo Priso's GANC to his government and adopted the demand for independence and reunification as a strategy for winning back the outlawed UPC to legality and making participation in his government acceptable to many southerners.

11 *Ahmadou Ahidjo*

Ahidjo quickly announced a programme which sought: effective independence within a limited period of time; national unity and the reunification of Cameroon in a federation of independent African states; and the solution to the UPC problem which had become more serious than ever before. Following discussions in France in March 1958, Ahidjo submitted to ALCAM a draft resolution for a timetable for advancement towards independence. On 12 June ALCAM approved the resolution and voted to ask France to recognise Cameroon's option for independence at the end of the trusteeship, and to transfer to Cameroon all powers relating to the management of internal affairs.

The French government of Charles de Gaulle replied favourably, and negotiations commenced between the two countries for a new Cameroon Statute. It was decided during the negotiations that an entirely new Statute embodying self-government for Cameroon be formulated, instead of merely making amendments to the Statute of 1957. The Statute that emerged from the negotiations proposed to turn over to Cameroon control all matters except foreign affairs, defence, monetary and foreign exchange policy. France also agreed to provide aid and assistance in certain spheres of activity as required, and to request the UN to terminate the Trusteeship whenever Cameroon wanted. In preparation for the promulgation of the new Statute which France was about to propose to it, ALCAM voted a resolution with some very important provisions on 24 October 1958. The resolution expressed Cameroon's desire for independence on 1 January 1960 and affirmed support for the reunification of British and French Cameroon before that date. It also invited the Ahidjo government to ask France to request the UN to abrogate trusteeship concurrently with independence, and rendered homage for France's work in Cameroon. On 22 November ALCAM accepted the new Statute proposed to it by the French Government and promulgated it into law on 30 December. The new Cameroon Statute came into force on 1 January 1959.

Ahidjo had taken up and succeeded in executing the entire UPC programme, but had not yet won the outlawed party to legality. Towards the end of 1958 the situation changed. The death of Um Nyobe on 13 September at the hands of a government patrol near his home village, led the rebels in the Sanaga-Maritime area under Theodore Mayi Matip, Um Nyobe's chief lieutenant and secretary, to abandon the *maquis* and declare their readiness to return to legal opposition. On 22 September Mayi Matip accepted Ahidjo's measures of amnesty and reconciliation and urged his fellow rebels to do the same. In doing so Mayi Matip and his companions concealed neither their membership of the UPC nor the part they had played in the terrorist campaign under Um Nyobe. In less than a month after the amnesty, more than 3000 UPC guerrillas laid down their arms in the Sanaga-Maritime region, thereby bringing the rebellion in that area to a virtual end. This surrender was immediately and vehemently condemned by the rebels under Dr Félix-Roland Moumie who continued their activities in the Bamileke region.

On 12 April 1959 by-elections were held in the Sanaga-Maritime to fill the empty ALCAM seats left by the assassination of candidates from the area who had won the December 1956 elections. The government allowed Mayi Matip and his friends tó win the elections, implying that the vote was rigged. Once elected, these UPC members carried on vociferous opposition both inside and outside ALCAM, but condemned those of their members who had refused to lay down their arms and accept the government's amnesty.

Meanwhile, on 1 January 1959, the new Cameroon Statute came into force. Under it, Cameroon acquired complete internal autonomy and was no longer represented in the French assemblies. Its elected authorities took over all powers of legislation, administration and justice, and Cameroon nationality was recognised internationally. On 12 and 14 March, the Trusteeship Council and the General Assembly of the UN supported Ahidjo's programme and voted to terminate the trusteeship on 1 January 1960 without new elections as demanded by Moumie's exiled wing of the UPC. On 30 October ALCAM elected a Consultative Commission to help the government to implement it. On 1 January 1960 the independence of Cameroon was proclaimed.

Economic and social advancement

During the interwar period French Cameroon made only moderate progress in the economic and social domains because the French did not want to invest heavily in a territory whose international status, as a mandate of the League of Nations, made its future relations with France uncertain. But during the trusteeship period, beginning in 1947, the French undertook measures to promote the economic and social advancement of the territory on a much larger scale.

In April 1946, the French National Assembly passed a law establishing an Economic and Social Development Investment Fund (FIDES), a long-term programme for the development and modernisation of France's overseas territories. The funds for the programme were to be made up in large part of contribution from grants from the French national budget and from the long-term and low-interest loans each territory acquired from the Central Fund for French Overseas Territories (CCFOM) for participation in its economic and social plans. Other investment funds were to be provided by private concerns. Total investments in Cameroon, public and private at all levels of government, from January 1946 to June 1959 stood at 95 424 200 000 CFA francs. Of this, the French state provided 39 698 000 000 francs as grants and 9 214 500 000 francs as loans. Private investors put approximately 21 000 000 000 francs into privately-held enterprises, and some 15 658 700 000 francs in semi-public enterprises in which the Governments of Cameroon and France also participated. Cameroon's contribution at the territorial and communal levels of investment stood at 9 873 000 000 francs.

The investment funds were used for financing projects in the two four-year economic plans which together lasted from 1947 until 1959. The first economic plan concentrated on developing the infrastructure of the territory. A considerable part of the work undertaken involved major construction works such as the extension and modernisation of the Douala seaport, the building of bridges, including the splendid Bonaberi bridge over the Wuri river complete with a railway linking the Douala – Yaounde and the Douala – Nkongsamba lines, the development of telecommunications, the renovation of railway equipment, the building of airfields, and the improvement of the road network, especially between Douala and its hinterland, which would permit the transportation of products to the internal and overseas markets. The second plan was intended to deal more directly with the welfare of the Cameroon people. It devoted greater attention to such social aspects of development as schools, health facilities in the rural areas, agriculture and technology.

Among some of the major economic projects sponsored by the French Government in Cameroon under the two Four-Year Economic Plans was the impressive technological electrical and metallurgical complex, Alucam, established in Edea. This hydro-electric industrial complex was built to provide electricity for the city of Douala and for the aluminium industry. The project involved the building of a dam on the Sanaga river and generators to provide electricity, and the construction of a plant for the processing of aluminium. Work on the complex cost an estimated 26 000 000 000 CFA francs and employed 2000 – 3000 Cameroonian workers, although it was expected to employ only 600 Cameroon and 100 French technical and managerial staff when completed. It was hoped at the time of construction that since the electricity generated by the plant would be far more than Alucam would consume, the surplus would serve as the basis for the industrialisation of the entire region. Alucam became fully operational in 1956 and was expected to produce 45 000 tons of aluminium per annum.

Cameroon also made rapid progress in the development of the production of export and commercial crops. The three most important export crops from which the territory drew most of its income were cocoa, coffee and bananas. These crops accounted for a full 70 per cent of the value of export crops. Cocoa alone accounted for 50 per cent of the total export earnings of Cameroon, while coffee and bananas together accounted for 20 per cent. The remaining crops, namely timber, cotton, rubber, palm products, groundnuts and tobacco, accounted for 30 per cent of the value of exports. While cocoa cultivation was almost entirely in the hands of Cameroonians, the coffee and banana production until well after the Second World War was a monopoly of white farmers. Cameroonians, mainly the Bamileke, were only able to force their way into the production of these two crops and to gain an equal share in the export markets with the

whites in the 1950s. Cocoa production, which was vigorously promoted by the administration in all areas with the requisite soil and climatic conditions, was most successful in the centre-south region from the Yaounde area south to Ebolowa and Ambam. More than half a million inhabitants of the region were dependent on the crop. The banana crop was principally grown in the Mungo region, and *arabica* coffee was cultivated mainly in the western highlands of the Bamileke and Bamum areas.

In the region of social advancement, France undertook many measures to improve health, the status of women, and working conditions. But the most significant advances were in the field of education. Many schools were opened and many more children went to school than was the case during the mandate period. The literacy rate in the territory rose so rapidly that by 1956, an estimated 50 per cent of the population of the south under 40 was literate. It was hoped that every child of primary school age in Cameroon would be able to go to school before the end of the trusteeship.

As a result of the increased efforts in education, primary school enrolment rose from approximately 119 000 in 1947 to 330 988 in 1959, and secondary and technical school enrolment from less than 1000 in 1948 to 2815 in 1959. There were about 1000 or more Cameroon students studying in the various institutions of higher education in France in any given year from 1956 to 1960. But France's educational policy continued to be assimilationist, seeking to inculcate in the Cameroonian loyalty to France and to French culture. Mission schools, which were more numerous than government schools and taught the overwhelming majority of Cameroon children, were also urged to promote assimilation.

It is worth remarking, in conclusion, that the economic and social advances made by Cameroon from 1946 to 1959 had both positive and negative consequences. On the positive side, the economic advances raised the standard of living of many Cameroonians to new heights. There also emerged in the Cameroon society significant numbers of people belonging to such economic and social groups as small producers of export crops, salaried workers, a small middle-class engaged in agriculture or commerce, and a civil service class. Investments and the rapid increase in the number of wage-earning Cameroonians led to the growth of labour unions with an accompanying extension of French social legislation and social security benefits. The rapid spread and knowledge of the French language through educational institutions enabled Cameroonians of different ethnic and linguistic backgrounds to communicate easily and to develop a feeling of unity and nationalism.

On the negative side, French investments in Cameroon were concentrated in an area of about one-tenth of the entire territory, the so-called 'fertile crescent' or the region of the territory served by the railroad, with Douala as the centre. This was the region in which the major Cameroon export crops were produced. Secondly, the economic and social advances were more urban than rural. This kind of situation stimulated a movement of the rural unemployed to the towns and cities, principally Douala and Yaounde, leading to the rapid growth of these towns and to such social problems as overcrowding, inadequate housing, and electricity and water shortages. Lastly, except in the production of cocoa, few efforts were made to facilitate the entry by Cameroonians into commercial agriculture and the import-export trade and internal commerce. In the commercial sector, large colonial trading firms controlled the greater part of the whole-sale and retail trade, while the *colons*, the Greeks and the Lebanese controlled both the retail trade and trade in agricultural produce. The banks were unwilling to make loans available to Cameroonians to enable them enter into competition with the whites in these areas. Only the economically dynamic Bamileke were able to render the discriminatory policies of the credit agencies of little significance by using *njangi* and other traditional financial devices to force their way into the import-export trade and retail markets.

Questions

1. Why was the French Constitution of 1946 important for Cameroon?
2. Why did the ARCAM elections of December 1946 and January 1947 arouse a great deal of enthusiasm in French Cameroon?
3. Discuss the emergence of political parties and trade unions in French Cameroon.
4. Why is the UPC described as Cameroon's first coherent political organisation?
5. Why did the UPC movement revolt against the French administration in 1955? What were the consequences of the revolt?
6. Who was Reuben Um Nyobe and what role did he play in the formation of trade unions in Cameroon?
7. Why was the administration of Ahmadou Ahidjo more successful than that of André-Marie Fouda before it?

Further reading

Alain Bockel, *L'Administration Camerounaise* (Berger-Levrault, Paris, 1971).

David E. Gardinier, *Cameroon: United Nations Challenge to French Policy* (OUP, London, 1963).

Richard Joseph, *Radical Nationalism in Cameroon* (OUP, Oxford, 1977).

Bertrand Lembezat, *Le Cameroun* (Editions Maritimes et Coloniales, Paris, 1954).

Victor T. LeVine, *The Cameroons From Mandate to Independence* (University of California Press, Berkeley and Los Angeles, 1964).

Edward Mortimer, *France and the Africans 1944 – 1960* Faber & Faber, London, 1969).

Engelbert Mveng, *Histoire du Cameroun*, Tome II (CEPER, Yaounde, 1985).

Chapter ten
British trusteeship in Cameroon: 1946-61

British Southern Cameroons witnessed virtually no significant political and administrative changes until the period of trusteeship from 1946 to 1961. It was then that the territory gradually changed its status from a province of the Eastern Region of Nigeria to a separate entity within Nigeria. It was only after 1954 when the territory was accorded some form of regional status that it acquired some legislative, administrative and budgetary autonomy with some self-supporting economic provision from the Nigerian and British governments. Northern Cameroons continued to be administered from Kaduna as an integral part of the three Northern Nigerian provinces of Bornu, Adamawa and Benue. We shall discuss the situation in that territory in Chapter 11 where independence and the plebiscites are studied.

Constitutional developments

During the greater period of trusteeship, British Cameroon continued to be administered as an integral part of the Federation of Nigeria. The Governor-General of the Federation continued, as was the case under the mandate, to be responsible for the implementation of the Trusteeship Agreement in the Trust Territory on behalf of the Government of the United Kingdom. This meant that all political and administrative arrangements which were introduced in Nigeria directly or indirectly influenced developments in Cameroon. The first of such arrangements was the Richards Constitution of 1946.

The Richards Constitution (named after Sir Arthur Richards who was Governor-General of Nigeria from 1943 to 1947) was conceived in 1945, arbitrarily introduced in 1946, and came into effect on 1 January 1947. According to Sir Arthur, it had three objectives: to promote the unity of Nigeria, to provide adequately for the diverse peoples of Nigeria, and to secure greater participation by Nigerians in the discussion of their affairs. It was, however, introduced without discussion with the Nigerians. Insofar as the Southern Cameroons was concerned, it represented a backward step for the territory. While it broke important new ground in establishing a legislative council for all Nigerians in Lagos, it did not provide for any representation for Southern Cameroons in that central legislative council. Instead Cameroon was deprived of its lone seat which Chief Manga Williams of Victoria had occupied in the Lagos Legislative Council since 1942, and was offered only two native authority seats in the thirteen-member Eastern Regional House of Assembly. The two native authorities concerned were Chief Manga Williams of Victoria and Galega, the Fon of Bali. The Richards Constitution evoked widespread opposition all over Nigeria and Cameroon since it did not seem in any substantial way to advance the trend towards self-government. Under it, British Cameroon was destined to remain an integral part of Nigeria.

In April 1948 Sir John Macpherson replaced Sir Arthur Richards and promised the disgruntled Nigerian politicians that a constitutional conference to revise the Richards Constitution would be held in Ibadan. Avoiding the mistake of his predecessor, Sir John indulged the Federation in two years of protracted negotiations on the form the new constitution should take.

Preparations for the Ibadan Conference led to the holding of several political meetings by the Southern Cameroons politicians, leaders of youth organisations, and representatives of ethnic groups at Mamfe, Victoria and even Lagos. Meetings were held at the village, divisional and provincial levels. These meetings resolved that the British Trust Territory of Cameroon should be accorded a separate regional status with its own House of Assembly to be directly responsible to the Trusteeship Council of the UN.

The resolution was introduced at the Regional preparatory meeting at Enugu in July 1949. It was rejected on two grounds, namely that it would be financially unsound to grant Cameroon regional status and that, even if that was done, it would be politically difficult to organise the region in view of the fact that part of that territory was administered from the Eastern Region and part from the Northern Region. The Enugu meeting instead recommended that the Southern Cameroons be represented in both the Regional House of Assembly and the Executive Council at Enugu, and in the Central Executive and Legislative Assembly in Lagos.

In January 1950 the general Constitutional Conference at which Cameroon was represented by two delegates met at Ibadan to review the Richards Constitution. From the Conference came the Macpherson Constitution which was warmly welcomed. It offered greatly increased regional autonomy within a united Nigeria; it gave Nigerians a full share in the shaping of government policy and direction of executive government action in a Central Council of Ministers and Regional and Executive Council; it provided for larger and more representative Regional legislatives with increased powers.

As far as Southern Cameroons was concerned, the Conference confirmed the Enugu recommendations, and the territory continued to form part of the Eastern Region. Under the new system, Southern Cameroons was to be represented by 13 elected members in the 80-member Eastern House of Assembly, by at least one member in the Eastern Regional Executive Council, and by 7 out of 34 members from the Eastern House of Assembly to the newly-created House of Representatives at Lagos. Cameroon was also to have one Regional Minister at the Enugu assembly, and one of the four representatives from the Eastern Region to the Council of Ministers in Lagos.

The Macpherson Constitution received the general approval of the British Colonial Secretary in 1951 and came into effect in January 1952. Despite the fact that it was much more in keeping with the desires of the Nigerians than its predecessor, it was however destined for a short life. Breakdown resulted largely from party antagonisms. The hostile disagreement between Northern and Southern Nigeria over the question of self-government in 1956, and the sharp discord between members of the National Council of Nigeria and the Cameroons (NCNC) over the Constitution in the Eastern House of Assembly in 1953, led to its collapse. At the time, pressure was already building up in Cameroon for separate institutions of its own. The crisis in Eastern Nigeria led to the immediate dissolution of the House. The Southern Cameroons members of the House seized the opportunity to break off their relations with the Eastern Region and to demand a separate Regional House for Southern Cameroons. The political situation in the whole Federation soon convinced the British Colonial Secretary, Oliver Lyttleton, of the need to redraw the Nigerian Constitution in order to provide for greater regional autonomy. In April 1953 he announced that a Nigerian Constitutional Conference would be held in London in August of the same year.

In August 1953, delegates from all the political parties of the three Regions of Nigeria gathered in Lancaster House, London, for the Conference which was presided over by the Colonial Secretary, Mr Lyttelton (later Lord Chandos), himself. Southern Cameroons was represented by two delegates from the two political parties, namely Dr E.M.L. Endeley of the Kamerun National Congress or KNC and

N.N. Mbile of the Kamerun People's Party or KPP. The KNC stood for administrative autonomy in the Southern Cameroons, while the KPP stood for continuous association with the Eastern Region of Nigeria. Endeley's demand for regional autonomy in the Southern Cameroons was reflected upon in London. It was concluded that if the forthcoming elections were won in the Southern Cameroons on the basis of an appeal for a separate status for the territory, the resumed Conference in Lagos in January 1954 would respect the wishes of the Cameroonians and make the necessary changes. This condition was satisfied when the KNC captured all the six seats allocated to the Southern Cameroons in the Federal House of Representatives and, eventually, twelve of the thirteen seats in the Southern Cameroons House of Assembly. Hence, the Lagos Conference in January 1954 announced that Nigeria would become a full Federation of three Regions, a federal capital and the quasi-federal territory of the Southern Cameroons.

Southern Cameroons was thus separated from the Eastern Region and was accorded its own House of Assembly and its own Executive Council. The House of Assembly was empowered to raise taxes, and to share with Federal authorities legislation on subjects on the 'concurrent list' and residual matters in terms of the Nigerian Constitution. In other words, both the Nigerian Federal Legislature and the Federal Executive Council were to have some power in the Southern Cameroons in respect of matters within their competence. The Governor-General of Nigeria would have to give his assent to all laws passed by the Southern Cameroons House of Assembly. The new status acquired by the Southern Cameroons under the Lyttelton Constitution enabled the territory to be accorded the post of one Federal Minister from the House of Representatives in Lagos. Dr Endeley, whose party had been instrumental in the acquisition of the new status, became Leader of Government Business in the Executive Council presided over by the Commissioner of Southern Cameroons. The Southern Cameroons House

of Assembly met at Buea for the first time on 26 October 1954 with 13 elected members, 6 nominated Native Authority members, 2 appointed Special Members, and 3 Ex-officio members.

In May – June 1957 delegates from Nigeria and Cameroon again met in London to revise the 1954 Constitution. The three prominent Southern Cameroons political parties also sent delegates. The KNC was represented by Dr E.M.L. Endeley, Fon Galega of Bali, J.T. Ndze and V.E. Mukete. The KPP was represented by P.M. Kale and N.N. Mbile, while the Kamerun National Democratic Party or KNDP was represented by J.N. Foncha and A.N. Jua.

During the Conference, the British Colonial Secretary held discussions with the Southern Cameroons delegation on several issues which were to be laid on the table in the general Conference. The outcome of these discussions and of the deliberations at the Conference was further constitutional advancement for Southern Cameroons. The Cameroon delegation returned home with a promise of a full regional status in the near future, a ministerial system of government, and a House of Chiefs. The Governor-General of Nigeria was to be the High Commissioner of Southern Cameroons, responsible for all trusteeship matters in the territory. The elected members of the House of Assembly were to be increased from 13 to 26, and the Native Authority representation would be abolished. The House would have a Speaker, and the High Commissioner would appoint Ministers on the recommendation of the Premier. Each of the six Divisions of Southern Cameroons would be represented by at least three members in the House of Chiefs which was to be created.

The Conference did not finish its work of revising the Nigerian Constitution and was scheduled to resume on 29 September 1958. Meanwhile, back in Cameroon, Endeley's party suffered a major setback when two of its members crossed the carpet and joined the KNDP in the Opposition. The reason for this was that Dr Endeley was now against the reunification, which the KNDP continued to support. The KNC was thus forced into an alliance with the KPP to maintain its leadership in the House of Assembly and its place in the Executive Council. In May 1958, Dr Endeley resolutely introduced the ministerial system of government in the Southern Cameroons and became the territory's first Premier. But Cameroon was not yet a full Region and would not be self-governing until 1959.

Back in London in September – October 1958 for the resumed Conference, Cameroon made many more constitutional advances. The Cameroon delegation returned home with many resolutions to implement after the general elections scheduled for January 1959. The Commissioner of Southern Cameroons was to cease to be a member of both the Executive Council and the House of Assembly. The post of Financial Secretary was to be converted to that of Minister of Finance. The number of Ministers in the cabinet, including the Premier, was not going to be less than four nor more than seven, and there was provision for the appointment of Parliamentary Secretaries. Southern Cameroons was to have a separate Public Service with an advisory Public Service Commission. The House of Chiefs was to be established.

But before these provisions could come into effect, Nigeria's independence date had already been fixed for 1 October 1960. French Cameroon was going to be independent even earlier, on 1 January 1960. The UN was already discussing the question of the status of British Cameroon. These events turned the January 1959 general elections into a decisive factor in determining whether the people of Southern Cameroons wanted to secede from Nigeria or not. When the votes were counted, the KNDP, which campaigned for secession, was victorious and J.N. Foncha replaced Dr Endeley as Prime Minister. Foncha immediately announced that the Federal elections of 1959 would not take place in the Southern Cameroons. From then on, steps began to be taken for Southern Cameroons to separate from Nigeria before that country achieved independence in October 1960. Foncha also began to discuss reunifica-

tion with the authorities in French Cameroon before and after that territory became independent in 1960.

General administration

The British trusteeship administration in the Southern Cameroons from 1946 to 1954 was fully integrated with the administration of the Eastern Region of Nigeria. The main agents of that administration were the Commissioner for the Southern Cameroons, Residents for the Bamenda and the Cameroons Provinces, District Officers, Assistant District Officers, and departmental officers. The Commissioner for the Southern Cameroons was responsible to the Lieutenant-Governor of the Eastern Region for local administrative matters, and to the Governor-General for trusteeship affairs in the territory. Departmental officers were directly responsible to their heads of departments in Lagos in strictly technical matters, and to the Lt-Governor for the execution of approved policy within the Region.

Southern Cameroons continued to constitute only one province until July 1949 when Bamenda became a province and had its own Resident. The two provinces and the office of Resident were abolished in 1954 when Southern Cameroons became a quasi-federal territory. The creation of the Bamenda Province in 1949 resulted in the creation of two new divisions with headquarters in Wum and Nkambe. These received their full divisional status on 1 April 1951. District Officers appointed to the different divisions were instructed to reorganise the Native Authorities in their divisions by encouraging the formation of Federated Native Authorities. These Federated Native Authorities were to continue to be responsible for the maintenance of order and good government in the areas under their jurisdiction. The local British officials were there to advise, assist and improve the efficiency of the local administration and to maintain a form of control which was to be progressively relinquished.

From 1954 to 1961 when the Southern

Cameroons reunified with East Cameroon, the affairs of the six administrative divisions of the territory were controlled direct from Buea. The Lyttelton Constitution of 1954 had made Southern Cameroons a quasi-federal territory with its own legislature and an executive council. The former could raise taxes and pass laws, although these still required the assent of the Governor-General. In 1957, the powers of the Governor-General to disallow legislation in the territory were reduced and those of the Government at Buea were increased. In 1958, the Southern Cameroons House of Assembly passed a resolution requesting the implementation of full regional government in the territory. This came into effect in 1959. It was followed by the creation of a bicameral system for the legislature, with the introduction of the House of Chiefs. The Commissioner of Southern Cameroons ceased to be a member of the Executive Council which now had an unofficial majority and was led by a premier. The Southern Cameroons Executive Council became the principal organ of policy for the territory, while the Commissioner had only reserved powers similar to those exercised by governors of the Regions of Nigeria. The Governor-General of Nigeria, in his capacity as the High Commissioner for Southern Cameroons, continued to be responsible for all trusteeship matters in the region.

Law and order in the territory was maintained by the police force. Recruitment into the Southern Cameroons Police Force was local, although the recruits received their training in Enugu, later Lagos, in Nigeria. The most senior police officer in the territory was the Superintendent of Police. He had under him two Assistant Superintendents of Police at Bamenda and Victoria, and officers in charge of the police detachments in the various districts of the territory.

As concerns the judiciary, two sets of Courts were organised to function side by side in the territory. These were the Supreme Court and the Magistrates' Court which primarily administered English law, on the one hand, and the Native Courts which dealt with native law and custom on the other hand. The Supreme Court had appellate jurisdiction to hear and determine all appeals from the Magistrates' Court in civil and criminal matters and also appellate jurisdiction to hear appeals from Native Courts and from decisions of Magistrates on appeals from Native Courts. While the Magistrates were appointed by the Governor and assigned to their districts by the Chief Justice of Nigeria, Native Courts were established by the Resident to exercise jurisdiction within the area defined in the warrant.

The era of political parties and elections

The trusteeship period witnessed a great deal of political activity and the formation of political parties in the Southern Cameroons. But the emergence of real parties did not begin until 1951, after the Macpherson Constitution had provided the representation of Southern Cameroons in both the Eastern House of Assembly at Enugu and the House of Representatives in Lagos. Before then, however, political organisations in the form of pressure groups were already active and spearheading the political affairs of the territory.

The first of such political pressure groups was formed in Victoria (now Limbe) at the beginning of the Second World War in 1939 and became active in 1940. It was termed the Cameroon Welfare Union or CWU. Led by a veteran schoolmaster, G.J. Mbene, the CWU established branches in almost all the Divisions of Southern Cameroons and in Lagos. During its short existence, the CWU petitioned the Nigerian and British authorities for Cameroon representation in the Nigerian Legislative Council in Lagos. This demand was granted, although none of the three candidates proposed by the organisation for consideration was taken. Instead, the Nigerian Government nominated Chief J. Manga Williams as representative of the Cameroons Province in the Legislative Council. The CWU failed to replace Chief Manga Williams and became defunct.

The disintegration of the CWU led to the formation of the Cameroons Youth League or CYL in Lagos on 27 March 1940. The new organisation, which was modelled on the Nigerian Youth Movement, was led by Peter M. Kale as president, E.M.L. Endeley as secretary, and J.N. Foncha. Its main concern was the protection of a distinctive Cameroonian identity in Nigeria. Although the headquarters of the organisation was in Lagos, the CYL had branches all over the Southern Cameroons and in most Nigerian colleges where there were three or four Cameroon students. The CYL kept its members informed about the activities of the organisation and developments concerning Cameroon through the publication of a newsletter. In 1944, the organisation presented a challenging memorandum on education in the Southern Cameroons to the Elliot Commission for Higher Education which visited the territory. The CYL also initially championed the case for a separate or autonomous legislature for the Southern Cameroons. In 1946 it played the most important part in the campaign against the Richards Constitution which had completely annulled Cameroon representation in the Nigerian Legislative Council by urging home rule for Cameroon. After a decade or so of its existence, the CYL faded into insignificance partly because the population of Cameroonians in Lagos, the headquarters of the organisation, had dwindled so much and partly because its members who were students had graduated from the colleges and were absorbed into a civil service plagued with transfers. But the organisation had 'blazed the trail' for real political parties in the Southern Cameroons.

Another political pressure group in the Southern Cameroons which lasted only for a couple of years was the Cameroons Federal Union or CFU. The CFU was a loosely-knit organisation that grew out of the CYL and several ethnic associations like the Bakweri Improvement Union and the Bakweri Land Committee. Led by E.M.L. Endeley, the CFU became the first political pressure group in the Southern Cameroons to formally advocate the reunification of the British and French Cameroon, although Endeley's real concern was for greater administrative autonomy and separate regional status for the Southern Cameroons within the Nigerian framework. The organisation called for the teaching of both English and French in the two Trust Territories, the establishment of free trade between the British and French Cameroon, and the creation of a joint constitutional assembly. The CFU, which functioned principally among the Westernised elite working in Lagos and Enugu, existed between 1947 and 1949.

The Cameroons National Federation or CNF emerged out of the May 1949 Conference in Kumba. The Kumba Conference was attended by the CFU and about eighteen political groupings of various ethnic improvement unions, including a union of French Cameroonians (French Cameroons Workers Union) residing in the British Trust Territory. The leaders of the CNF were E.M.L. Endeley, N.N. Mbile, S.T. Muna and Sampson A. George. In 1949 the organisation submitted the first written petition for Cameroon reunification to the UN Visiting Mission to Cameroon. The CNF memoranda often demanded the removal of all restrictions on the frontiers between the British and French Cameroon, and the teaching of English and French in the schools of the two Trust Territories.

But the political pressure exerted by the CNF was weakened by the division among its members over the prime objective of the organisation. While some members wanted to focus on the reunification of Cameroon, Endeley and others wanted the creation of an autonomous Cameroons Region to be the first priority. The feeling by the first group that the Endeley-led faction was either faltering or insincere in its support for reunification led to the collapse of the CNF.

Those who wanted reunification decided to found the Kamerun United National Congress or KUNC in August 1951 under the leadership of R.J.K. Dibonge and N.N. Mbile. This group became a really outspoken unificationist organisation in the Southern Cameroons. It made several contacts with the UPC leaders in 1951 and 1952, but soon became disenchanted with the UPC's communist connections. In 1953, KUNC combined with the Endeley-led CNF to form the Kamerun National Congress or KNC.

All the aspiring Southern Cameroons politicians who were leaders or members of the various political pressure groups were members of the National Council of Nigeria and the Cameroons or NCNC led by Wnamdi Azikiwe. In fact, P.M. Kale, E.M.L. Endeley, N.N. Mbile and others from the Southern Cameroons participated in the founding of the NCNC on 21 August 1944. In 1951, the first general elections into the three Nigerian Regional Houses of Assembly (Eastern, Northern and Western) were held. The Southern Cameroons was allocated thirteen of the eighty seats in the Eastern House of Assembly. All the seats, that is, two each for Victoria, Kumba, Mamfe, Nkambe and Wum and three for Bamenda were won on the NCNC platform. While in Enugu, the thirteen Cameroon Assemblymen formed themselves into a bloc and began to look for an opportunity to found a purely separate Southern Cameroons political party.

Their chance came in April 1953 during a serious political crisis in the Eastern House of Assembly. On 5 May the Lt-Governor of the Region decided to end the row by proclaiming the dissolution of the Eastern house. Following this act, nine of the thirteen Cameroon Assemblymen addressed a message to the Cameroon electorate, declaring that the deliberate disregard of the wishes of Cameroonians in the Eastern House had forced them to break their relations with the Eastern Region. They declared it their immediate duty to press their demand for a separate Region, and advised the people to boycott any future elections to the Eastern House of Assembly. They themselves would stay at home until a Cameroons House of Assembly was created.

In May – June 1953, the nine members of the Cameroon bloc of thirteen in the Enugu House of Assembly, together with the Endeley-led CNF and the Dibonge-led KUNC agreed to amalgamate into one political party. The outcome of that amalgamation was the birth of the Kamerun National Congress or KNC, the first real Southern Cameroons political party. R.J.K. Dibonge was elected President-General of the party and Dr E.M.L. Endeley became head of the parliamentary wing.

In August 1953 and January 1954, the KNC delegates to the Nigerian constitutional conference in London and Lagos respectively demanded a separate Cameroons Region and returned with the promise that the request would be granted if the party won the forthcoming elections on the basis of such appeal. In 1954 elections were held in the territory for both the new House of Representatives in Lagos and the Regional House of Assembly. The KNC won both elections. On 1 October 1954 Southern Cameroons became a quasi-federal territory with its own Executive Council and a House of Assembly. Dr E.M.L. Endeley became Leader of Government Business in the Executive Council. In October and November 1954, the Southern Cameroons House of Assembly held its first session and adopted an interim budget for the services of the territory until 31 March 1955.

The KNC continued to form the government of Southern Cameroons from 1954 to 1959. In 1955, two prominent members of the party, J.N. Foncha and A.N. Jua, resigned their membership because the KNC was no longer advocating secession from Nigeria and ultimate reunification with the French Cameroon, and formed the Kamerun National Democratic Party or KNDP (see Figure 9). In the elections of 1957 the KNC won only six of the thirteen seats in the Southern Cameroons House of Assembly and had to establish a working alliance with another party, the KPP (see Fig. 9), in order to form the government. The two parties then agreed to campaign for the independence of British Cameroon within the Federation of Nigeria.

Following the implementation of a new Nigerian Constitution which accorded Southern Cameroons a full regional status and enlarged

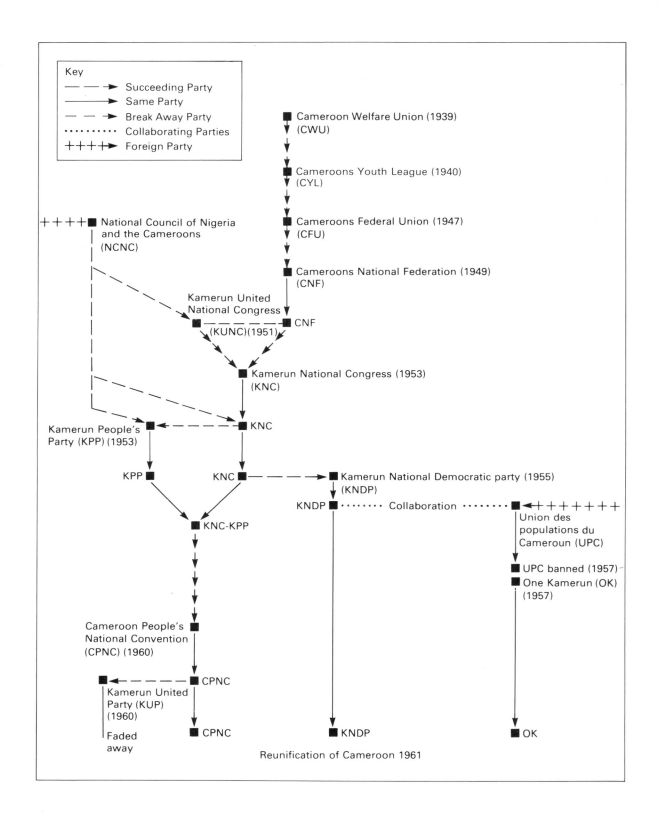

Figure 9 *Pressure groups and political parties in the Southern Cameroons, 1939–61*

the House of Assembly from 13 to 26 elected members, new elections were called for January 1959. The KNDP won 14 seats, the KNC 8 seats and the KPP 4 seats. John N. Foncha and his KNDP were able to form the government, although one of its members (J.N. Boja from Wum) later crossed the carpet to the KNC. The KNC – KPP alliance, which now formed the Opposition, decided to merge into one party in May 1960 and thereafter became known as the Cameroons People's National Convention or CPNC.

The Kamerun People's Party or KPP emerged in June 1953 from and against the newly formed KNC. It was led by P.M. Kale, N.N. Mbile and P.N. Motomby-Woleta. The primary objective of the KPP was continued association with the NCNC and the Eastern Region of Nigeria, although eventually it began to advocate regional autonomy and secession from Nigeria when the latter became an independent country. During the first elections into the Southern Cameroons House of Assembly created under the 1954 Constitution, the KPP won only one seat. In 1957 it won two seats, and in 1959 it won only 4 of the 26 seats. In 1960 the KPP merged with the KNC to form the CPNC.

The KNDP was formed in March 1955, and soon became the third major Southern Cameroons political party. This new party, led by J.N. Foncha, stood for the severance of political ties with the Federation of Nigeria and the administration of the territory as a separate dependency under the British Colonial Office. The KNDP also desired ultimate reunification with the French Cameroon with which British Cameroon would be politically associated on a federal basis. During the 1957 elections into the Southern Cameroons House of Assembly the KNDP won 5 seats, and in the course of the year increased its seats as a result of the defection of S.T. Muna from the KNC. In 1959 the KNDP won 14 of the 26 seats in the Assembly elections and ably formed a government which it led to independence and reunification in 1961.

The three other political parties in the Southern Cameroons worth mentioning were the UPC, the One Kamerun or OK Movement, and the Kamerun United Party or KUP. The UPC began to operate permanently in the Southern Cameroons after it was banned by the French in their trust territory in July 1955 and its leaders fled to the British territory where they were able to establish its headquarters in Kumba. The party soon made common cause with the KNDP. But collaboration with the KNDP did not last long, and the relationship between the two organisations became permanently estranged. In July 1957, the UPC was banned by the British and its leaders deported from the Southern Cameroons. Almost immediately after this incident, the OK Movement led by Ndeh Ntumazah was established in place of the UPC. But the OK, though considered to be the old UPC in disguise, was more indigenous to the Southern Cameroons than was the UPC. The main objective of the OK was immediate independence and reunification without qualification. The OK won no seats in any Southern Cameroons elections before reunification and independence. The only seat it managed to secure in the December 1961 elections, just after reunification, was soon lost when the member declared for the KNDP shortly after the results were proclaimed. The OK dwindled in significance thereafter. The KUP was a minor party formed and led by P.M. Kale for the sole purpose of campaigning for independence as the third alternative in the 1961 UN plebiscites. Unfortunately, the UN rejected the independence alternative, possibly because neither Foncha nor Endeley had proposed it, and the KUP disintegrated.

Economic advancement

The British declared in 1946 that their general economic objective in the Southern Cameroons was to do everything that was deemed expedient in the interest of the economic advancement of the territory. Their aim was to raise the general standard of living and to encourage every form of economic development among the indigenous inhabitants. But, on examination, the economic record of the British in Cameroon from 1946 to 1961 shows that neither of these goals was rigorously pursued in the territory. As will be seen, the economic development of the territory during the period was one-sided. Southern Cameroons depended on the plantation lands leased to the Cameroon Development Corporation or CDC. There was very little substantial economic activity elsewhere in the territory outside the plantations.

The CDC was created in 1946 as a statutory corporation to take over and administer most of the plantations confiscated from the Germans in 1939 for the benefit of the inhabitants of the Trust Territory. In fact, the plantations were acquired by the Governor-General of Nigeria on behalf of the Government at the end of the war from the Custodian of Enemy Property for £850 000 and leased to the CDC for 60 years at a nominal rent.

Among its many functions spelt out in the Ordinance setting up the Corporation, the CDC was to cultivate economic crops, raise stock and deal in merchandise and produce of all kinds as producer, manufacturer, exporter or importer. Its major economic crops were the palm tree for oil and kernels, banana, rubber, cocoa and, eventually, tea. The corporation was heavily dependent on the Nigerian Government for capital after 1947, and increasingly on Britain for its export and import markets.

The CDC was not only the main employer of labour in the Southern Cameroons; it also played a crucial role in the remainder of the economy. In its heyday it contributed about two-thirds of the territory's export tonnage and more than one-half of its export earnings. It made important contributions to the ports and transport system through the taxes it paid to the government. The Corporation's net profit, after taxes and payment of certain charges, was to be paid to the Governor-General of Nigeria for the benefit of the inhabitants of the Trust Territory. In 1948, for example, the Corporation allocated £54 352 for expenditure on the people of British Cameroon. Of this sum £22 352 was allocated to British Northern Cameroons and £32 000 to the Southern Cameroons. Of the Southern Cameroons allocation £5000 was spent on reading rooms, £2000 on secondary school scholarships for boys and girls in Cameroon and Nigeria, and the rest on various schemes like community halls and maternity homes put up by the territory's provincial committees. After 1954 when Southern Cameroons became a quasi-federal territory with its own government, the Corporation's net profits were paid directly to it.

The valuable contribution of the CDC to the Southern Cameroons financial structure was adversely affected by the Corporation's irregular record of profitability. The CDC's net profits dropped from a maximum of £60 000 in 1953 to less than one-third of that sum in 1954, and only three times exceeded £25 000 in the remainder of the period up to 1961. As a result, the Southern Cameroons government found it increasingly necessary from 1954 to seek direct budgetary assistance from Nigeria.

1948	£54 352	1955	nil
1949	£22 544	1956	£15 117
1950	no data	1957	£38 028
1951	£55 559	1958	£16 078
1952	no data	1959	nil
1953	£60 285	1960	£25 788
1954	£19 204	1961	£47 620

Table 10.1   CDC net profits 1948 – 1961

The extent to which Southern Cameroons was, or could be, self-supporting was given attention for the first time after 1954, when it became a separate administrative unit within Nigeria. Before then, the territory was only covered in the budget allocation for Eastern Nigeria with which it was administratively integrated, and the public accounts kept for that Region. Revenues accruing from the Southern Cameroons were included without distinction in the budgets of the Eastern Region, and expenditures were allotted to it not on the basis of its overall needs, but on the basis of the need of the whole Region.

This arrangement made it difficult to accurately determine the capacity of Southern Cameroons to finance its own projects. It was simply assumed that Nigeria was putting more into the Trust Territory than it was getting out. As a matter of fact, the Nigerian Government claimed that during the period from 1943 to 1959 it subsidised Cameroon by more than one million pounds sterling. It was only when the CDC began large-scale production in 1948 that Southern Cameroons for the first time had a surplus of revenue over expenditure. This led to the creation of a special fund into which £1 163 000 was deposited over the next six years to be used for the benefit of the trust territory as a whole.

Despite the surpluses, a fiscal commission which studied the Southern Cameroons financial situation in 1954 reported fairly accurately that the territory could not be viable without external financial assistance. In fact, the budget of the new Government for the first full year showed a deficit of about £285 000. To guard against future deficits a special formula, known as the 'Chick formula', was worked out by Sir Louis Chick, the Financial Secretary in the Nigerian Government, for stabilising the finances of the Southern Cameroons government. Under this formula, a federal constitutional grant was instituted to pay back to the Southern Cameroons Government every penny the Federal Government got out from the territory but did not spend on federal services for the territory. In addition, a special advance of £300 000 was made to the new government to provide it with working capital. The 'Chick formula' was based on the assumption that the CDC would continue to be a major source of revenue. But the poor showing made by the Corporation in 1954 and in the subsequent years made it difficult for the region to finance its own programmes.

A new arrangement designed to guarantee the Southern Cameroons a fixed minimum of revenue was worked out in 1955 to replace the 'Chick formula'. Under this system, the Federal government accepted the obligation to guarantee that the revenues the Southern Cameroons would receive annually over a period of three years from the Federation would not be less than £580 000. In other words, if the normal grant of some £300 000 plus the CDC's net profit fell short of the £580 000, the Federal Government would make up the difference. This system was still deemed unsatisfactory. During the two fiscal years from 1956 to 1958, Federal grants to Southern Cameroons were £450 000.

It now required a careful investigation into both the actual and estimated financial situation in the territory before a formula similar to that applied in the other Regions of the Federation could be worked out for the Southern Cameroons. The study was entrusted to the Raisman Commission during the fiscal years from 1956 to 1959. The Commission's recommendations, which were applied in the 1958 – 59 allocations to the Southern Cameroons, assigned to the territory the proportion estimated to be due to it from the import and excise duties imposed by the Federal Government as well as receipt of the entire revenue from all personal income tax, mining royalties and certain miscellaneous revenues raised within the territory itself. In addition to the new allocation, debts totalling £700 000 and the accrued interest made under the old system of revenue allocation were cancelled by the Nigerian Government. All the same, Southern Cameroons still suffered a deficit of some £200 000 in the first budget estimates in which the new formula was applied. It was only through unexpectedly high revenues that the 1958 – 59 budget was finally balanced.

There were also, as earlier indicated, capital grants to the Southern Cameroons by both the United Kingdom and Nigeria, including an annual grant of about £300 000 by Nigeria from 1955 to 1958, and an expenditure of £1.2 million on the Victoria – Bamenda road in 1959. In 1956, the British Colonial Office made a grant of £1.3 million for various aid projects including roads, technical education, agriculture, communications and other development projects. An outright British grant of £450 000 was also made in early 1958 to help

12 *The first Southern Cameroons Executive Council, 1954, with Dr E.M.L. Endeley as Leader of Government Business*

meet the territory's bugetary deficits. Nevertheless, there was always a feeling among the Southern Cameroonians that their territory was not receiving the financial attention it deserved from the British Government, or its just share of Nigerian revenues. Those who were dissatisfied with the income allocated to the territory by Nigeria were convinced that Southern Cameroons would do better if it could operate its own finances. This belief received a boost in 1959 when a study showed that under certain circumstances Southern Cameroons might prove to be potentially viable, although the territory would not be able to stand on its own feet as an independent country.

The Endeley and Foncha Governments

Dr E.M.L. Endeley, whose bloc in the Eastern House of Assembly espoused the cause of separate regional status for the Southern Cameroons was named Leader of Government Business in the Southern Cameroons House of Assembly on 1 October 1954, after the territory secured its distinctive 'quasi-federal' status. At the time, the head of the Southern Cameroons Executive Council was the British Commissioner of the Southern Cameroons. Dr Endeley and his colleagues in both the Executive Council and the House of Assembly continued to lead the campaign to see the Southern Cameroons of the future as a self-governing region.

After the Constitutional talks in London in 1957, Dr Endeley introduced a ministerial system of Government in the Southern Cameroons on 15 May 1958. He became the first Southern Cameroons Premier on that date, holding in addition the Portfolio of Minister of Local Government, Land and Survey. The members of his cabinet were V.T. Lainjo as Minister of Social Services, F.N. Ajebe-Sone as Minister of Natural Resources, N.N. Mbile as Minister of Works and Transport, and Rev. Andoh Seh as Minister of State.

In his policy statement on his government's attitude towards the French Cameroon, Premier Endeley almost completely abandoned the reunification goal. He declared on 29 May 1958 that although ultimate reunification was still desirable, the intervening events and circumstances had removed the question from the realm of urgency and priority. Dr Endeley said that his government was convinced that reunification should only be achieved when an independent Nigeria, of which the Southern Cameroons would form a part, was to explore the possibility of a union as part of the movement towards the creation of the United States of West Africa.

In September 1958, the Constitutional talks resumed in London, where Endeley and his KNC – KPP alliance advocated that Southern Cameroons would attain her independence as part of independent Nigeria. The Opposition KNDP led by Foncha opposed the idea. But the various delegations returned from London with a promise of a full regional status after an election and a definite establishment of a House of Chiefs. On 24 December 1958 the Southern Cameroons House of Assembly was dissolved on the recommendation of Premier Endeley, and new elections into the enlarged Assembly were scheduled for 24 January 1959.

The 1959 elections were taken as a determining factor on whether or not the Southern Cameroons would secede from Nigeria. By this time, the reunification movement championed by Foncha's KNDP and other parties had gained much ground in the territory. When the election votes were counted, the KNDP had captured 14 seats, thereby narrowly defeating the KNC – KPP alliance which had won a total of 12 seats. John Ngu Foncha was named Prime Minister, replacing Dr Endeley. On 11 March 1960 the KNC – KPP alliance now in the Opposition induced J.N. Boja to leave the KNDP, thereby bringing the state of the parties in the House of Assembly to KNDP 13, KNC – KPP 13. But the KNDP was still able to hold on to the government, and Foncha continued as Prime Minister.

Prime Minister Foncha's cabinet in 1959 included among others A.N. Jua, S.T. Muna, W.N.O. Effiom and J.M. Bokwe. Almost immediately after Foncha and his Ministers were sworn in on 30 January, he and Dr Endeley left for New York to plead their respective positions before the UN General Assembly on the future of the British Trust Territory. At the UN, where the idea of a plebiscite was agreed upon for 1961 or 1962, Foncha wanted the electorate to decide only between continued association with Nigeria or secession from it. Endeley wanted the decision to be between continued association with Nigeria and reunification with the French territory. The inability of Foncha and Endeley to agree on anything specific led the UN to decide on two separate plebiscites for Northern Cameroons and Southern Cameroons. The UN General Assembly also decided to postpone the decision on the questions to be posed to the electorate in the Southern Cameroons. But, since Nigeria's independence was already set for 1 October 1960, it was necessary to introduce interim constitutional reforms which would allow for a separate administration for the Southern Cameroons pending the plebiscite.

The new Southern Cameroons constitution which came into force on 1 October 1960, as the Southern Cameroons Constitutional Order in Council, did not differ very much from the Nigerian constitution under which the territory was administered. The new Constitution retained the form and size of the House of Assembly and the House of Chiefs, re-established the form of responsible government under a Prime Minister, and maintained the British Commissioner of Southern Cameroons as head of the administration. Britain of course remained accountable to the UN as the Administering Authority in the Trust Territory. The new constitution also initiated a new and separate judiciary for the Southern Cameroons, gave the territory control over the police and

13 *J.N. Foncha, Prime Minister of Southern Cameroons in 1959*

14 *Sembum (Sem) III, Fon of Nso, Member of the House of Chiefs*

other territorial affairs, and introduced a set of fundamental rights and liberties which were justifiable before the courts of law.

The date for the Southern Cameroons plebiscite was soon set for 11 February 1961. Foncha held several discussions with Prime Minister, later President, Ahidjo in late 1959 and in 1960 when the French Cameroon became independent on the question of reunification. Prime Minister Foncha finally accepted the fact that his KNDP would have to campaign on the definite alternative of reunification with the independent Cameroon Republic and not a period of intervening independence. The UN had decided on only two questions for the Southern Cameroons plebiscite: integration with Nigeria or reunification with Cameroon. Foncha had tried but failed to persuade the British government to agree to interpret a vote in favour of reunification as one which implied a preparatory period of independence for the Southern Cameroons. When the votes of the plebiscite were counted in February 1961, the result was a KNDP landslide. On 1 October 1961 Cameroon reunified.

Further reading

Edwin Ardener, Shirley Ardener, A. Warmington, *Plantation and Village in the Cameroons* (OUP, Oxford, 1960).

S.H. Baderman, *The Cameroons Development Corporation: Partner in National Growth* (CDC, Bota, 1968).

Michael Crowder, *The Story of Nigeria* (Faber & Faber, London, 1962 and 1966).

Simon J. Epale, *Plantation and Development in Western Cameroon 1885-1975* (Vantage Press, New York, 1985).

Ndiva Kofele-Kale (ed.), *An African Experiment in Nation Building: The Bilingual Cameroon Republic Since Reunification* (Westview Press, Boulder, 1980).

Stanford Research Institute, *The Economic Potential of West Cameroon* (California: The Institute, Mendo Park, 1965).

Willard R. Johnson, *The Cameroon Federation* (Princeton University Press, Princeton, 1970).

P.M. Kale, *Political Evolution in the Cameroons* (Buea, 1967).

Victor T. LeVine, *The Cameroons From Mandate to Independence* (University of California Press, Berkeley and Los Angeles, 1964).

Neville Rubin, *Cameroon: An African Federation* (Praeger, New York and London, 1971).

Questions

1. What political and administrative arrangements were introduced in the British Cameroons from 1946 to 1961?
2. Discuss the emergence and importance of political parties in the Southern Cameroons from 1946 to 1961.
3. Why was the establishment of the CDC in 1946 a major economic achievement for the Southern Cameroons?
4. Discuss the rise to power and fall of Dr E.M.L. Endeley and the emergence of J.N. Foncha as Prime Minister of the Southern Cameroons in 1959.

Chapter eleven

Nationalism, independence and reunification

This chapter studies the political developments which led to the attainment of independence and the reunification of Cameroon in 1960 and 1961. Political parties, trade unions, political revolts and elections in French and British Cameroon have been dealt with in sections of the previous two chapters. But these themes are again touched upon in this chapter in order to emphasise their contribution to the struggle for independence and reunification. The struggle for the attainment of these two objectives was spearheaded by the nationalists, that is Cameroonians who demanded the right of the people of this country to be free to make their own decisions and supported the movement for the recreation of the nation within the framework of the pre-1916 German Protectorate of Kamerun. Independence and the re-establishment of the Cameroon nation would then lead to the true union of all the diverse peoples of the national territory.

Latent nationalism

It is difficult to say exactly when nationalism in Cameroon began, but it is certain that the nationalist sentiments began to be expressed shortly after the partition of the territory in 1916. It is from then that we can begin to trace the development of modern Cameroon nationalism.

Since the word 'nationalism' means a strong devotion or loyalty to one's own nation, it stands to reason that there can be no nationalism without the existence of a nation. The two questions that come immediately to mind are: What is a nation? Was the colonial territory of Cameroon a nation? The answer to the first question is simple. A nation is defined simply as a 'large community of people usually speaking a single language and usually having a political character or political aspirations'. But the answer to the second question is not as simple as that. We all know that there was no nation or country known as Cameroon before the colonial era. Our country of Cameroon was carved out by the Germans who first colonised it. Even after Cameroon had been defined, the territory did not constitute a community of people speaking the same language and having a political character or political aspiration. The various peoples of the territory continued to belong to their ethnic groups or states rather than being immediately transformed into a nation-state. In other words, Cameroon was not a nation. On what then, we may ask further, is Cameroon nationalism based?

Cameroon nationalism was rooted more in the terms *Cameroon* and *Cameroonian* rather than in the myth of a German-created nation. Surely, the inhabitants of the territory that was delineated and named Cameroon were not immediately conscious of belonging to one new country. They did not even attach any importance to that fact. But they began to be aware of it after thirty years of hardship under one colonial authority, when efforts began to be made to divide them. It was then that devotion to the initial colonial territory that was described as *Cameroon*, rather than to the power which had created it, began to take on a national character. For, indeed, the term *Cameroon* became the symbol of the unity of the territory, the term *Cameroonian* the foundation of the unity of existence of its inhabitants, and both were the basis of Cameroon nationalism.

It is easy to prove that the basis of Cameroon nationalism was the fact of belonging to that territory and being a Cameroonian from 1884 to 1916. Although the territory was partitioned by the British and the French, and administered separately for more than forty years, the people never ceased to think of themselves as one or to associate as brothers. It was very seldom that the distinction was made between a Cameroonian from the British territory and his fellow countryman from the French territory. No Cameroonian from the one or the other sector was considered a foreigner by the peoples indigenous to the sector. On the other hand, no Cameroonian from the British Cameroon ever considered himself a Nigerian despite the forty-four years of close political, administrative and cultural association with Nigeria. Besides, in spite of the partition of the territory, the imposition of the mandate and trusteeship systems of administration, and the further partition of the British section into North and South, every part of the initial territory as carved out by the Germans was still called Cameroon. No matter whatever the enemies of the territory did, they failed to eliminate that one word *Cameroon*.

The First World War was a remote stimulus to the rise of nationalism in Cameroon. It was the war that led to the repartition following the defeat and expulsion of the Germans from the territory. The repartition made many Cameroonians become aware, within a relatively short space of time, not only of the oneness of their territory but also of their peoples who had borne the brunt of the harsh German rule together. It developed in them a new national consciousness. Indeed, the general opinion of the people in both the British and French spheres was overwhelmingly against the repartition.

Throughout the period between the two world wars, individual Cameroonians and groups seized every opportunity to petition or demonstrate against the repartition of their country and continued colonial rule. In 1919, Prince Alexander Douala Manga Bell of Douala raised his voice against the repartition. During the Paris Peace Conference, he began his reunification and independence campaign. He appealed to traditional rulers and leaders of the people in both the French and British spheres to support the idea of an uprising against the repartition and against the British and French administrations. In August of the same year, a group of Duala people petitioned the Paris Peace Conference pleading that the Anglo-French provisional partition of Cameroon should not be confirmed. Rather, they urged that the whole territory of Cameroon should be entrusted to the protection of one of the Allied powers. Other similar petitions to the newly-formed League of Nations urged the suppression of the mandate, the removal of all barriers placed in the way of relations between Cameroonians in the British and French spheres, and the reunification and independence of the territory.

Petitions and demonstrations in favour of reunification and independence continued in the 1920s and the 1930s. In 1922 – 23 the whole town of Douala, supporting an expelled Cameroonian pastor of the Native Church, Pastor Alfred Lotin Same, revolted and paraded the streets of the township singing anti-colonial songs. They called for the independence of Cameroon, urging that Africa be left to the Africans. Many of the demonstrators did not fail to recall the good old days˙ when Cameroon was one indivisible country. In December 1929 another petition from the Duala to the permanent Mandates Commission denounced the cupidity of all colonial powers who could not tolerate the idea of national autonomy among the people entrusted to their care. They called for the independence of Cameroon, arguing that the new state would evolve according to the conceptions of Cameroonians. In the 1930s the struggle for national reunification led to the idealisation of the German colonial period when Cameroon was one and to the establishment of pro-German clubs and organisations. Some of the clubs and organisations began to work secretly for the return of the German administration in the hope that such an outcome would result in the reunification of the territory.

What is to be noted about nationalism in Cameroon between the two world wars is that it was either ethnically based or the concern of a few individuals. No attempt was made to coordinate the activities of these individuals. No attempt was made to coordinate the activities of these individual nationalists from different parts of the territory or to form nationalist movements to which all would belong. It was not until after the Second World War that real nationalism began in Cameroon.

Nationalism in the French Cameroon

Cameroon nationalism from the 1940s moved from the stage of individual concern or the concern of a handful of people from a single ethnic group, and wishful thinking, to the stage of organised mass movements to exert effective pressure on the colonial powers and concerned bodies. The political movements that emerged during this period, the activities of nationalist leaders and their followers, the contacts between nationalists in British and French Cameroon, and the significant political events at home and abroad, especially at the UN, affected Cameroon's advance towards independence and reunification. The principal ideas in all the nationalist programmes included self-government, independence and reunification.

The political nursery from which post-Second World War nationalist movements emerged in the French Cameroon was Jeucafra founded in 1938. Jeucafra survived the war as the only quasi-political association through which Cameroonian nationalists might address themselves to political matters. The members of the association hoped that the postwar era would establish a new relationship between French Cameroon and France free of all vestiges of colonialism. In 1943 the association asked for a number of political reforms, particularly the suppression of the mandate and the right of Cameroonians to elect their own representatives.

But nationalists began to be more active and outspoken from 1944, following the legalisation of trade-union activity in the territory. The freedom to form trade unions led immediately to the establishment of the Cameroon Trade Union Federation, the USCC, which embarked on a mass propaganda campaign designed to enlist membership and bestir political feeling. The union leadership intended to use trade union activities to bring about the establishment of a sovereign Cameroon state. After challenging France's overseas labour laws, the USCC inspired a series of wildcat strikes which degenerated into the bloody Douala riots of September 1945. In the same year another movement, Unicafra, a successor organisation to Jeucafra, began to plead both the Cameroon cause and devotion to France. In 1947 an attempt by the leaders of Unicafra, the USCC and several other smaller groups to discuss joint prospects led to sharp disagreement between extreme and moderate nationalists.

Meanwhile in 1946 the Representative Assembly, ARCAM, was created and became a tribune for the most able of the Cameroon politicians and nationalists. The representatives of the Assembly who had won their first election on personal appeal began casting about for organisational bases on which to build more solid political support. They were aware that what the country needed were genuine Cameroon political parties with nationalist programmes. But it was from outside the Assembly that a real nationalist movement was formed. In April 1948 the trade union leaders who had been discredited by the Douala riots of 1945 founded the UPC, the first true nationalist party in Cameroon. The UPC leaders, who included among others Ruben Um Nyobe, Felix Moumie, Ernest Ouandie and Abel Kingue, announced the party's programme, which contained essentially the complete independence of Cameroon under the terms of the UN Charter and the reunification of the two Trust Territories. The UPC quickly gained the support of the Duala, the Bamileke and the Bassa from whom many of its leaders were drawn, and to a lesser extent among the Bulu and Ewondo; it also gained the support of the *Ngondo*, the Duala traditional council of notables, and the *Kumsze*, a traditional Bamileke secret society.

Soon after its formation, the UPC established and maintained contacts for many years with the Southern Cameroons political groups. The UPC even assisted in the formation of the French Cameroon Welfare Association (later Union) with the dual purpose of mobilising the inhabitants of French Cameroon resident in the British territory, and spreading the unification idea. The UPC at one time or another supported the aims of most Southern Cameroons political leaders. It participated in several conferences of nationalist groups from both the British and French Cameroon at which reunification and independence were always discussed. Indeed, frequent participation by the UPC in the Southern Cameroon political meetings made the reunification issue a permanent factor in the politics of the territory. In 1955, the UPC leadership, fleeing from arrest after the party was banned in French Cameroon, established its headquarters in Kumba in a sympathetic atmosphere. It soon made common cause with the KNDP leadership, although the friendship did not last for long. In 1957 it participated in the election into the Southern Cameroons House of Assembly although it won no seat. Later in the year it was banned by the British from the territory and its leaders, who had been under police surveillance since 1955, were deported. But by the time the UPC was banned it had made every Southern Cameroonian aware of reunification. It left behind a nationalist group indigenous to the Southern Cameroons, the OK, to continue

to beat the drum of reunification and independence in their own territory.

In the French Cameroon, the UPC moved quickly to structure itself on a nationwide basis through establishing branches everywhere and creating subsidary and complementary organisations. By 1949 when the first UN Visiting Mission arrived in Cameroon, the UPC had become the best-organised nationalist movement in the territory.

Between 1948 and 1955, a number of nationalist organisations, some of them with ethnic referent and all in opposition to the UPC, had representatives in the Cameroon legislative Assembly. Most of these organisations initially favoured only legislation which would convert Cameroon into a semi-autonomous state. In order to gain the popularity which the UPC seemed to enjoy, many of these political organisations began to adopt the UPC programme of independence and reunification but without allying with that party. By 1955 almost all the parties had accepted as their goals the eventual independence of the country and the reunification of the two Trust Territories.

Events in Cameroon soon overtook the UPC and drove it into a campaign of terror and violence after 1955. This followed the decision of the French administration to take an offensive against the party. In April 1955, the UPC and its affiliated labour union demanded in a joint statement the termination of Cameroon's trusteeship status and the establishment of a sovereign state. The following month, violence erupted in several towns and districts in which many casualties were recorded and houses and property destroyed. On 13 July 1955 the administration ordered the dissolution of the UPC and its affiliates, and arrested some of their leaders. Other leaders fled into exile in the British territory.

In the meantime, constitutional reforms which gave Cameroon its first push towards independence were being worked out in France. These reforms created the office of Prime Minister as head of a ministerial government. When Ahidjo succeeded Mbida as Prime

Minister in 1958 he began immediately to hold talks with the French in Paris to see how independence should be worked out. In October 1958 the French government signified its assent to Cameroon's independence on 1 January 1960.

The UPC meantime continued underground where it directed acts of violence, sabotage and terrorism in the territory. It also sent spokesmen to the UN to attack both the Ahidjo and French designs in Cameroon. Later in 1958 Um Nyobe, the UPC leader, was killed by a government patrol in Bassaland. Following this disaster for the UPC, a significantly great number of the party's followers in the Sanaga-Maritime region and elsewhere surrendered to the government. In June 1959, Ahidjo began contacts with Foncha, the pro-reunification Prime Minister of Southern Cameroons, on the nature of Cameroon reunification. On 1 January 1960 the French Cameroons acquired her independence and became the Republic of Cameroon. Talks between Ahidjo and Foncha became more frequent until reunification was achieved in October 1961.

Nationalism in the Southern Cameroons

At no time did British colonial authorities intend to administer their Trust Territory of Cameroon as a separate entity from Nigeria. Reactions to this policy led to the emergence of organised nationalism in the Southern Cameroons. Southern Cameroons nationalism was initially directed toward the status of an autonomous region within the Nigerian Federation. The first step in this direction was taken by the leaders of the newly-formed Cameroon Welfare Union (CWU) who in 1939 requested representation for the Southern Cameroons in the Nigerian Legislature at Lagos. Only the three Regions of Nigeria (Eastern, Northern and Western) were represented in Lagos in their own right and, as Southern Cameroons was administered as an integral part of the Eastern Region, it did not have this status. The request

was therefore seen as tantamount to a demand to grant the territory equal political rights to the other Regions of Nigeria. It was rejected by the British, although in 1942 they named a Southern Cameroonian, Chief Manga Williams, as one of the representatives from the Eastern Region to the Legislative House in Lagos. The struggle for an autonomous Region and a possible Cameroon nation was taken over by the Cameroons Youth League (CYL) after 1940. In 1946 the CYL took part in the agitation against the Richards Constitution, which made no provisions for a separate Southern Cameroons Region.

From 1949 Southern Cameroons nationalism made still greater advances following the formation of more nationalist groups, principally the Cameroon National Federation (CNF). The CNF had three main political objectives, namely, to assert the identity of Cameroon, to unite the two sections of British Cameroon into a single political entity, and to bring about the reunification of the British and French Trust Territories. The CNF denounced the system of administering the British Cameroon as an appendage to Nigeria to the first UN Visiting Mission to Cameroon in the same year as not in the best interests of the inhabitants of the territory. They asked that the two parts of the British-administered territory be united and made into a distinct region, and that steps be taken to reunite all of Cameroon as it existed before 1914. The nationalists also proposed that Cameroon should either be administered directly by the UN or accorded independence. In 1952 when the UN Visiting Mission came for the second time, the CNF and other organisations which had the opportunity to address the Mission, pressed for an autonomous Cameroon Region separate from the Eastern and Northern Regions of Nigeria. The thirteen Cameroon members of the Eastern House of Assembly and the KUNC also demanded the reunification and creation of a greater Cameroon nation.

In 1953 two of the leading Nigerian nationalists, namely, Nnamdi Azikiwe and Obafemi Awolowo, supported the right of Cameroon nationalists to self-determination. Azikwe (Zik) gave his weight to Cameroon aspirations for separate regional status, including a separate legislative assembly with full budgetary autonomy, and the reunification of Cameroon as it existed before 1914. Awolowo also supported the concept of a separate Cameroon legislature and the right to self-determination to remain in or outside Nigeria.

Following the dissolution of the Eastern House of Assembly in May 1953, a conference of all the Southern Cameroons politicians, nationalists, traditional authorities and cultural groups was held at Mamfe to reach a decision on the future of the territory. The Conference resolved to petition the British government for a separate state and autonomous legislature for the Southern Cameroons. Dr Endeley, who was the acknowledged leader, was immediately dispatched to London to submit the petition to the Secretary of State. Later in 1953 and in January 1954, at the All-Nigerian Constitutional Conference, the British for the first time recognised explicitly the separate identity of the Southern Cameroons. The Southern Cameroons became a Quasi-Region, separate from the Eastern Region but unequal in all respects to the other Nigerian Regions. The territory acquired its own House of Assembly and could also elect its own representatives to the House of Representatives in Lagos. The new status was a landmark in the political history of the Southern Cameroons. Henceforward, the Southern Cameroons nationalists were to be faced with three alternative major political objectives, namely: full autonomy as a Region in the Nigerian Federation or integration into Nigeria; full separation and independence for British Cameroon or secession from Nigeria; and secession from Nigeria and immediate reunification of the two Trust Territories.

Another outcome of the Mamfe Conference was the creation of the first real Southern Cameroons political party, the KNC out of the CNF and the KUNC, with Endeley as leader. Later in 1953 the KNC won all the six Southern Cameroons seats into the Federal House of Representatives, and in 1954 twelve of the thirteen seats into the Southern Cameroons House of Assembly in Buea. Endeley became Leader of Government Business (not Premier as in the other Regions) in the Southern Cameroons House of Assembly. But soon after the acquisition of the quasi-regional status, Endeley began to pay less and less attention to secession and began to perceive the Southern Cameroons developing into a self-governing region within an independent Nigerian Federation. He began to relegate the unification of the two sections of the British and French Cameroon to the background and to work for the integration of Southern Cameroons into Nigeria. Endeley's policy shift soon led to a split in the KNC. John Ngu Foncha decided to break with the party and to form the KNDP, which began to champion the case for secession and reunification.

In 1955 the UN Visiting Mission was again in Cameroon, for the third time. Foncha's KNDP demanded that the British Northern Cameroons and the Southern Cameroons be merged and administered as a single entity and that the two Trust Territories be reunified. Endeley's KNC and the KPP made the same request but less forcefully. A few months later, in 1956, Endeley changed his mind completely, and went to the UN at New York to denounce secession from Nigeria and the reunification of the British and French Cameroon. He now demanded 'rapid constitutional advancements' to bring the Southern Cameroons 'to the status of a fully self-governing region within the Nigerian context'. Foncha and the KNDP rapidly countered Endeley's demands and joined hands with the UPC (which was already established and active in the Southern Cameroons) in championing the course of secession, reunification and independence. The KNDP later severed relations with the UPC when it was discovered that the latter party had strong communist connections and was prone to violence. In 1957 the British banned the UPC from the Southern Cameroons and outlawed it with its members for fear that the party might resort to violence in order to achieve its political

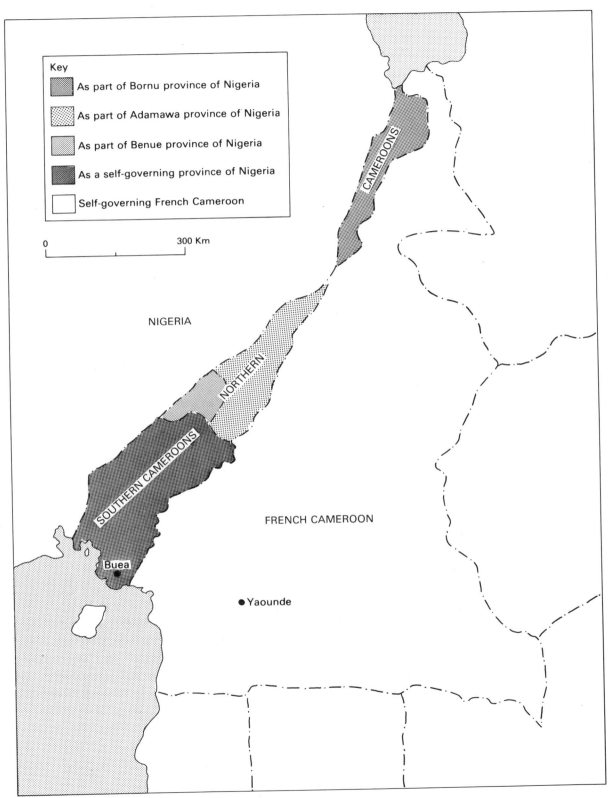

Figure 10 *Administration of Cameroon in 1959*

objective. The party was immediately resuscitated under the disguised name of OK, with a totally new leadership indigenous to the Southern Cameroons.

In 1957 the British promised full autonomy in the form of a Region for the Southern Cameroons, within Nigeria. In 1958 Endeley became Premier in the first ministerial government in the territory. Later in the year, Southern Cameroons was granted self-government, to come into effect after the general elections of January 1959. Endeley's KNC, which was in alliance with the KPP, lost the elections, which the KNDP narrowly won. John Ngu Foncha became Prime Minister of the self-governing Southern Cameroons Region and Endeley became Leader of the Opposition in the House of Assembly.

In late 1958 the UN Visiting Mission made its final visit to Cameroon and was addressed by the nationalist groups and the traditional authorities. Foncha and his KNDP demanded that the British Trust Territory be set free from its entanglement with Nigeria as the first step towards the reunification of Cameroon. Endeley's alliance wanted the Southern Cameroons to continue 'its already assured progress as a self-governing state in the Nigerian Federation'. The OK asked for immediate reunification and independence. Traditional authorities wanted secession from Nigeria but not reunification with the French Cameroon. Efforts by the nationalist leaders, particularly Foncha and Endeley, to reach agreement on the questions of integration, secession and reunification failed. In October 1960 the British Trust Territory was separated from Nigeria on the latter's attainment of independence, to prepare to decide between integration and reunification in a UN-supervised plebiscite.

Cameroon and the United Nations Organisation

The United Kingdom and France were granted responsibility as Administering Authorities over the Trust Territories of Cameroon by the UN. In doing so, the UN established separate Trusteeship Agreements with the two Administering Authorities for the proper administration of the territories. The UN undertook to supervise the administrations through its Trusteeship Council.

There were three principal ways by which the Trusteeship Council exercised its supervisory powers over the British and French administrations in Cameroon. Firstly, the Council required each Administering Authority to submit annual reports which it studied thoroughly; it posed oral and written questions on specific aspects of the administration; and it made observations and recommendations. Secondly, the Council monitored adherence to the UN Charter and the Trusteeship Agreements by periodically sending Visiting Missions to Cameroon to make on-the-spot investigations and submit reports embodying observations and recommendations. Finally, the General Assembly gave the politicians and nationalists of the Trust Territories the opportunity to visit and address the UN and its organs on various issues concerning Cameroon, including economic advancement, self-government, independence and reunification.

The UN began exercising its supervisory powers over the administrations in Cameroon in 1949 when it first examined the annual reports submitted to it by the French and the British. The Administering Authority always sent a special representative to the Trusteeship Council to present the report, answer questions on specific issues, and defend the soundness of its policies. The annual reports were based on the questionnaire issued by the Trusteeship Council. The procedure for examining the reports was for the Trusteeship Council to discuss it in general terms and then allow its Special Committee to draft a report comprising the Council's observations and recommendations. The ensuing report was then sent to the General Assembly of the UN, which in turn referred it to its Fourth Committee for trusteeship and non-governing territories where each member country of the UN had a representative. The Fourth Committee then voted resolutions and made recommendations to the full Assembly for action on specific issues. The representative of the administration was allowed to defend the report before the Special Committee of the Trusteeship Council and again before the Fourth Committee of the UN. In exercising its powers of supervision, the UN was always careful not to turn supervision into intervention in either the French or British administration.

The UN objected to the French policy of assimilation in Cameroon and to its decision to administer the territory as part of the French Union. It criticised the representation of the territory in the institutions of the French Republic, the lack of Cameroonians in key positions in the territorial administration, and the assimilationist aspects of the educational policy, which placed a great deal of emphasis on French culture and virtually ignored African culture. The UN from 1949 regularly requested France to increase the powers of the territorial assembly and to develop institutions of local government. Above all, the UN wanted France to maintain the separate status of Cameroon as a Trust Territory which should eventually acquire self-government or independence.

In addition to studying annual reports submitted to it, the UN sent periodic Visiting Missions to Cameroon to conduct investigations and submit reports. These occurred at three-yearly intervals (1949, 1952, 1955 and 1958) prior to the termination of the trusteeship status for French and British Cameroon on 1 January 1960 and 1 October 1961 respectively. The prospect of a Visiting Mission stimulated much activity and preparation in the territory. Each Mission listened to and received copies of addresses, petitions and complaints from various political, cultural and ethnic associations regarding self-government, independence, reunification, customs and boundary restrictions between the British and French Cameroon, and various alleged colonial malpractices.

The first Visiting Mission arrived in Cameroon in November 1949. In the French Cameroon it received petitions listing a number of demands including proposals for various political reforms, for the industrialisation of the territory, for the protection of the economic interests of Cameroonians, and for the improvement of such matters as education and health services. There were demands for the greater participation of Cameroonians in the economic and political affairs of Cameroon. In the Southern Cameroons there was the demand for an end to the system of administering the British Cameroon as an appendage to Nigeria. Everywhere in the British territory the Mission encountered the cry for more and better education and health services. In both territories there was demand for reunification, principally by some Southern Cameroons nationalist groups and the UPC. In their report to the UN after this visit, the Mission dismissed petitions for reunification on the grounds that it was not a real issue in the two territories.

In 1952 many political groups in French Cameroon protested to the Visiting Mission and to the Trusteeship Council over the retention of the dual electoral college system, especially in view of its abolition in Togo, France's other Trust Territory. There were political demands including full regional status for British Cameroon and the reunification of the two Trust Territories. In 1955 French Cameroon politicians continued to object to the inadequacies of French rule and to plead for the greater participation of Cameroonians in the affairs of the country. The UPC group organised demonstrations against French rule, demanding independence and the reunification of the British and French territories.

The last Visiting Mission was in Cameroon from October to November 1958. This Mission was instructed to investigate the ways and means of implementing the request for the termination of the trusteeship in French Cameroon and the granting of independence in 1960. It was also to study the various complex political situations in the British Southern Cameroons which involved demands for the creation of a self-governing region within the independent Nigerian Federation, or secession from Nigeria and independence as an entity in its own right, or reunification with the French territory. In its report on the French Cameroon, the Mission recommended the termination of trusteeship, and independence by 1 January 1960 without any necessity for elections in the territory beforehand. For the British Cameroon, the Mission recommended a plebiscite to settle the political demands in the territory. Both recommendations were approved by the Trusteeship Council and the UN.

The third and final way by which the UN exercised its supervisory authority and monitored the activities of the Administering Authorities in Cameroon was through listening to petitioners, politicians or nationalists who cared to write or to travel to New York to address the world body in person.

In December 1952 Reuben Um Nyobe requested and became the first nationalist politician from the French Cameroon to be granted the first of several annual appearances before the UN General Assembly. He claimed that he was the spokesman for many organisations including his party the UPC, the Trade Union Organisations, the Babimbi Solidarity Movement, the Association of Ex-Servicemen, the Union of Cameroon Students in France, the Women's Organisation, and the nationalist groups in the British Cameroon. In his address Um Nyobe stressed the deficiencies of the French administration and asked that a time-limit be set for Cameroon's independence and that political reforms be undertaken with the ultimate aim of reunifying the French and British Cameroon. The French Government vigorously criticised the UN decision to grant Um Nyobe a hearing.

Following Um Nyobe's appearance before the General Assembly, the French colonial administration hastened to ensure that moderate Cameroon political leaders were also heard by the world organisation. Among those sent in 1952 to counteract Um Nyobe's testimony were Prince Douala Manga Bell, Charles Okala, Daniel Kemajou and Jules Ninine.

This attitude of the colonial administration and of Um Nyobe to appear before the UN every year opened the gates to a flood of visits and petitions from political groups in Cameroon to New York. Appearances were made before, and petitions received by, the Trusteeship Council, the Secretary General of the UN, the General Assembly and the Fourth Committee of the General Assembly. Besides raising economic, ethnic and social problems and the deficiencies of the Administering Authorities, the petitioners and visitors to New York also argued for or against the political options for Cameroon, namely, self-government, independence and the reunification of the French and British Cameroon. Southern Cameroons politicians also included the options of complete secession from Nigeria or complete integration as a full self-governing Region of the Nigerian Federation. The case for the reunification of Cameroon was much stimulated by the visits to the UN.

In 1959 almost every French Cameroon politician who could gather sufficient funds for the trip went to the UN session on Cameroon which opened on 20 February. In all, some 28 political and nationalist groups were represented. All who wanted to speak were heard. Prime Minister Ahmadou Ahidjo who brought with him the new self-governing 1959 Statute of the Cameroon, and the very favourable 1958 UN Visiting Mission's Report spoke eloquently and convincingly. He assured the UN that all the elected members of the Cameroon Legislative Assembly, ALCAM, had endorsed independence, which was going to be complete and unconditional. He convinced the world body that the new Republic of Cameroon would not be integrated into the French community. The UPC and other petitioners wished independence to be delayed until certain conditions were met, including the dissolution of ALCAM and the holding of new elections. They were unconvincing. The UN finally adopted the resolution approving independence for 1 January 1960, and endorsing the prospective admission of Cameroon into the Organisation. In the same year Prime Minister Foncha,

Endeley and other Southern Cameroons politicians, who in 1958 had accepted the idea of a plebiscite to determine the future of the British territory, were again at the UN to draw up the plebiscite questions. After very lengthy discussions and negotiations, Foncha and Endeley at last arrived at a compromise agreement. Consequently, the UN adopted a resolution stating that the plebiscite in the British Cameroon would require the voters to choose between attaining independence by joining either the independent Federation of Nigeria or the independent Republic of Cameroon.

French Cameroon becomes independent

André-Marie Mbida's government collapsed in February 1958 primarily because he was against the independence of Cameroon in the near future and also against the reunification of the French and British territories at any time in the future. Shortly after succeeding Mbida as Prime Minister, Ahmadou Ahidjo embarked upon the road to independence and reunification which had won the support of almost all the political parties in the French territory. In March Ahidjo went to Paris to negotiate a timetable for advancement towards independence. In May his government submitted to ALCAM a draft resolution in which Cameroon requested France to recognise Cameroon's aspiration to independence, transfer all powers relating to the domestic affairs of the territory, and to maintain the trusteeship until the proclamation of independence. ALCAM voted in favour of the resolution in June and on 24 October solemnly proclaimed the desire of the people of Cameroon to see their country attain independence on 1 January 1960. It then invited France to inform the UN General Assembly about the date of independence so that the abrogation of the trusteeship could be timed to coincide with it. ALCAM also demanded the

reunification of the British and French Trust Territories before the attainment of independence.

The French Government notified the UN on 28 October 1958 of Cameroon's desire to attain independence on 1 January 1960 and for the revocation of the trusteeship to coincide with it. The UN then acted quickly and instructed its last Visiting Mission to Cameroon to sound the opinion of the population on independence. Meanwhile, on 12 November ALCAM adopted a new Statute of Cameroon proposed to it by France. Under it the territory acquired complete self-government and ceased to be represented in the French Assemblies. On 1 January 1959 the new Statute of Cameroon came into force.

Back in New York at the end of 1958, the UN Visiting Mission reported that the overwhelming majority of the population of Cameroon was clamouring for independence. During the UN session in February and March 1959 Ahidjo, not wishing to jeopardise progress towards the independence of French Cameroon, suggested that the reunification of the two territories of Cameroon should come after independence and after a plebiscite in the British zone. On 12 March 1959, the Trusteeship Council and the General Assembly voted in favour of Cameroon's independence as proposed. Thus on 1 January 1960, in the presence of the UN Secretary General, Dag Hammarskjöld , the independence of Cameroon was proclaimed. It became a republic completely outside the French community. On 21 February 1960, a new independence constitution was ratified by the new state in a referendum in which the 'Yes' vote was 797 000 and the 'No' vote 531 000. On February 25 the government of the Republic repealed the decree of 13 July 1955 banning the UPC and then called for elections on 10 April. The governing UC won 51 of the 100 seats and 49 seats were divided between the five Opposition parties and independents. On 5 May 1960, Ahmadou Ahidjo was elected the first President of the Republic of Cameroon. Ahidjo now embarked upon the reunification programme.

The plebiscite in the Southern Cameroons

In 1955 the Southern Cameroons political leaders who supported the reunification of the British and French Trust Territories urged the UN to go ahead and effect the policy of reunification without consulting the people. In 1956 the KNC–KPP alliance opted out of the reunification while the KNDP suggested that the Southern Cameroonians be consulted on the issue through their elected representatives. Between 1956 and 1958 the gap between the political programmes advocated by the integrationists, secessionists and reunificationists widened so much that the idea of consulting the people to determine the future political status of the territory became an important and lively issue for discussion. It gained impetus from the British suggestion to the UN in 1958 that a plebiscite be held in their sphere of Cameroon. When the UN Visiting Mission came to the territory towards the end of that year, and again when the political leaders were at the UN in early 1959 to explain their programmes, the notion of a plebiscite as the best form of consultation was fully endorsed.

Even after agreement in principle had been reached, several technicalities remained undetermined. Decisions had to be made on what questions were to be put to the voters, who should qualify to vote, and when exactly the vote should be recorded. Long discussions were held by the Southern Cameroons political leaders both in Cameroon and at the UN to answer these questions. The alternative questions suggested by the different political parties included: integration with Nigeria versus separation from Nigeria and the determination of the future of the territory at a later date, self-government within Nigeria versus independence through reunification, and association with

15 *The Southern Cameroons Delegation to the UN talks in 1960, led by J.N. Foncha and E.M.L. Endeley*

Nigeria versus joining the Cameroon under the French administration. A compromise agreement was at last arrived at by Foncha and Endeley at New York in the presence of the British representative and the representatives of the African states at the UN. The agreement was adopted and put out as a Resolution of the General Assembly.

The questions to be put at the plebiscite would be:

(a) Do you wish to achieve independence by joining the independent Federation of Nigeria?

(b) Do you wish to achieve independence by joining the independent Republic of Cameroon?

Only persons born in the Southern Cameroons were to vote in the plebiscite. The arrangements for the plebiscite were to begin on 30 September 1960 and end not later than March 1961. Polling day was fixed for 11 February 1961. By narrowing down the political alternatives the agreement simplified the issue and opened the way for the campaign for the two alternatives to be put at the plebiscite to begin. In fact campaigning began in earnest even before 30 September 1960. The CPNC Opposition backed the first proposition, namely integration with Nigeria, while the KNDP Government supported the second proposition or reunification with the Cameroon Republic. During the campaign, accusations and counter-accusations were levied by both sides against each other. These allegations included refusal to register and give the vote to people of a particular area because they supported the other proposition, bribery and corruption to win over the voters, hooliganism and violent intimidations, and refusal to tell the population the real meaning of the proposition campaigned for.

During the lead-up to the plebiscite five fundamental but controversial realities in the Southern Cameroons emerged. These, according to Willard R. Johnson, were: a deepseated antipathy toward Nigerians and particularly the Ibo ethnic group by most Southern Cameroonians; a general attachment to 'British ways'; a feeling of community with certain groups in either Nigeria or Cameroon Republic; a general antipathy against 'French ways'; and a fear of terrorism in the Cameroon Republic. Each side had to juggle perceptions of these realities in order to produce favourable attitudes.

The KNDP based its campaign upon the idea of being a Cameroonian in Cameroon. Its principal argument, which the Opposition found difficult to destroy was that 'Cameroonians are not Nigerians'. Those opposed to reunification were easily labelled as traitors to the Cameroon nation. The KNDP also tried to equate support for reunification with loyalty to the government. Indeed, as Dr Endeley confirmed later, 'the plebiscite was generally understood only as an issue between those ethnic groups controlling the government and those groups whose leaders were in the Opposition and who wished to unseat the government.' The CPNC, on the other hand, based its campaign on emphasising 'British ways' and the assurance of the security of the rule of law in Nigeria. The party appeals were almost wholly devoted to unfavourable comparisons between the terror-stricken Cameroon Republic and a peaceful, well-intentioned Nigeria. The CPNC concentrated almost all its campaign efforts in Victoria, Kumba and Nkambe Divisions, in the belief that the remaining three Divisions were already lost to the KNDP.

A total number of 349 650 people registered to vote in the plebiscite. Of these 331 312 people or 94 per cent cast valid votes. As can be seen in the table of results, the results of the vote revealed that only Kumba and Nkambe Divisions voted for the Nigeria proposition, while the region as a whole voted for the Cameroon proposition. In all 97 741 voted for integration with Nigeria and 233 571 voted for reunification with the Cameroon Republic.

Some people from the ethnic groups along the Southern Cameroons frontiers voted for the one or the other proposition on the basis of cultural, linguistic and ethnic affinities and continuities with groups in either Nigeria or

Administrative Divisions	Plebiscite Districts	Votes for Nigeria	Votes for Cameroon
Nkambe Division	Nkambe North	5 962	1 917
	Nkambe East	3 845	5 896
	Nkambe Central	5 095	4 288
	Nkambe South	7 051	2 921
		21 917	15 022
Wum Division	Wum North	1 485	7 322
	Wum Central	3 644	3 211
	Wum East	1 518	13 133
	Wum West	2 137	3 449
		8 784	27 115
Bamenda Division	Bamenda North	8 073	18 839
	Bamenda East	1 822	17 856
	B'da Central West	1 230	18 027
	B'da Central East	529	18 193
	Bamenda West	467	16 142
	Bamenda South	220	19 426
		12 341	108 485
Mamfe Division	Mamfe West	2 039	8 505
	Mamfe North	5 432	6 410
	Mamfe South	685	8 175
	Mamfe East	1 894	10 177
		10 070	33 267
Kumba Division	Kumba North-East	9 466	11 991
	Kumba North-East	14 738	555
	Kumba South-East	6 105	12 827
	Kumba South-West	2 424	2 227
		32 733	27 600
Victoria Division	Victoria South-West	2 552	3 756
	Victoria South-East	1 329	4 870
	Victoria North-West	4 744	4 205
	Victoria North-East	3 291	9 251
		11 916	22 082
	GRAND TOTAL	97 741	233 571

Table 11.1   Results of the Southern Cameroons plebiscite

Cameroon Republic. And there were more groups with affinities and continuities in the Cameroon Republic than in Nigeria. Many who voted against reunification said that they abhorred the idea and dreaded the thought of uniting with a people whose customs, education, language, system of government and way of life differed from anything they had known. Despite the irregularities, the suspicions and the accusations involved in the campaign

and conduct of the plebiscite, everyone appeared enthusiastic about the vote. That the plebiscite was a KNDP landslide has been attributed to the deep-seated commitments to the idea of a Cameroon nation, if only within the context of Southern Cameroons.

The situation in Northern Cameroons

During the period of trusteeship, British Northern Cameroons continued to be administered separately from the Southern Cameroons, and the various sections of that territory continued to be tied to the Northern Nigeria provinces of Bornu, Adamawa and Benue. Thus, the Northern Cameroons political developments were entirely separate from those of the Southern Cameroons. After 1948, the territory qualified for representation in the bicameral Northern Regional Council. In 1955 a special Ministry for Northern Cameroons Affairs was set up in Kaduna, the capital of the Northern Region. But, throughout the period of trusteeship, no separate budgets were prepared for that part of the British trust territory, and public accounts were undifferentiated from those of the Northern Region of Nigeria. Of course the British hoped that Northern Cameroons would eventually integrate with Northern Nigeria.

As the date for Nigeria's independence, set for 1 October 1960, approached, the British informed the Trusteeship Council that they would like to terminate their trusteeship in Cameroon on that day. They wanted a decision on the future of the territory to be made before independence. Following the recommendations of the UN Visiting Mission to Cameroon in 1958, the idea of a plebiscite to decide the political future of British Cameroon was adopted by the UN. But the plebiscites would be conducted separately for Northern and Southern Cameroons. The one for Northern Cameroons would be held before Nigeria became independent.

Accordingly, 7 November 1959 was chosen as the UN plebiscite day for Northern

Cameroons. The voters were required to decide whether they wanted to be part of the Northern Region when Nigeria attained her independence on 1 October 1960, or whether they would like to decide their future at a later date. It was taken for granted in both Kaduna and Lagos that the vote in favour of Northern Nigeria would be a landslide. But when the ballots were counted, 70 546 out of 113 859 of the electorate who voted, or 61.5 per cent, favoured deciding their future at a later date. The result stunned the Northern Regional Government in Kaduna. There was no possibility of organising a definitive plebiscite before Nigeria's independence on 1 October 1960. Instead, arrangements began to be made to separate Northern Cameroons from the Northern Region in particular and from Nigeria in general before the latter achieved independence.

On 1 October 1960, Northern Cameroons was, in theory, separated from Nigeria and restructured as a Trust Territory Province, independent of Bornu, Adamawa and Benue provinces. Under special arrangement with Nigeria its administration was headed by a very senior British administrator 'within the body politic of an independent Nigeria.' Its district and provincial officials, including the DOs and the Resident, continued to be responsible to the Northern Nigerian Government.

A final UN plebiscite was soon organised for the Trust Territory Province on 11 and 12 February 1961, to be conducted separately from that in the Southern Cameroons on 11 February. The two questions asked were the same as in the Southern Cameroons plebiscite: whether they wished to achieve independence by joining the independent Republic of Cameroon or by joining the independent Federation of Nigeria. The Republic of Cameroon under Ahmadou Ahidjo expected an overwhelming vote in favour of reunification, considering the vote against becoming part of Nigeria in 1959. But an all-out campaign by the Kaduna Government, coupled with all sorts of intimidations and unequivocal warnings to those who voted against Nigeria, produced a vote in favour of integration with Nigeria. Northern Cameroonians voted 146 296 out of 244 072, or 60.40 per cent, in favour of independence within the independent Federation of Nigeria. Nigeria was delighted with the results, which shocked the Cameroon Government in Yaounde. Ahidjo's Government was furious at Nigeria's intervention in the conduct of the Northern Cameroons plebiscite, and doubted the accuracy of the results. Ahidjo carried his protest to the UN, which rejected it.

Plebiscite area	1959 plebiscite				1961 plebiscite			
	Total vote	Vote for Nigeria	Vote against Nigeria	Percentage result for Nigeria	Total vote	Vote for Nigeria	Vote for Cameroon	Percentage result for Nigeria
Dikwa North	14 671	7 575	7 197	52.48	33 327	22 765	10 562	68.32
Dikwa Central	19 879	8 891	11 988	43.57	52 900	28 697	24 203	54.46
Gwoza	10 129	3 356	6 773	33.67	20 669	18 115	2 554	88;12
Madagal/ Cubunawa	14 065	4 247	9 818	30.70	30 266	16 904	13 299	56.44
Mubi	19 654	6 120	13 578	30.70	34 930	23 798	11 132	68.32
Chamba	16 191	4 539	11 651	28.72	34 881	9 704	25 177	28.72
Toungo/ Gashaka	4 351	2 252	2 099	52.48	8 161	4 999	3 108	62.38
Mambila	10 118	2 747	7 353	27.73	20 990	13 523	7 467	65.35
United Hills	3 152	3 063	89	97.3	7 984	7 791	157	98.2
TOTAL	113 859	42 788	70 546	38.62	244 072	146 296	97 659	60.40

Table 11.2   The plebiscites in Northern Cameroons 1959 and 1961

Source: A.H.M. Kirk-Grene, *Adamawa Past and Present*.

On 1 June 1961, the British trusteeship of Northern Cameroons was terminated as the territory definitively became part of Nigeria. Shortly after the territory was named Sardauna Province in honour of the Premier of Northern Nigeria. In Cameroon, 1 June was declared a day of national mourning. The date was observed for some years before relations with Nigeria improved and the declaration abrogated.

The reunification of Cameroon

Prime Minister Ahidjo and Prime Minister Foncha began to hold talks concerning the reunification of Cameroon in 1959. In that year they met twice, in New York in February – March and in Buea in July, to discuss the form which the union would take and the system of government to be adopted. These talks were intensified when the French territory became independent in January 1960 and Prime Minister Ahidjo became President of the Republic in May of the same year. In that year the two leaders held talks in January in Yaounde, in April in Nkongsamba, and in May, November and December in Yaounde. At these pre-plebiscite talks, Ahidjo and Foncha were able to agree that their territories would join neither the French Community nor the British Commonwealth and that their own federal institutions would be responsible initially for foreign affairs, defence, public liberties, nationality, higher education, immigration, posts and telecommunications, and the federal budget. Other powers of the federal institutions as well as the powers of the two federated states would be elaborated after the Southern Cameroons had voted for reunification in the plebiscite.

The results of the plebiscite in the Southern Cameroons solved all the doubts about reunification. Ahidjo and Foncha resumed their talks on a note of self-satisfaction, although both were disappointed by the results of the separate plebiscite in the British Northern Cameroons

16   *Ahidjo and Foncha bid farewell to the British Administration, October 1961*

where the majority of the voters decided in favour of integration with Nigeria. Following discussions in April 1961, a Constitutional Conference was held at Fumban from 17 to 21 July between representatives of the Republic of Cameroon and those of the Southern Cameroons to resolve the differences between the Ahidjo and Foncha conceptions of the nature of the forthcoming federation. The Fumban Conference was followed by another meeting in August in Yaounde. The outcome was a draft federal Constitution. It was soon approved by the legislatures in both territories, and 1 October 1961 saw the end of the Southern Cameroons trusteeship. Simultaneously the Federal Republic of Cameroon came into existence. The former Southern Cameroons became the State of West Cameroon and the former Cameroon Republic became the State of East Cameroon. Ahamadou Ahidjo became the President of the Federal Republic and John Ngu Foncha, while remaining Prime Minister of West Cameroon, became Vice-President of the Federal Republic.

Further reading

Bongfen Chem-Langhëë, *The Kamerun Plebiscites 1959 – 1961: Perceptions and Strategies* (Ph.D. Thesis, University of British Columbia, 1976).

James S. Coleman, *Nigeria: Background to Nationalism* University of California Press, Berkeley and Los Angeles, 1958).

David E. Gardinier, *Cameroon: United Nations Challenge to French Policy* (OUP, London, 1963).

Arthur Hazlewood (ed.) *African Integration and Disintegration* (OUP, Oxford, 1967).

Richard A. Joseph, *Radical Nationalism in Cameroun* (OUP, Oxford, 1977).

P.M. Kale, *Political Evolution in the Cameroons* (Government Press, Buea, 1968).

Ndiva Kofele-Kale, *An African Experiment in Nation Building: The Bilingual Cameroon Republic Since Reunification* (Westview Press, Boulder, 1980).

Victor T. LeVine, *The Cameroons From Mandate to Independence* (University of California) Press, Berkeley and Los Angeles, 1964).

Engelbert Mveng, *Histoire du Cameroun*, Tome II (CEPER, Yaounde, 1985).

Claude E. Welch, Jr, *Dream of Unity: Pan-Africanism and Political Unification in West Africa* (Cornell University Press, Ithaca, 1966).

Questions

1. What is nationalism? Discuss the origin of Cameroon nationalism.
2. How did French Cameroon become independent?
3. What is a plebiscite? Why and how were the plebiscites in the British Northern and Southern Cameroons organised?
4. How was the reunification of the British and French Cameroon achieved?
5. Why was June 1 declared a day of national mourning in Cameroon in 1961?
6. What was the role of the UNO in the advancement of Cameroon towards independence?

Chapter twelve
The Cameroon Federation

President Ahidjo and Prime Minister Foncha met on several occasions before the plebiscite in the Southern Cameroons to discuss the framework of the government of the united Cameroon in the event of a vote in favour of reunification. They came to a vague agreement that the union should be federal and loose, with a minimum number of items subject to the federal authority. After the plebiscite the two leaders and members of their respective governments and advisers met at Foumban in July 1961 to work out a Constitution defining the formal structure of the Federal Republic of Cameroon. That Constitution became the basis of the government from 1 October 1961 to 20 May 1972. In this chapter we shall study the content of the Federal Constitution, the political and administrative developments during the

period of federation, and also the economic development of the territory. I am greatly indebted to Victor T. LeVine and other sources included in the Further reading section at the end of this chapter.

The Constitution of the Federal Republic

The Foumban Constitutional Conference was summoned for 17–21 July 1961. In preparation for this very important meeting, the Southern Cameroons political leaders and traditional authorities held a Convention at Bamenda in June at the instance of Prime Minister Foncha to draft a comprehensive set of proposals as a basis for negotiation with the

17 *The Southern Cameroons Delegation to the Foumban Constitutional Conference, 1961*

delegation from the Cameroon Republic. The Bamenda proposals advocated a loose federation and upheld the principle of each future Federated State preserving its local autonomy and political power. In contrast to those of the Southern Cameroons, the draft proposals of the Ahidjo government were in the form of a complete constitution which advocated a clear preponderance of federal over state institutions. Unfortunately, these two conflicting documents were not available for scrutiny before the two parties assembled in Foumban.

The Foumban Conference was held in an atmosphere of inhibited gaiety and celebration. There were twenty-five delegates from the Southern Cameroons and twelve from the Cameroon Republic. Ahidjo and Foncha opened the Conference on notes of caution, realism, and family spirit. Both leaders stressed their commitment to a federal form of government in view of the linguistic, administrative,

economic, and cultural differences which the two territories were inheriting from their colonial past.

Once the opening formalities were through and the delegations got down to business, it became clear that the Southern Cameroons delegation was not in a position to deal intelligently with the comprehensive and unfamiliar set of propositions advanced by the Cameroon Republic delegation. The Foncha delegation was therefore forced to hold long discussions *in camera* to consider the Ahidjo proposals point by point and to attempt to form a position on them. The task took them nearly the whole five days of the Conference. Given the circumstances, one wonders why the Southern Cameroons delegation did not ask for adjournment. As a result, the official joint Conference of both delegations extraordinarily lasted only 95 minutes.

During the five days at Foumban and the

18 *President Ahidjo and Prime Minister Foncha arriving for the opening of the Foumban Conference*

subsequent meeting at Yaounde which produced the final content of the Federal Constitution, most of the efforts of the Southern Cameroons delegation were devoted to obtaining alterations which would lessen the impact of the extremely centralised administration on the existing institutions of the future Federated State of West Cameroon. The overall framework of the Federal Constitution followed the model presented by the Ahidjo government.

The document of the Federal Constitution of Cameroon, which became effective on 1 October 1961, laid down the structure of the Federal Republic of Cameroon. It was divided into eleven parts and contained a total of 60 Articles. Part 1, made up of Articles 1 to 4, designated the Federated States of East and West Cameroon, declared the Federation's adherence to the Universal Declaration of Human Rights and the Charter of the UN, the official languages, the motto, the national flag, the anthem, the seal and the citizens of the Federal Republic. It vested the sovereignty of the Federation in the people, authorized the free and democratic participation of political parties in elections, and accorded the exercise of Federal Authority to the President of the Federal Republic and the National Federal Assembly.

The remaining 56 Articles from 5 through to 60 can be divided into Federal Organs, Federated States, Amendment of the Constitution, and the Transition and Special Dispositions. The Federal Organs were covered in Parts II to VIII, from Articles 5 to 36, under the titles Federal Jurisdiction, the President of the Federal Republic, the Federal Legislature, Relations Between the Federal Executive and Legislature, the Judiciary, Impeachment, and the Federal Economic and Social Council. The Federated States were covered in Part IX, Articles 38 through 46. Part X, with only one Article, concerned the Amendment of the Constitution, while Part XI from Articles 48 to 60 covered Transition and Special Dispositions.

The Federal Republic of Cameroon was to

19   *Dr John Ngu Foncha, Vice-President of the Federal Republic of Cameroon*

be headed by an executive President who was to be assisted by a Vice-President. Both members could not come from the same State. The President was both the Head of State and the Head of the Federal Government. As an interim measure, Ahmadou Ahidjo, who was President of Cameroon Republic, and Prime Minister John Ngu Foncha, who was Prime Minister of Southern Cameroons, were to hold the positions of President and Vice-President of the Federal Republic respectively, until May 1965 when Ahidjo's mandate under the 1960 Cameroon Republic Constitution expired and the first Presidential elections were held.

The President was empowered by the Constitution to select his ministers from among the nationals of the two Federated States without specifying that they be members of the Federal Assembly nor that they be divided in any particular proportion between the two States. He was empowered to appoint the Prime Ministers of the Federated States after consultation with the State Legislature and the cabinets of the Federated States on the recommendation of the Prime Minister of the State concerned. The President was also empowered to intervene where necessary if the Federated State Government did anything which was likely to affect the life of the Federation. In the event of such a development, according to Article 15, he was to proclaim by decree a state of siege and take all necessary measures to bring the situation under control.

The Federal Constitution did not assign any functions to the Vice-President. It merely stated that he was to assist the President who might by Decree delegate any part of his functions to him. In the event of vacancy (by reason of death, resignation or other) of the Presidency, the powers of President of the Federal Republic were to devolve upon the Vice-President until election of a new President. The offices of President and Vice-President were not to be held concurrently with any other office, although as an interim measure John Ngu Foncha would be both Vice-President of the Federation and Prime Minister of the Federated State of West Cameroon until the Presidential elections in May 1965. Later in the decade, S.T. Muna was to hold the two offices of Vice-President and prime Minister together from 1970 to 1972 in contravention of Article 9 of the Federal Constitution.

The Federal Constitution defined the composition and powers of the Federal Legislature and also established the Federal Courts as well as the Federal Economic and Social Council. The Federal National Assembly was to be composed of 50 Members or Deputies, forty from the Federated State of East Cameroon and ten from the Federated State of West Cameroon. Each Deputy represented approximately 80 000 inhabitants. The life of the Legislature was fixed at five years, meeting annually in two sessions, each session lasting 30 days. One of the sessions had to be devoted to the study and approval of the Federal Budget. A Bill passed by the Federal Legislature would be adopted only if the majority of the Deputies of each of the Federated States voted for it. The President of the Federal Republic had 15 days within which to promulgate a Bill passed by the Federal Assembly into law.

The Constitution established two exclusively Federal Courts, namely, the Federal Court of Justice and the Federal High Court of Justice. The Federal Court served as a final Court of Appeal for Federal cases arising in State Courts or cases between the Federated State and the Federation, while the Federal High Court was especially established to try cases of high treason or conspiracy against the Federal Republic. The Federal High Court was the only Court empowered to try the President, Vice-President, Ministers, Prime Ministers, Federated State Ministers, and other officers of the Federal Republic charged with conspiracy or treason. Finally, the Constitution created a Federal Economic and Social Council, although it did not spell out its functions. The Economic and Social Council which was set up in 1963 served as a consultative body incorporating representatives of industry, labour, management, agriculture, businessmen, and so on and so forth.

The scope of Federal power as defined by the Constitution appeared to be very broad. It provided Federal jurisdiction under two categories, one in which Federal organs were to operate immediately and the other listing areas which would come into force after the period of transition. Article 5 enumerated such matters as nationality, national defence, currency and money, foreign affairs, press and broadcasting, and so on as immediately falling under Federal control, while Article 6 listed areas originally under State control such as secondary education, local judicial organisation and administration as subject to Federal authority after a period of transition. By 1963 most areas listed under Article 6 had fallen under *de facto* Federal jurisdiction. The Constitution did

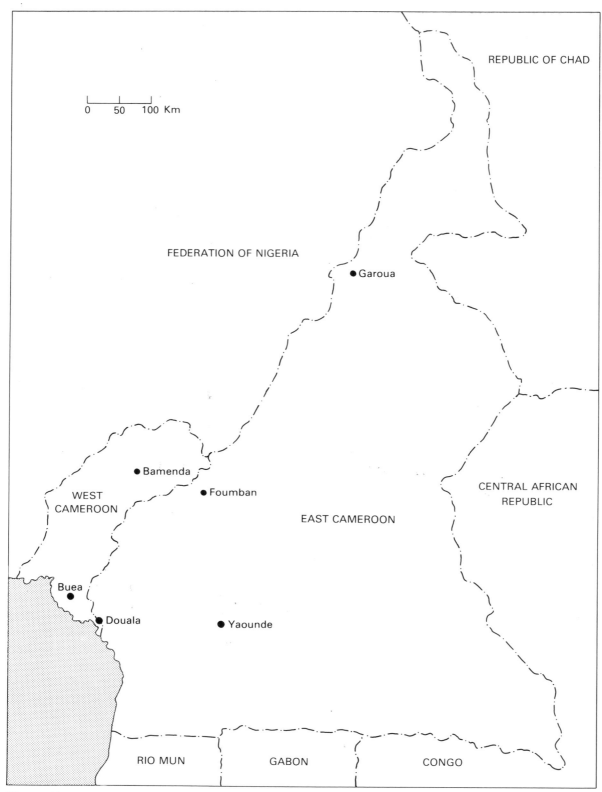

Figure 11 *The Federal Republic of Cameroon*

preserve the two entrenched rights of the Federated State of West Cameroon, namely, customary law courts and the House of Chiefs. Concerning the Federated States and Federal State relations, the Constitution said very little beyond defining the powers of the President in respect to the selection and termination of State governments and in relation to laws passed by the State assemblies. The West Cameroon House of Assembly was enlarged from its earlier 26 to 37 seats by the Constitution, and the East Cameroon House of Assembly was to have 100 representatives.

Political developments in Cameroon 1961-72

The period of Federation witnessed significant developments in party politics in Cameroon, both in the Federated States and at the national level. The basis for these developments was President Ahidjo's call in November 1961 for the creation of a grand national unified party in Cameroon. From then until 1966 it became the most widely talked-about political issue, and it opened the way for changes in party cooperation and inter-party relations in West and East Cameroon. The path of development was different for each State, although both moved in the direction of the merger of all political parties at the national level.

The first political event in West Cameroon after reunification was the general election into the State Legislative Assembly on 7 January 1962. In that election the KNDP captured 25 of the 37 seats, thereby winning an absolute majority, while the CPNC won 10 and the OK and independent candidates won one seat each. The OK and Independent candidates immediately declared their support for the KNDP when the new Assembly was convened. In 1962 the KNDP and the Opposition CPNC declared their readiness to join a true national party of which the UC – KNDP 'Unity Group' in the Federal Assembly was the model. (The UC and KNDP ruling parties in the East and West Cameroon were the only two parties repre-

sented in the Federal Assembly.) The CPNC wanted the merger to begin at the State level and be preceded by the dissolution of both the KNDP and the CPNC. The KNDP argued differently that the CPNC should dissolve and join the KNDP in order to be associated with the 'Unity Group', the UC and the future unified national party. These arguments prevented the merging of the two parties in the West Cameroon House of Assembly.

In 1963, with the prospect in view of a successor to Foncha in the post of Prime Minister of West Cameroon, clashes of personalities and personal ambitions precipitated a rift within the governing KNDP. The competition for Foncha's position began in mid-August at the ninth KNDP Convention at Bamenda with the unspoken assumption that

20   *Augustin Ngom Jua, Prime Minister of West Cameroon in May 1965*

whoever was elected First Vice-President, the second position in the party's hierarchy, would be Prime Minister whenever the post became vacant. A.N. Jua and S.T. Muna, respectively West Cameroon Secretary of State for Finance and Federal Minister of Transport, Posts and Telecommunications, vied with one another for selection. Muna lost and, with E.T. Egbe (who contested and lost the party's secretary-generalship to Nzo Ekah-Nghaky), was unrepentant after the Convention. In May 1965 when Foncha finally vacated the Prime Minister's office and was succeeded by Jua, Muna along with Egbe and six others who supported them were expelled from the KNDP for challenging the party's democratic and constitutional decisions. Foncha even tried without success to convince President Ahidjo to discharge Muna and Egbe from their positions as federal ministers. Muna, Egbe and their six allies immediately formed the Cameroon United Congress or CUC in order to have a voice in both the Western House of

Assembly and in the impending all-party talks for a unified party. The KNDP responded to the Muna — Egbe intransigency by forming a coalition government with the CPNC.

By the end of 1965 West Cameroon had three political parties preparing to merge at the national level with Ahidjo's UC from the East. On 1 September 1966 the four parties, namely UC, KNDP, CPNC and CUC, finally and formally united and became known as the Cameroon National Union or CNU. The new party became the single organisation that effectively controlled men and politics in both the Federation and the Federated States. It postponed for one year the West Cameroon Assembly elections that were due at the end of 1966. When the elections finally took place on 31 December 1967, the CNU National Political Bureau nominated the 37 contestants and presented them to the voters as a single slate. Shortly after the electoral endorsement in January 1968, Ahidjo surprised everyone in West Cameroon by naming Muna to succeed

21 *Prime Minister Solomon Tandeng Muna's government in 1968*

Jua as Prime Minister. Muna in turn reduced his cabinet from 14 to 8, retaining only two members of the last government. In 1970 Ahidjo again shocked the West Cameroonians by selecting Muna to replace Foncha as Vice-President in the single-slate Federal Presidential elections. Ahidjo's authority in the CNU and in the State of West Cameroon was now invincible.

The political situation in East Cameroon was less complex and much more direct than in West Cameroon. Between 1961 and 1962 the UC's leadership towards the goal of creating a unified party convinced some parties like the MANC, the *Front Populaire L'Unité et la Paix* or FPUP, and many from the DC, to agree to fuse or collaborate with the ruling party and so they were absorbed by the UC. On 16 June 1962 four opposition leaders, namely, Okala of the PSC, Mayi-Matip of the UPC, Mbida of the DC and Dr Marcel Beybey Eyidi of the *Parti Travailliste Camerounais* or PTC (then newly formed) rejected Ahidjo's concept of a unified party. Speaking as members of a loose coalition known as the *Front National Unifié* (FNU) the four leaders, while affirming their willingness to work toward the formation of a real national party, argued that Ahidjo's unified party would sabotage other parties for the benefit of the UC. Within two weeks of their statement the four leaders were arrested, and on 11 July they were tried and convicted on charges of inciting hatred against the government and disseminating news prejudicial to public authorities. They were tried under the provisions of an anti-subversion law promulgated only two months earlier.

Following the imprisonment of the 'gang of four' President Ahidjo again, on 11 November 1962, called for the formation of a great unified national party, and began to employ coercive methods to create national unity. Opposition parties were frequently intimidated and prevented from organising party meetings or conferences. As a result only the UC remained active and East Cameroon soon became, for all intents and purposes, a one-party state. Many opposition leaders and organisations, having concluded that it was only a matter of time before they were dissolved by the government, began to switch allegiance. By the end of 1962 many opposition members in the Eastern House declared for the UC, including 5 UPC, 2 PSC and 1 DC deputies. Other well-known opposition leaders outside the legislature, as well as entire traditional organisations like the *Ngondo* of the Duala and the ethnic unions of Ntem and Kribi, also switched allegiance. By the time of the East Cameroon State elections in 1965, only the UC was able to present candidates on a single slate to the voters. The march towards a single-party government in East Cameroon was now complete. All that remained was the creation of a national party. In the same year, 1965, the four jailed leaders were released, probably to give them an opportunity to reconsider their positions and join the movement for a unified party.

Political activities at the national level began in 1961 with the 'Unity Group' coalition of the UC and KNDP in the Federal House of Assembly. Ahidjo and Foncha hoped that sooner or later the 'Unity Group' would really be the merger of the two parties. From 1962 Ahidjo continued to emphasise the need for the creation of a great national party. His wish was that the process of realising such a party should commence with the fusion of all the political parties in each Federated State. As early as 1962 Ahidjo had substantially achieved that goal in East Cameroon. Foncha never achieved it in West Cameroon where the party system was fragmented into three strong factions following the KNDP crisis of 1965. For this reason the 'Unity Group' never became a UC – KNDP merger, despite repeated pledges by Ahidjo and Foncha to make it so.

On 11 June 1966 President Ahidjo summoned to his presidential palace in Yaounde the leaders of the three West Cameroon parties, together with the Prime Ministers of the two Federated States, and urged them to decide on the issue of a national party on the spot. During the two days of their meeting, the four leaders agreed to dissolve their political organisations and create a new national party to be known as the Cameroon National Union or CNU. They agreed to inaugurate the new party before the end of August. The four party leaders then immediately set up a Steering Committee of thirty members to oversee the transition, and a Working Committee of twelve to prepare the new party's Statutes. The draft of the Statutes was approved on 23 July by the Steering Committee, which proceeded to set up a provisional Executive to lead the new party.

President Ahidjo was to head the party, Foncha and Prime Minister Tchoungui of East Cameroon became respectively First and Second Vice-Presidents, Samuel Kamé became Secretary-General, and Moussa Yaya, Ekah Nghaky and Egbe became Assistant General-Secretaries. Prime Minister Jua of West Cameroon, Dr Endeley, Dr Bernard N. Fonlon and Henry Elangwe were included as general members. During the month of August each of the four parties, beginning with Ahidjo's UC, held extraordinary convention, dissolved and willed their assets to the new party. On 1 September 1966, the CNU came into being. Shortly afterwards Okala's PSC and Mbida's DC dissolved and merged with the new party. In 1968 the legal UPC under Mayi-Matip also joined the CNU. Thus, as of 1966 there was no formal opposition to the single party, the CNU, in both the Federal and State legislatures. In 1969 the CNU held its first Congress in Garoua, during which it elected a new Political Bureau of 35 to replace the provisional Executive named in 1966.

The Cameroon administration 1961-72

The French and the British left their respective territories of Cameroon with well-organised and relatively well-functioning bureaucracies. Both colonial powers created full-fledged administrative frameworks on both the territorial and local levels long before the era of independence and reunification. But independence and reunification brought many unantici-

pated problems, principally because the operating core of bureaucracy composed of foreign (mainly European) expatriates and Nigerians departed from both Federated States in large numbers.

The administration of the Federation was formally organised on two levels, corresponding to the constitutional division of powers. The first was the federal organisation operating separately from the state system, but cooperating with the local ministries in areas of parallel or joint jurisdiction. The second were the two state systems which, theoretically, were expected to maintain a liaison through the appropriate federal ministries.

The cornerstone of the federal administrative system was the six Federal Administrative Inspectorates whose Administrative Inspectors were direct representatives of the Federal Executive or President. These Federal Inspectors, whose powers were almost plenary in character, reported directly to the President through the Minister-Delegate at the Presidency in charge of Federal Territorial Administration. One of the six Administrative Inspectorates into which the federal territory was divided corresponded with the region of the Federated State of West Cameroon. The other five Inspectorates fell within East Cameroon, one each for the north, east, centre-south, littoral and Bamileke regions.

Federal Inspectors of Administration supervised, coordinated, investigated and kept track of the work, correspondence and activities of all the federal officials and departments within their regions. They might call upon the police and the armed forces to carry out an investigation. By so doing, the Administrative Inspectors guaranteed the centralised nature of the federal system. Because West Cameroon constituted only a single Administrative Inspectorate, the powers of the Administrative Inspector were frequently seen by the Federated State authorities as challenging those of the State Prime Minister.

The federal territory was divided into 39 administrative Divisions, 9 in West Cameroon and 30 in East Cameroon. Each Division was divided into Sub-Divisions, some of which were again divided into Districts according to need or population. In all there were 128 Sub-Divisions and 38 Districts, with 22 Sub-Divisions and 1 District in West Cameroon. The lone District in West Cameroon was Bali in Bamenda.

Each Division was headed by a Senior Divisional Officer or SDO (Préfet in East Cameroon), each Sub-Division by a Divisional Officer or DO (Sous-Préfet), and each District by a District Head. These administrative officers were appointed by presidential decree, understandably on the recommendation of the State Government. They performed the dual roles of Federal and State officers, sending their reports to the Federal Minister-Delegate at the Presidency in charge of Territorial Administration and to the appropriate State ministries. They applied both Federal and State laws within their areas of jurisdiction.

Within each Division in the Federated State of West Cameroon, local administration and budgetary control was provided by a popularly-elected Divisional Council. The Divisional Councils were empowered to control the operations of subordinate District Councils, also popularly elected, whose sizes varied from Division to Division. Many of these subordinate Councils tended to be founded on existing traditional institutions such as the powerful grasslands kingdoms of Nso, Kom, Bali and Bafut. In the larger towns of Bamenda, Mamfe, Kumba, Buea and Victoria, full-fledged municipal governments composed of elected Municipal Councils and officers were instituted. All these local government institutions were the agents of tax collection, particularly the income and poll taxes levied by the Federated State Assembly. They also collected fees and penalty payments enacted by Native Authorities. While part of the collections went to the State Government, certain varying percentages were kept by the area or town Council for developmental projects and the payment of salaries of their own staffs.

In East Cameroon, local government was based on a complex system of urban and rural communes, and an array of minor and major chiefs. Urban and Rural Communes had Councils elected from common rolls, although they were classified as having full or limited powers. Councils with full powers were headed by elected mayors and had complete control over municipal finances and services, while those with limited powers were headed by nominated mayor-administrators. Both were established by government decree. The Communes with full powers were found in such urban centres as Douala, Yaounde and Nkongsamba. In places like Ngaoundere and Garoua, mixed Urban Communes with limited powers were established. These were different from Urban Communes with limited powers in that if their population was ethnically mixed it might require special rules to determine the selection and composition of the Municipal Council. There was, again, a special form of local government known as a Mixed Rural Commune which could be of any size, although usually coterminal in area with Sub-Divisions and which were headed by mayors appointed by the Minister-Delegate at the Presidency in Charge of Territorial Administration. Mixed Rural Communes might co-exist with Urban Communes, in cases where the latter were physically located within Rural Communes. Finally, the East Cameroon system allowed traditional authorities such as the lamibe, the emirs, the sultans, the *fons* and so on to continue to play an important role in local government. Some of these chiefs, particularly those in the northern administrative Divisions continued to enjoy considerable authority.

The entire local government system in Cameroon was under the Ministry Delegate at the Presidency in Charge of Territorial Administration. Locally it was controlled by the officials of the Divisional Office and regionally by the Inspectorates of Administrations.

As far as the judiciary was concerned, each State continued to operate the judicial system it inherited from the colonial administration although the Constitution placed the judicial organs under the Federal government. Each

State had its own Supreme Court and one or more subordinate system of Courts of Appeal. The Supreme Court in West Cameroon, unlike in the East, combined the functions of the High Court and the Court of Appeal. At the bottom of the judicial ladder in West Cameroon were the Magistrate and Customary Law Courts. The bottom of the ladder in East Cameroon was occupied by the Courts of First Instance and Customary Courts. There were also some Special Military Courts established during the early days of independence and reunification to apply summary justice for those caught and convicted of involvement in the UPC rebellion. These Special Military Courts were different from the Military Court permanently established in Yaounde and the several Military Tribunals that might move about the country to try cases falling within their jurisdiction. A Special Criminal Court with nationwide jurisdiction was set up in Yaounde to hear cases involving embezzlement and misappropriation of public funds. Finally, there were Labour courts and Conciliation Boards to judge labour cases or arbitrate between employers and their workers.

The Bamileke problem

Before and during the period of the Cameroon Federation, relations between the Bamileke and other groups became the most hostile in the country. The Bamileke problem as it came to be known, was caused by many factors. The Bamileke were, and still are, among the most energetic and resourceful peoples of west-equatorial Africa, compared only with the enterprising Igbo of Nigeria, and reputed for being ruthless in acquiring wealth and other advantages for themselves. They were generally more successful in securing employment and other undertakings than other peoples in Cameroon. From the early 1930s to the 1950s overpopulation and its consequent pressure on the available traditional land forced many Bamileke to migrate in massive numbers from their region to other areas, mainly in southern Cameroon. The Bamileke emigration was also deliberately encouraged by the French administration. It was soon to impinge socially and economically on the host groups. In many places the Bamileke bought land and put pressure on the local people, for example the Duala, who were soon eclipsed numerically. By the time of independence and reunification, none of the Southern Cameroon towns of any size had been spared the influx of the Bamileke. As a result, hostility developed between them and their host groups. In 1956 a major riot broke out between the Bulu and the Bamileke in the town of Sangmelima. Bamileke market stalls were burnt and pillaged and many Bamileke were beaten up and wounded. In January 1960, the month of independence, the Bamum, who are neighbours to the Bamileke, crossed the Nun and razed the Bamileke village chiefdom of Bamendjin, killing more than 100 people before calm was restored. They alleged they were reacting against a Bamileke terrorist attack on a Bamum village in Foumbot, but more truly they were provoked by long-standing Bamileke encroachments on their land. Also in 1960, a fight between the Bamileke and the Duala broke out in the economic city of Douala. Almost a quarter of the city which was heavily inhabited by the Bamileke was plundered and burnt down. At least 19 people were killed, many more wounded, and more than 5 000 Bamileke were left homeless. Minor clashes between the Bamileke and the host groups continued to occur in different parts of the Cameroon.

The most bloody reaction against the Bamileke influx occurred in Tombel in Bakossi country in the State of West Cameroon. The incident has since been referred to as the Tombel or Bakossi massacre. On 31 December 1967 a mob of Bakossi in Tombel ran riot and slaughtered as many as 236 Bamileke and wounded hundreds more. They were reacting against the robbery and murder of four Bakossi, including a school teacher, by a group of bandits, widely assumed to be Bamileke, shortly before Christmas. The Bakossi, whose relations with the Bamileke were already very strained because of what they considered was a Bamileke invasion of their country, interpreted the work of the bandits as a deliberate act of provocation against them. In any event, the government immediately sent troops into the area and clamped down on movement and communication for fear that the people from the Bamileke homeland and elsewhere would rush to the area to assist their ethnic brethren. Within a couple of days tension had abated and order was restored, although heavy security continued to be maintained in the area for a very long time. Investigation led to the arrest of 143 Bakossi who were accused of participation in the massacre. At a subsequent trial before a Military Tribunal, 17 were sentenced to death, 37 were to be detained for life, 38 received life imprisonment, 10 were imprisoned for ten years in jail, 4 were to be detained for twenty years, and 36 were set free. One person died during the trial.

Another aspect of the Bamileke problem during the period of federation was the UPC guerrilla campaign, which lasted from 1955 until the 1970s. The insurgents were mainly Bamileke. The campaign, which often resulted in massive property damage and loss of lives, made both the government and non-Bamileke peoples associate all Bamileke with terrorism.

There were also overtones of the Bamileke problem in both the 'Victor Kanga affair' and the 'Ndongmo affair'. Victor Kanga, who had risen rapidly in the Ahidjo government, was suddenly dismissed from his ministerial job on 22 November 1966, and arrested a week later on charges of publishing and distributing a seditious pamphlet in league with some four other Bamileke functionaries. Many Bamileke were eventually arrested because of the Kanga affair. In the subsequent trial Kanga himself was convicted and sentenced to four years' imprisonment. The 'Ndongmo affair' involved the Roman Catholic Bishop of Nkongsamba, Mgr Albert Ndongmo. Bishop Ndongmo and Ernest Ouandie, both of them Bamileke, were arrested in August 1970, tried and found guilty of subversion and conspiracy to overthrow the government and kill President Ahidjo. Ouandie

22   *Bishop Albert Ndongmo*

was sentenced to death and executed on 15 January 1971. Bishop Ndongmo's death sentence was commuted to life imprisonment, partly through the intervention of the Pope, who asked for clemency on his behalf. Ndongmo was soon released and called to Rome for other assignments from the Church. He lived in exile until he was pardoned by the government of President Paul Biya and allowed to return to his country in 1985, on the occasion of the visit of Pope John-Paul II to Cameroon.

Economic development

During the period of federation the government of Cameroon was essentially preoccupied with integrating the economies of the Federated States and with the development of the whole country's economy. Before studying the economic development of the country as a whole, let us look at what was done to integrate the economies of the two States.

The first action aimed at integrating the economies of the reunified Cameroon was the adoption of the franc, which was used in East Cameroon as a common currency for the country. West Cameroon, which formerly belonged to the sterling area, was brought to the franc CFA (*Communauté Financière Africaine*) zone. Secondly, from the 1962 – 63 financial year, the federal budgets in which the joint enterprises of East and West Cameroon were funded were promulgated. Thirdly, a branch of the Cameroon Development Bank, a federal-loan agency, was opened in West Cameroon. Fourthly, the British imperial system of weights and measures hitherto used in West Cameroon was replaced by the metric system then current in East Cameroon. The federal government also created statistical services in West Cameroon.

Other activities undertaken to integrate the economies of East and West Cameroon were the expansion of inter-state air services and the completion in 1969 of the branch of the Douala – Nkongsamba railway from Mbanga in East Cameroon to Kumba in West Cameroon. In the same year, the first practical road-link between the country's economic capital of Douala and the Tiko – Victoria – Buea complex was opened. This road-link not only reduced the hundreds of kilometres roundabout route from Victoria through Kumba, Loum and Mbanga to Douala to a mere 56 kilometres, but also united the modernised coastal-belt economies of East and West Cameroon. All these developments put an end to the long economic isolation of West Cameroon.

As concerns the economic and industrial development of the country as a whole, two short-term economic plans designated the First Five-Year Plan (1960 – 65) and the Second Five-Year Plan (1965 – 70) were undertaken. The general framework of the two plans was the older Twenty-Year Plan, substantially revised, worked out for East Cameroon at the time of independence. The First Five-Year Plan was produced without consideration either for reunification or for West Cameroon featuring in the federal economy. It was therefore an unrealistic plan for the country. Its achievements only partially corresponded to its stated aims. In areas such as road-building, railways, public education, health and housing, the objectives of the plan were realised and even surpassed. But very little progress was made in agriculture on which the federal economy was almost entirely based. In this domain, it can only be said that the first plan permitted the creation of structures for the success of the second plan.

The Second Five-Year Plan was elaborated under Cameroon auspices and with the Federal Republic as a whole in mind. A total investment of 165 thousand million francs CFA, more than three times the sum that was scheduled in the first plan, was envisaged. It was hoped that 50 per cent of this amount would come from the federal budget, grants and loans and that the other 50 per cent would come from external sources and private funds. The major aspects of the plan were agriculture, industrialisation, the north – south railway axis and other areas of the infrastructure.

As far as agriculture was concerned, the second plan was called the 'Peasant Plan' because it laid particular emphasis on accelerating the commercialisation of the agricultural sector, agricultural reform and reorganisation. An important facet of the plan involved the radical improvement of peasant export production through the diversification of cash crops. The major export crops such as cocoa, coffee, banana and cotton were increased significantly, and wood, meat and livestock were also exported in greater quantities. Efforts were made to increase the production of tea, rubber and palm products. Most export crops were marketed by the cooperatives, which had witnessed a remarkable growth and effectiveness in both East and West Cameroon. In addition, the federal government created Agricultural Modernisation Centres in the five geographical areas of the country to coordinate development, research and technical aid relating to the principal crops grown in the areas served by the five centres. The plan called for the establishment of regional development societies which would combine plantations and agro-industrial complexes in addition to supervising the creation of rural development funds and distributing agricultural credit.

The whole agricultural plan rested upon the assumption that prices and markets for the country's principal exports would remain relatively stable. They did better than that. By 1968 the value of Cameroon exports was reported to have increased faster than that of imports, and by 1969 the international market price of cocoa had risen to new heights. Thus the federal government was able to raise salaries in the private sector to offset inflationary pressures that had been building up since reunification.

The country's industrial development was directed toward the creation of small-scale industry, designed to serve the local markets. Such enterprises as meat-canning, flour-milling and biscuit production as well as the manufacture of matches, shoes, soap, plywood, cement and plastics had utility within the range of Cameroon's limited economic potential.

The extension of the Douala – Yaounde railway line northward to Ngaoundere represented the most important development project in Cameroon during the federal period. The first phase of the project, Yaounde to Belabo, a distance of about 300 kilometres, was to cost 36.3 million dollars which was obtained from a consortium of French, American and Common Market sources. The same sources financed the second phase, Belabo – Ngaoundere, at an estimated cost of 44.9 million dollars. The project was completed after the Cameroon Federation had been replaced by the United Republic following the national referendum on 20 May 1972. The Douala – Yaounde – Ngaoundere railway was essential for the development of the north of Cameroon by providing a new and profitable means of access to the sea for a huge area of the national territory.

Educational development

Articles 5 and 6 of the Federal Constitution placed higher education and scientific research as well as secondary and technical education under the jurisdiction of the Federal Government. The Federal Government also stimulated and enforced reforms at the primary level, although the Federated State authorities who had jurisdiction over primary education were often responsible for administering the changes. An early attempt at reform was the reduction of the primary course in West Cameroon from eight to seven years as a first step toward bringing the system in line with what prevailed in East Cameroon. The second step which would have brought the system at par with the six-year course in East Cameroon was never taken because of the resistance to it in West Cameroon. At the secondary level, where both systems lasted seven years of training in two cycles of unequal length in each state, nothing was done to standardise them. Examinations and certificates continued to follow their colonial models, although the course of study faced important reforms. Such reforms were directed to the content of the subjects taught, especially in the field of history and geography, which were given a Cameroon and African flavour.

Still at the secondary level, the learning of the two official languages was introduced and made compulsory as early as 1963. This development created a few problems in West Cameroon where, unlike in the East, all the secondary schools were run by the missions. Except the Cameroon Protestant College, Bali, which already taught French, the missions in West Cameroon found it difficult to provide adequate teaching staff to meet the demands of the double-language programme. Besides, there was also the fear in the West that the scheme would negatively affect proficiency in English if French was taught fully as well. There were no great obstacles to the scheme in East Cameroon where a large number of secondary schools run by the state had always taught English and other European languages.

In 1967 it was officially laid down that the syllabuses in all the secondary schools in the federation should be identical. This development reflected the successes registered by the Federal Bilingual Secondary Grammar School at Man-O-War Bay, Victoria (later moved to Molyko near Buea), the only designated 'bilingual' school in the Federation.

The difference in the educational traditions in the two States was reflected in the predominant role played by private education (i.e. mission schools) in West Cameroon. More than 85 per cent of students in West Cameroon attended mission schools whereas most schools in East Cameroon were state-run. The main effect of this disparity was the emphasis laid on religious instruction and the less rigorous system of supervision in the West than was the case in East Cameroon. No attempt was made to do away with the religious content of education in West Cameroon at either the primary or secondary level. In fact, attempts to harmonise the educational system were always accompanied by the fear in West Cameroon that a process of assimilation was involved and that the state's distinctive cultural features would ultimately disappear.

The development of education in general favoured East Cameroon. Statistics of enrolment in primary and secondary schools in 1969, for example, stood for East Cameroon at 567 000 and 37 237 respectively, and for West Cameroon at 162 000 and 4531. The number of secondary school students remained depressingly low for West Cameroon with a population of more than a million, although there was substantial increase in the figures over those for the first year of reunification. A similar imbalance existed in technical education where East Cameroon had at least six state-run technical colleges in 1969 as against one for West Cameroon.

At the level of the Federal University which was established in Yaounde in 1962, fewer than 7 per cent of the student population came from West Cameroon. Although the University was envisaged as a bilingual institution which would bring together and promote not only the two official languages but also the African traditions in Cameroon, no such achievements were made during the period of federation. The language of instruction and the teaching staff were French. With the exception of the English Department in the Faculty of Arts and a few courses on the West Cameroon legal system, no attempt was made to teach in English. No African language was taught. The result of this one-sided concentration of the French system was that the small number of West Cameroon students in the University alone became really bilingual. Neither the students from East Cameroon nor teachers from France bothered to learn or use English.

External relations

Cameroon pursued her external relations with other countries and organisations on a very selective basis. France occupied the first place in Cameroon's external relations. The basis of Franco-Cameroon special relations was the Treaty of Cooperation signed between the two countries on 13 November 1960, and extended to the entire Federal Republic of Cameroon by a protocol in November 1961 after reunification. Under the provisions of the Treaty, France represented Cameroon in those states and organisations where Cameroon did not have her own representatives. France also aided in the training and organisation of Cameroon's diplomatic corps. The Treaty of Cooperation also established very close cultural and commercial ties between Cameroon and France. France steadily gave Cameroon the support she needed at the international level. Additionally, the support which countries such as Ghana, Guinea and other Communist-inclined countries gave to the UPC rebellion in Cameroon and to exiled UPC leaders contributed to stronger ties between Cameroon and France.

Relations with African states were based on good-neighbourliness. Cameroon participated in the Organisation of African Unity (OAU), the African and Malagasy Common Organisation (OCAM), and the Central African Economic and Customs Union (UDEAC). Cameroon's commitment to OCAM was based both on the members' common and special ties to France and on the looseness of the Organisation, which permitted each member country a wide degree of individual freedom of action. In general terms, Cameroon's external relations with African countries were geared toward such goals as economic, social and political cooperation among African states. However, she faced two major obstacles. The first, as already mentioned, was the assistance which Ghana and Guinea gave to the exiled UPC leadership and rebellion in Cameroon. Because of their support for instability in Cameroon, relations with the two countries remained strained for a long time. In fact relations with Ghana were normalised only after the overthrow of President Nkwame Nkrumah in 1966, and with Guinea only in the 1970s. The second concern was the Nigerian civil war of 1967–70. The civil war became a problem not only because the secessionist region of Nigeria lay directly on Cameroon's southwestern frontier, but also because thousands of refugees from the so-called state of Biafra sought shelter in Cameroon at the height of fighting. The heavy Igbo population from Biafra that was resident in Cameroon before and during the civil war, as well as most Cameroonians, made no secret of their sympathies for the Biafran cause. But in spite of all these considerations, the government of the Federal Republic of Cameroon maintained a posture of support for, and cordial relations with, the Nigerian central government throughout the period of the civil war. In addition, Cameroon sought in various ways to mediate in the dispute between Nigeria and Biafra, and was directly involved in the efforts by the OAU and the UNO to bring the conflict to an end. When the civil war ended in January 1970, Cameroon played a major role in reconciling Nigeria with Gabon and the Ivory Coast, the two OCAM states which had recognised and supported Biafran secession.

Cameroon's external relations were largely limited to western Europe, North America, the Vatican, the Sovereign Order of Malta, and the UN and its affiliated organs. By 1971 forty-five states had accredited missions in Yaounde, twenty-three of them with established embassies. Nine countries with embassies in Yaounde also had consulates variously in Yaounde, Douala or Buea. Relations with western Europe were principally with the member states of the European Economic Community (EEC) of which Cameroon was an associate member, and with the United Kingdom. Cameroon developed relations with the United States and Canada in 1960, and with the Soviet Union in 1962. Relations with communist China, which had actively supported the UPC rebellion, began only in 1971.

The end of the Cameroon Federation

The Cameroon Federation lasted exactly ten years and eight months, before being supplanted by the United Republic. During these years, it was realised that the federal structures were a handicap to the rapid development of the country. The functioning of three governments, namely, the Federal Government and the two State Governments, as well as four assemblies, namely, the Federal Assembly, the two State Assemblies and the West Cameroon House of Chiefs, involved considerable expenditure which could be used in the economic, social and cultural domains. Besides, the State of West Cameroon was continually unable to balance its budgets, despite the fact that most services had been federalised and balancing subsidies amounting to about three-quarters of the budget always made to the State. The country needed constitutional and administrative changes which would allow for one, not three, governments and one, not four, legislative assemblies. Such a unitary state would not only consolidate national unity but would also accelerate the economic and social development of the country.

On 9 May 1972, President Ahidjo informed the Federal National Assembly that he would consult the Cameroon people 'who are sovereign and masters of their destiny' on the question of instituting a unitary state. They would be asked to approve or reject the institution of one and indivisible United Republic of Cameroon.

The referendum took place almost immediately, on 20 May 1972. Participation was 85 per cent of the country's eligible voters. Of the total 3 226 280 ballots cast, only 176 voted against a unitary state, and 99.9 per cent in favour. Following this massive support, President Ahidjo supplanted the Federal with the Unitary Constitution, and decreed that henceforth, 20 May would be Cameroon's National Day.

Further reading

David Birmingham and Phyllis M. Martin (eds), *History of Central Africa,* Vol. 2 (Longman, London and New York), 1983.

David E. Gardinier, *Cameroon: United Nations Challenge to French Policy* (OUP, London, 1963).

Pierre F. Gonidec, *La République Fédéral du Cameroun* (Berger-Levrault, Paris, 1969).

Willard R. Johnson, *The Cameroon Federation* (Princeton University Press, Princeton, 1970).

Ndiva Kofele-Kale, *An African Experiment in Nation Building: The Bilingual Cameroon Republic Since Reunification* (Westview Press, Boulder, 1980).

Victor T. LeVine, *The Cameroon Federal Republic* (Cornell University Press, Ithaca and London, 1971).

Engelbert Mveng, *Histoire du Cameroun,* Tome II (CEPER, Yaounde, 1985).

Neville Rubin, *Cameroon: An African Federation* (Praeger, New York, 1971).

Questions

1   How was the Foumban Constitutional Conference of July 1961 organised?
2.   Why was the Foumban Conference a total victory for the delegation from East Cameroon?
3.   How was the CNU formed and why was it possible for it to absorb all other political organisations?
4.   Discuss Cameroon's foreign policy during the period of Federation.
5.   How and why did the Cameroon Federation come to an abrupt end?

Chapter thirteen

Cameroon since the Unitary Constitution of 1972

In this concluding chapter we shall recount the constitutional, administrative, economic and social developments since the advent of the United Republic of Cameroon in 1972. We shall also describe the voluntary and peaceful transfer of presidential power from Ahmadou Ahidjo to Paul Biya in 1982, as well as the abortive *coup d'état* of April 1984.

Constitutional and administrative developments

The Constitution of 1972 abolished the state system of government and created seven provinces each headed by a Governor appointed by the President of the Republic. Five of the seven provinces, namely Centre-South with headquarters in Yaounde, East with headquarters in Bertoua, Littoral with headquarters in Douala, North with headquarters in Garoua, and West with headquarters in Bafoussam, superseded the Administrative Inspectorates of the defunct federated State of East Cameroon. The former State of West Cameroon, which had constituted only a single Administrative Inspectorate, was divided into the North-West and South-West Provinces with headquarters in Bamenda and Buea respectively. On 22 August 1983 three new provinces, namely Adamawa with headquarters in Ngaoundere, Extreme-North with headquarters in Maroua, and South with headquarters in Ebolowa were carved out of the North and Centre-South provinces, making a total of ten provinces. The unitary state Constitution also abolished the office of Vice-President and designated the Speaker of the National Assembly as successor in the event of death or inability of the President of the United Republic to exercise his powers and functions. The Honourable Solomon Tandeng Muna, who was Vice-President under the defunct Constitution, became Speaker of the 120-member National Assembly in 1973. Muna held the office of Speaker for three consecutive terms (fifteen years) until he retired from politics. In 1983 the number of parliamentarians was raised to 150 (though not implemented) and in 1988 effectively to 180. The new national Assembly, elected in April 1988, selected the Hon. Lawrence Shang Fonka from Nso in Bui Division as the new Speaker, after S.T. Muna.

Between 1973 and 1988, several amendments were made to the unitary Constitution. In 1975 the office of Prime Minister of the Republic was created and Paul Biya, then Secretary-General at the Presidency, was named to it. The Prime Minister, whose principal function was to coordinate the activities of the various government departments, could neither form nor head the government. In 1979 a further modification designated the Prime Minister (not the Speaker of the National Assembly) as successor to the President of the Republic in the event of the death, physical incapacity or resignation of the latter. The Prime Minister

Figure 12 *The ten provinces of Cameroon*

in assuming the office of President would, however, not call a Presidential election until the end of term of office of his predecessor. This clause was eventually removed during further modifications in the Constitution in 1983.

The 1983 modifications in the Constitution, for the first time since independence and reunification, allowed for the possibility of multiple candidates in the one-party system for the office of President. This modification specified, however, that each contestant for the office of the President of the United Republic would have to furnish evidence of national support for his candidature. The evidence would be a list of 500 supporters (50 from each of the ten provinces) from among such persons as district officers, governors, municipal administrators, traditional rulers, members of the Central Committee of the Party, members of the Economic and Social Council, members of the National Assembly, and other people holding elective office. It would appear from the presidential elections of 1984 and 1988 that the incumbent President seeking re-election, or rather the official Party candidate, was not expected to furnish evidence of national support. Any candidate for President must have been resident in the country for at least five years.

On 4 February 1984, further modifications were made in the Constitution. The name of the State was changed from United Republic to simply Republic of Cameroon. President Biya explained in a later publication that 'the change ... from the Federal Republic to the United Republic and finally to the Republic of Cameroon indicates the desire of the Cameroonian State to solve a problem which was created by colonization and which has served as a springboard for political action during the past quarter of a century.' The modifications also abolished the post of Prime Minister and again empowered the Speaker of the National Assembly to fully assume the powers of President in the event of death, resignation, impeachment or inability of the occupant to attend to his duties as duly ascertained by the Supreme Court. The Speaker, as interim President of the Republic, however, may not propose an amendment to the Constitution, make a cabinet-reshuffle, organise a referendum or be a candidate for the Presidential elections which must take place within 20 – 40 days after the vacancy. But where the President is temporarily unable to discharge his duties, he must name a minister of his choice and authorise him to discharge such duties 'within the scope of an express delegation of powers.'

From Ahmadou Ahidjo to Paul Biya

Ahmadou Ahidjo accepted nomination for the Presidency of the Republic for the fifth consecutive five-year term in April 1980. In some of the earlier elections it was often speculated that he might not accept renomination; in 1980, however, everyone wanted Ahidjo for President. Those selected by the Central Committee of the Party to lead the election campaign described Ahidjo as the 'father of the nation', a symbol of peace, stability, progress and national unity. As Professor Bernard Nsokika Fonlon put it two years earlier, 'Cameroonians of all ranks, of all origins, of all creeds, of all tendencies acknowledge his worth: some lovingly, some grudgingly, but all boundenly.' Ahidjo was re-elected with 99.9 per cent of the votes cast. He continued to lead the nation for more than two years without demonstrating any sign of fatigue or ill-health.

But on the evening of 4 November 1982 Ahidjo stunned the nation by announcing his resignation from the highest office in the state in a broadcast on state networks. Without giving reasons for his sudden and unexpected resignation, President Ahidjo called on all Cameroonians to place their full confidence in and give whole-hearted support to his constitutional successor, Paul Biya. He said that Biya merited the confidence of all both at home and abroad. Ahidjo informed the nation that the transfer of power would take place on 6

23   *President Ahidjo (in white) at the National Day celebrations, 20 May 1982*

November 1982. Fear reigned over the Cameroon nation that night and the following day. Many believed that Ahidjo had resigned under duress.

On Saturday 6 November, at exactly 10.00 a.m., Paul Biya, then Prime Minister, was sworn in as the new President of the Republic by the Speaker of the Assembly, in the presence of members of Parliament and of the Supreme Court. Within an hour of the swearing-in ceremony, Ahidjo received and conferred with the new leader at the Unity Palace before vacating the presidential residence for good. The transfer of power from Ahidjo to Biya had indeed taken place smoothly, peacefully and voluntarily. There was no sign anywhere that the change of leadership was a result of a silent *coup d'état*. Ahidjo later explained that he had resigned because he was tired and needed more rest and because he was advised by his medical doctors to do so.

Paul Biya, the second Cameroon head of state and government since independence and reunification, is a Roman Catholic Christian from the south of the country. He is a native of the Beti group, Bulu, which spans the Centre and South Provinces. Born on 13 February 1933 at Mvomeka near Sangmelima, he acquired his post-primary education at the junior seminaries in Edea and Akono. He later studied at the Lycée Leclerc in Yaounde before proceeding on a scholarship to France where he obtained a bachelor's degree in Law, a post-graduate diploma in Public Law and a diploma in Political Science. He returned to Cameroon in 1962 and was employed as Chargé de Mission at the Presidency of the Republic. Between 1964 and 1975, when he became Prime Minister, he was Personal Assistant to the Minister in the Ministry of National Education, Youth and Culture, Secretary-General in the same Ministry, Director of the Civil Cabinet at the Presidency, and Secretary-General at the Presidency. He succeeded the former President, Ahmadou Ahidjo, when the latter resigned, in accordance with the Cameroon Constitution, on 6 November 1982.

President Biya announced his new Cabinet on the evening of the same day he assumed office. He named Bello Bouba Maigari, a

Muslim from the north, as Prime Minister to occupy his former office. Earlier, in an address after he was sworn in, Paul Biya pledged to continue with the policies of his predecessor in office. However, he declared that he would inject those policies with rigour, integrity and moralisation. His 'New Deal' administration would reject irregularities, lateness, laxity, wastefulness and irresponsibility in the conduct of public affairs and would condemn misappropriation of public or private funds, corruption, fraud or illegal acquisition of wealth and moral depravity. Many Cameroonians who were unsure of the future of their country when Ahidjo announced his resignation, prayed and hoped that Paul Biya would prove equal to the task of leading the Cameroon nation which had been entrusted to him.

Some years later, in 1987, Paul Biya propounded his political philosophy, 'communal liberalism', in a widely-read volume with the same title. In it President Biya prescribed objectives which Cameroonians must attain collectively in order to achieve efficiency, solidarity and respect for human personality. He advocated the increasing movement of Cameroonians within their country and the formation of inter-tribal unions as a means of facilitating fraternity and national unity. He argued that a 'Charter of Liberties' was necessary so that every Cameroonian should clearly know his rights and obligations. He called for a major decentralisation of decision-making in order that the people of any particular locality be made aware of their responsibilities and develop their sense of participation. Concerning the economy, President Biya argued that the sole motivation in determining priorities should be the general interest of all Cameroonians; no effort should be spared in seriously improving agricultural techniques in order that agriculture should continue to remain the mainstay of the economy. He said that it was essential that rural areas be opened up in order to stimulate the interest of the people in agricultural development and eliminate the drift of young people to urban centres. On social welfare he called for appropriate measures to enable every Cameroonian worker to own a house, and for the improvement of the standard of living of people in the rural areas. In foreign relations, he argued that Cameroon 'should seek unrestricted and equitable economic and cultural cooperation while doing everything in its power to consolidate the united front of the Third World.'

The retired President Ahidjo, after a short stay abroad, returned to Cameroon and undertook a tour of six provinces to solicit total and unconditional support for President Biya and to bid farewell to the people. He was enthusiastically received by every Cameroonian not only because he was still Chairman of the ruling party, the CNU, but more importantly because he had voluntarily and peacefully surrendered the reins of government to his constitutional successor. Ahidjo readily dismissed one of his close collaborators and Vice-Speaker of the National Assembly, Moussa Yaya and six others from the party, because they had opposed his resignation and were allegedly stirring up opposition against President Biya in the North and West Provinces. Their attitude was considered intolerable for the unity of the party.

Discord, subversion and an abortive coup d'état

As already indicated, Ahmadou Ahidjo, in abdicating the office of President of the Republic, did not equally resign his position as Chairman of the ruling CNU party. He instead named the new President, Paul Biya, Vice-Chairman of the Central Committee of the party. Shortly after his abdication, he not only began to summon and preside over party-meetings frequently, but also continued to make important political pronouncements. Many people began to sense that sooner or later the powers of the Chairman of the party would clash with those of the President of the Republic if Ahidjo did not resign his position as Chairman. On 31 January 1983 Ahidjo announced that it was the role of the CNU to define the nation's policy while the government implemented it. This in effect meant that the party was superior to the state and the government. President Paul Biya disagreed but did not make a public statement about it immediately. Later, however, he stated in an interview that it was the President of the Republic who defined the nation's policy. Rumours began to circulate about political differences between the two leaders. Ahidjo dismissed them, pointing out that if he had not wanted Paul Biya to be President he would simply have terminated his function as Prime Minister and replaced him before resigning. Besides, he had just demonstrated his confidence in the President by touring the provinces and asking people to give him total and unalloyed support.

President Biya in his turn undertook a meet-the-people tour of all the seven provinces. In the North-West and the South-West Provinces he won the hearts of everyone by speaking to the population directly in the English language. In the North Province he visited Garoua, Maroua and Ngaoundere and made encouraging and heartening pronouncements. In the East, the Littoral, the Centre-South and the West provinces he captured the admiration and support of everyone. By the time the President had rounded off his tour he had indeed become the people's President. This was not pleasing to his political rivals.

Once President Biya had concluded his meet-the-people tour, relations between him and the Chairman of the party, Ahmadou Ahidjo, had deteriorated. On 18 June 1983 the President made a cabinet-reshuffle, apparently without the knowledge of either his party boss or his Prime Minister, Bello Bouba Maigari. In the reshuffle, all the closest collaborators of Ahidjo in the Government, with the notable exception of Maigari and Maikano Abdoulaye of Defence, were dropped. Ahidjo was furious and advised northerners in the new Government to resign *en masse*. Although all the Ministers from the North Province allegedly signed a letter of resignation, no resignations took place. From then on President Biya refused to attend party meetings summoned

and chaired by Ahidjo. Disgruntled at the way things were going, Ahidjo left Cameroon and went into self-exile in France before the end of June 1983.

On 22 August 1983 President Biya disclosed, in a nationwide radio broadcast, that plans to destabilise the Government and physically eliminate the President had been uncovered and arrests had been made. He then announced some military and administrative measures to safeguard national institutions. An Armed Forces General Staff was set up and the three new provinces were designated, two in the north and one in the south. Bello Bouba Maigari and Maikano Abdoulaye were dismissed from the Government in another reshuffle, and Ayang Luc, a northern Christian, was appointed Acting Prime Minister. On 27 August Ahidjo announced his resignation from the Chairmanship of the party. An extraordinary Congress of the party was immediately summoned to study recent developments and take decisions. On 14 September 1983 Paul Biya was unanimously elected Chairman of the CNU.

Having acquired the leadership of the party, President Biya called a new Presidential election on 14 January 1984, although he had until April 1985 to complete his predecessor's term which he had inherited. He was the sole candidate for the presidency. His victory was a landslide, 99.98 per cent of the votes cast. On 21 January he was sworn in as elected President for a five-year term of office. From 23 to 28 February the trial was conducted in Yaounde of Major Ibrahim Oumarou and Captain Salatou Adamou, aides of former President Ahidjo; they had been arrested in August 1983 and accused of conspiracy against the state. The two indicted persons confessed their guilt but pleaded for clemency. Together with Ahidjo, who was said to be at large, they were found guilty of treason and sentenced to death by firing squad. On Wednesday 14 March President Biya commuted the sentences to detention and ordered that other inquiries connected with this sad conspiracy should be stopped because of 'the higher interests of the state and fidelity to the highest moral values.'

Biya's magnanimous show of clemency did not discourage the enemies of the state from attempting a military coup d'état. Thus, at about 3 a.m. on 6 April 1984, rebel forces made up essentially of officers of the Republican Guard, some officials of the National Police Force and a few civilians, decided to overthrow the Government. They attacked and temporarily took control of the army headquarters, Brigadier-General Pierre Semengue's residence, the national broadcasting house, the Unity Palace (presidency), Yaounde Airport, the residence of the Minister of State in charge of the Armed Forces, the residence of the officer responsible for the defence of the national capital, and other strategic places. In a broadcast which, for technical reasons, failed to be heard nationwide, the rebel spokesman accused the Government of: undermining the fundamental rights of citizens, playing freely with the national Constitution, behaving as if their only goal was to enrich themselves fast, throwing discredit on the nation by the recent trials 'which were merely a parody of justice', and scandalously undermining the high values of liberalism, democracy and national integration. They then suspended all air, land and sea links with the outside world until further notice, suspended the Constitution, imposed a curfew on the entire nation, dissolved the National Assembly, suspended the CNU party, and dismissed the government and the provincial governors. The rebels also discharged all senior and field officers commanding operational units and ordered that the 'immediate subaltern officer with the highest rank and the longest serving in that rank should take over command.' While the rebels still had an upper hand, former President Ahidjo announced from southern France that if they were his supporters they were going to win. But the rebellion was shortlived.

Loyal forces from Yaounde, Ebolowa, Koutaba and Douala attacking from air and land were able to rescue the Government and to re-establish peace to the national capital. By 7 p.m. on Saturday 7 April, President Biya was able to broadcast a reassuring message to the nation. He said that calm had been restored over the national territory and paid 'resounding tribute' to the regular units of the national army 'for their commitment to the spirit of republican government.' By Sunday morning all that was left of the rebellion was the damage caused to military camps and vehicles and the corpses of rebel soldiers in their burnt vehicles. In all, 73 people, including five civilians and 11 loyal troops, died as a result of the attempted coup d'état. The ringleaders of the rebellion, including Issa Adoum, who was tipped to succeed President Biya, were arrested, tried and sentenced according to the degree of their involvement in the revolt. The rebellion failed because it was not nationwide and also because the security around President Biya was effective and loyal. Besides, the rebels were unable to immobilise the air force, which contributed to their defeat.

At the time of writing, the only other major political event of note since the disturbances of 1984 has been the Party Congress which was held in Bamenda on 21–24 March 1985. Referred to as the 'New Deal Congress' because of President Biya's cherished principles of rigour and moralisation, liberalisation and democratisation, responsibility and participation, it turned out to be the last CNU Congress. The name of the party was changed from CNU to CPDM, that is, Cameroon People's Democratic Movement. In his general policy address President Biya told the Congress delegates that Cameroonians of good faith 'need not go underground or into exile or desert their families to be able to express their opinions.' The CPDM party was opened to all Cameroonians irrespective of their ideology or opinions. President Biya was elected the first Chairman of the CPDM.

The Christian Churches in the 1970s and 1980s

Throughout the post-independence period, and especially in the 1970s and the 1980s, all the Christian Churches in Cameroon continued to make progress in their missionary and social work. The Protestant Churches, which had variously established their independence from their Mother Houses overseas, continued to establish new mission stations and to open medical and educational institutions in different parts of the country. Their greatest religious and academic institution was the Protestant Faculty of Theology which was opened in the 1960s and quickly signed a convention of association with the University of Yaounde. The Faculty of Theology was able to set up a printing press, Editions CLE (Centre de Littérature Evangélique) which was soon to become one of the best publishing houses on the African continent. The principal of the Faculty since the early 1980s is the intelligent and highly rated Pastor Michael Bame Bame who holds a doctorate degree in theology. The Protestant Churches of Cameroon also made a determined contribution to the continental ecumenical movement. They were instrumental in the founding, organising and functioning of the Organisation of all African Churches and in the convening of its conferences. One of the earliest presidents of the Organisation was Pastor Kotto of Douala. The Protestant Churches also made great strides in indigenising their religious services, particularly in their music.

The Catholic Church made much more progress, particularly after the 'Bishop Ndongmo affair' of 1970, than all the Protestant Churches together. This Church, which had about one million Christians and catechumens at the time of independence and the reunification of Cameroon, had a membership of about three million Christians in the late 1980s: Its number of dioceses rose from three in 1961 to eighteen in 1988, and it had more than twenty bishops and archbishops. In April 1982 the Papacy divided the country into four ecclesiastical provinces and named archbishops to head them. The Ecclesiastical Province of Bamenda, comprising the dioceses of Buea and Kumbo (1982) and the archdiocese of Bamenda, was headed by Archbishop Paul Verdzekov; Douala, comprising the dioceses of Nkongsamba and Bafoussam and the archdiocese of Douala, was placed under Archbishop Simon Tonye; Garoua, comprising the dioceses of Maroua-Mokolo, Yagoua and Ngaoundere and the archdiocese of Garoua, was led by Archbishop Yves Plumey; and Yaounde, comprising the dioceses of Mbalmayo, Doumé, Sangmelima, Bafia, Bertoua and Obala (1987) and the archdiocese of Yaounde, was guided by Archbishop Jean Zoa, Cameroon's first archbishop. In 1984 Mgr Yves Plumey of Garoua retired and was replaced by Mgr Tumi who had been named Co-Adjutor Archbishop in 1982.

A significant event for the Catholic Church in the mid-1980s was the visit of Pope John-Paul II to Cameroon, at the invitation of President Biya and the Bishops. During the four-day state and apostolic visit (10 to 14 August 1985) the Roman Catholic Pontiff visited all the four ecclesiastical provinces and delivered a total of fourteen discourses. Addressing Cameroonian intellectuals and university teachers and students, the Pope called for the establishment of a Catholic Institution (University) in Yaounde where different aspects of Faith, and its beginnings, 'as well as the relationship of this Faith with the rest of the culture' will be studied with the same scientific rigour as other disciplines.

One other significant development, the greatest for the national Catholic Church, was the naming of the first-ever Cameroonian cardinal. On 29 May 1988 the Holy Father named Archbishop Tumi of Garoua prince of the Church, alongside twenty-four other nominees around the globe. It is perhaps necessary to know a little more about Cameroon's first Cardinal, who was invested with the robes and ring of eminence by the Holy Father in Rome on 28 June 1988.

His Eminence Cardinal Christian Wiyghan Tumi comes from Nso in Bui division of the North-West Province. Born on 15 October 1930 in the village of Kikaikelaki near Kumbo town, he went to primary school at Shisong, Nso, before proceeding to Nigeria where he trained as a schoolteacher. He then decided to become

24 *President Paul Biya*

a priest and entered the junior seminary in Ibadan before moving to the senior seminary in Bodya and to the Bigard Memorial Major Seminary, Enugu, where he completed his training. He was ordained as a priest on 17 April 1966 at the Cathedral Church, Soppo, Buea. After serving as curate in Fiango and teacher at Bishop Rogan Minor Seminary, Soppo, Christian Wiyghan Tumi pursued further studies at the Catholic Faculty of Lyon, France, where he was awarded a licentiate in theology and philosophy. From Lyon he proceeded to Fribourg (Switzerland) where he earned a doctorate degree in theology before returning to Cameroon. From 1973 to 1979 he was Rector of the newly-established Major Seminary at Bambui. On 6 December 1979 he was appointed Bishop of Yagoua and consecrated by Pope John-Paul II in Rome on 6 January 1980. In 1984 he became Archbishop of Garoua and the following year was elected President of the National Episcopal Conference of Cameroon. He was re-elected for another three-year term in April 1988. Cardinal Tumi, who is also a member of the Sacred Congregation for the Evangelisation of Peoples, speaks his vernacular, Lamnso, and English, French, Hausa and Pidgin with mastery, and also has an excellent knowledge of Latin and German. As Cardinal he is a member of the Sacred College of the Church, which elects Popes and can himself be elected Pope.

Economic and social developments

The economy of Cameroon continued to make progress in the 1970s and 1980s before it was severely hit by the worldwide crisis of 1986. The mainstay of the economy continued to be agriculture, which employed more than 80 per cent of the country's manpower and whose commodities accounted for more than 60 per cent of the total export earnings. The principal export crops continued to be cocoa, rubber, groundnuts, coffee, palm products, banana, timber, cotton and tea. Gas and oil exploitation advanced from the initial stages in 1976 when the National Refining Company Limited, SO.NA.RA. (Société Nationale de Reffinage) in Limbe was incorporated to being a major income-earner in the 1980s. SO.NA.RA.'s output was expected to exceed 4 billion tons in 1985. In the mid-1980s natural gas liquidation was projected at Kribi and large quantities were estimated in the area.

The state network of roads improved considerably after 1972. The roads from Limbe to Kumba, Ngaoundere to Garoua, Bafoussam to Bamenda, Douala to Bafoussam, Yaounde through Bafia to Bafoussam, and Belabo to Bertoua were widened and excellently tarred. Work on the Kumba – Mamfe road was started and arrangements were underway for the construction of the first phase of the Bamenda Ring Road from Bamenda to Kumbo, when the country was hit by economic crisis. The Yaounde – Doula and the Yaounde – Ngaoundere railway lines were realigned, and the express train service introduced between the cities of Douala and Yaounde in 1987. The Douala and Garoua international airports were enlarged and modernised, and the Ngaoundere, Bertoua and Bamenda airports properly built and provided with facilities for all-weather landings and takeoffs.

In the arena of labour and social welfare, the Cameroon Government showed real concern for the employment of thousands of young people graduating from institutions of higher learning within and outside the country in 1982. From that year on until 1986 it made an extra effort, outside normal yearly employment, to recruit more than 1500 graduates each year. Opportunities were created for the education of every Cameroonian child at all levels of schooling by opening and equipping government primary schools, secondary and technical schools and high schools in every Sub-Division and Division and by establishing University Centres at Douala, Dschang, Ngaoundere and Buea. Enrolment at the University of Yaounde, which was enlarged and provided with additional lecture halls and administrative and teachers' offices, rose from about 10 000 in the mid-

1970s to more than 20 000 in the late 1980s.

Cameroon made outstanding progress in the arena of national and international sports. The country won several continental trophies in games and athletics at both the club and national team levels. In 1982 Cameroon's national football team, the Indomitable Lions, participated in the World Cup in Spain and emerged with England as one of only two countries that did not concede defeat. From 1984 to 1988 Cameroon always reached the finals of the bi-annual African Nations Cup, winning it twice in the Ivory Coast (1984) and in Morocco (1988). The same satisfactory progress was recorded in lawn-tennis where the Cameroon-born Yannick Noah, appearing as a French citizen, continued to be a star; in boxing, where Jean-Marie Emebe continued to vie for the world title; and in wrestling where Crosdel Eko and Super Makia won the world middleweight and Africa's heavyweight titles respectively.

Still in the field of social development, Cameroon's television, CTV, became a reality on 20 March 1985. Two years later it became, with the National Radio, a corporation known as Cameroon Radio Television, CRTV. As well as offering educational and entertainment programmes, the television covered live political and social events such as the Party Congress in Bamenda in 1985, the 20 May National Day celebrations since 1985, the Pope's visit to Cameroon in August 1985, the World Cup in Mexico in 1986, the African Nations Cup competition in Egypt and Morocco in 1986 and 1988, and the presidential and legislative election campaigns of April 1988.

Although the country's economic and social progress was seriously affected by the economic crisis which hit it in 1986, there was every indication that Cameroon would emerge from it stronger and better. The solution to the crisis lay in the proper management of the state finances. Some drastic measures were already being taken to fight the crisis. These measures included the reduction of the national budget from 850 billion CFA francs the preceding year to 650 billion in the 1987/88 fiscal year and to 600 billion in the 1988/89 fiscal year. There were also increases in taxes for hunting and car licences, identity cards, passports and travel papers, business documents, landed property, petroleum products, housing and publicity, beginning from July 1988. Unproductive state corporations were to be liquidated. The Government also decided to put an end to the rampant misappropriation of public funds by investigating cases of embezzlement and arresting and detaining embezzlers and possibly trying to recover the misappropriated funds. There was every reason to believe that the country would survive the crisis before the end of the decade.

Further reading

Henri Bandolo, *la flamme et la fumée* (SOPECAM, Yaounde, 1985).
Paul Biya, *Communal Liberalism* (Macmillan, London, 1987).
Englbert Mveng, *Histoire du Cameroun*, Tome II (CEPER, Yaounde, 1985).
Paul Verdzekov (ed.), *The Pope in Cameroon: Homilies and Addresses* SOPECAM, Yaounde, 1986).

Questions

1. Describe the Constitutional changes which were introduced in Cameroon from 1972 to 1988.
2. How did Paul Biya become President of the United Republic of Cameroon in 1982?
3. Why did President Biya and the Chairman of the CNU party, Ahmadou Ahidjo, disagree? What were the results of the discord between the two leaders?
4. Describe the events leading to and the course of the abortive coup d'état of 1984.
5. Describe Cameroon's economic and social developments from 1972 to 1988. What measures were being taken to fight the economic crisis of 1986?
6. Who is Christian Wiyghan Tumi? Explain his rise from the rank of priest to Cardinal in the Roman Catholic Church.

Appendix

Arrêté déterminant les infractions spéciales à l'indigénat par application du décret du 8 août 1924

LE COMMISSAIRE DE LA RÉPUBLIQUE FRANÇAISE AU CAMEROUN OFFICIER DE LA LÉGION D'HONNEUR

Vu le decrét du 23 mars 1921, déterminant les attributions du Commissaire de la République française dans les Territoires du Cameroun; Vu le decrét du 8 août 1924, déterminant au Cameroun l'exercice des pouvoirs disciplin-aires,

ARRÊTÉ

Article premier – Les infractions spéciales reprimées par voie disciplinaire sont les suivantes:

1. Actes de désordre;
2. Organisation de jeux de hasard;
3. Mise en circulation de bruits mensongers et de nature à troubler la tranquillité publique. Propos séditieux, actes irrespectueux a l'égard d'un représentant qualifié de l'autorité;
4. Aide donné à des malfaiteurs, à des agita-teurs, à des vagabonds, à des indigènes enfuis de leur village et à toute personne recherchée par l'administration. Complicité d'évasion;
5. Refus de prêter aide en cas de sinistre ou d'accidents, de tumulte ou d'arrestation d'un criminel ou d'un délinquant;
6. Port illégal d'insignes officiels, civils ou militaires;
7. Entraves à la circulation sur les voies publiques, routes, sentiers, cours d'eau. Mauvais état des secteur de routes dont l'entre-tien a été attribué à des villages;

8. Racolage, sur la voie publique, des convois de porteurs et porteurs isolés venus vendre des produits aux établissements fixes d'un centre urbain classé ou non;
9. Détérioration volontaire de matériel appartenant a l'administration;
10. Vagabondage;
11. Depart d'un circonscription administra-tive sans avis préable aux autorités;
12. Abandon de service, sans motifs valables, pour les porteurs, piroguiers, con-voyeurs, guides, ouvriers ou employés de chantier publics. Déterioration des charges ou du matériel qui leur sont confiés;
13. Pratique de sorcellerie quand les con-séquences n'ont pas entraîné la comparution devant les tribunaux;
14. Plaintes ou réclamations sciemment inexactes renouvelées auprès de l'administra-tion après une solution régulière, autrement que dans le cas d'appel à l'autorité supérieure;
15. Mauvaise volonté à payer les impôts, contributions et taxes de toute nature et à s'acquitter les prestations. Entraves à la percep-tion de l'impôt, au recensement de la popula-tion ou de la matière imposable. Dissumulation de la matière imposable et connivence dans cette dissimulation;
16. Insoumission aux réquisitions de l'administration pour travaux publics essentiels;
17. Brutalité des agents indigènes à l'égard des travailleurs enfuis des chantiers de travaux publics;
18. Tentative de simulation ou d'aggrava-tion de plaies ou blessures naturelles dans le but de circonvenir l'autorité aux fins de licencie-ment d'un chantier public;
19. Défaut d'obtempérer sans motifs

valables aux convocations de l'administration;

20. Contrebande dûment constatée sans prejudice des sanctions pécunaires douanières;

21. Adultération volontaire de produits. Mise en circulation de tous produits falsifiés;

22. Abatage dans les centres urbains, sans autorisation préalable, d'animaux de boucherie, pour les livrer á la consommation;

23. Abatage et exportation, sans autorisation préalable, des femelles de gros et petit bétail, susceptible de reproduire;

24. Divagation d'animaux nuisibles ou dangereux. Divagation d'animaux domestiques sur la propriété d'autrui;

25. Refus de recevoir les espèces de monnaie et billets français circulant légalement dans le territoire, selon la valeur pour laquelle ils ont cours;

26. Abatage sans autorisation des arbres à produits et des essences de bois durs. Détérioration des bois domaniaux;

27. Refus d'effectuer des plantations vivrières. Mauvais état d'entretien, sans motifs valables, de ces plantations;

28. Culture, vente et usage du chanvre ainsi que de tout produit toxique;

29. Détention de boissons distillées et de boissons alcooliques titrant plus de 14 degrés;

30. Fabrication et vente de boissons fermentée;

31. Divagation des individus atteints d'aliénation mentale, de maladies épidémiques ou contagieuses, de la maladie du sommeil ou de la lèpre. Abandon des individus atteints de maladie contagieuse;

32. Non déclaration des maladies contagieuses sévissant sur les hommes ou les animaux domestiques. Inexécution des mesures d'hygiène et de prophylaxie prescrites par l'administration. Pollution des eaux d'alimentation;

33. Inhumation hors des lieux consacrés et dans les conditions autres que celles prescrites par l'autorité locale.

34. Pratiques d'usages médicaux et utilisation de médicaments en dehors du contrôle de l'administration.

Art. 2 – Le présent arrêté qui abroge toutes les dispositions antérieures contraires et dans son entier l'arrêté du 14 mars 1917, sera enregistré et communiqué partout où besoin sera.

Yaoundé, le 4 octobre 1924

MARCHAND.

Bibliography

Books

Ajayi, J.F. Ade and Crowder, Michael (eds), *History of West Africa,* Volume 2 (London, 1974).

Annet, Armand Léon, *En Colonne dans le Cameroun: Notes d'un Commandant de Companie 1914 – 1916* (Paris, 1949).

Ardener, Edwin, *Coastal Bantu of the Cameroons* (London, 1956).

Ardener, Edwin, Ardener, Shirley and Warmington, A., *Plantation and Village in the Cameroons* (Oxford, 1960).

Ardener, Shirley G., *Eye-Witness to the Annexation of Cameroon 1883 – 1887* (Buea, 1968).

Aymerich, Joseph G., *La Conquête du Cameroun* (Paris, 1931).

Baderman, S.H., *The Cameroons Development Corporation: Partner in National Growth* (Bota, 1968).

Baeschlin-Raspail, Beat C., *Ahmadou Ahidjo: Pionnier de l'Afrique Moderne* (Monaco, 1968).

Baeta, C.G. (ed.), *Christianity in Tropical Africa* (London, 1968).

Bandolo, Henri, *La flamme et la fumée* (Yaounde, 1985).

Beer, George Louis, *African Questions at the Paris Peace Conference* (New York, 1923).

Benjamin, Jacques, *Les Camerounais Occidentaux: La Minorité dans un Etat Bicommunautaire* (Montreal, 1972).

Bentwich, N.C., *Le Système de Mandats* (The Hague, 1929).

Betts, Raymond F., *Assimilation and Association in French Colonial Theory 1890 – 1914* New York, 1961).

Billard, Pierre, *La Circulation dans le Sud Cameroun* (Lyon, 1961).

Billard, Pierre, *Le Cameroun Fédéral,* 2 vols (Lyon, 1968).

Birmingham, David and Martin, Phyllis M. (eds), *History of Central Africa,* Volume 2 (London and New York, 1983).

Biya, Paul, *Communal Liberalism* (London, 1987).

Bockel, Alain, *L'Administration Camerounaise* (Paris, 1971).

Bridgeman, John and Clarke, David E., *German Africa* (Stanford, 1965).

Brunschwin, Henri, *L'Expansion Allemande Outre-Mer du XV Siècle à Nos Jours* (Paris, 1957).

Buell, Raymond Leslie, *The Native Problem in Africa,* Vol. 2 (New York, 1928).

Bullock, A. (ed.), *Germany's Colonial Demands* (London, 1939).

Chazelas, Victor, *Territoires Sous Mandat de la France: Cameroun et Togo* (Paris, 1931).

Chem-Langhëë, Bongfen, *The Cameroon Plebiscites 1959 – 1961: Perceptions and Strategies* (Ph.D. Thesis, UBC, 1976).

Chilver, E.M., *Zintgraff's Explorations in Bamenda, Adamawa and the Benue Lands 1889 – 1892* (Buea, 1966).

Chilver, E.M. and Kaberry, P.M., *Traditional Bamenda: Precolonial History and Ethnography of the Bamenda Grassfields* (Buea, 1966).

Coleman, James S., *Nigeria: Background to Nationalism* (Berkeley and Los Angeles, 1958).

Costeodat, René, *Le Mandat Français et la Ré-organisation des Territoires du Cameroun* (Besançon, 1930).

Crowder, Michael, *The Story of Nigeria* (London, 1966).

Crowder, Michael, *West Africa Under Colonial Rule* (London, 1968).

Delavignette, Robert, *Freedom and Authority in French West Africa* (New York, 1957).

Duchène, Albert, *La Politique Coloniale de la France* (Paris, 1928).

Elango, Lovett Z., *The Anglo-French Condominium in Cameroun 1914 – 1916: History of Misunderstanding* (Yaounde, 1987).

Epale, J. Simon, *Plantation and Development in Western Cameroon 1885 – 1975* (New York, 1985).

Eyongetah, Tambi and Brain, Robert, *A History of the Cameroon* (London, 1974).

Fage, J.D., *An Atlas of African History* (London, 1958).

Fage, J.D., *A History of Africa* (London, 1978).

Fage, J.D., *A History of West Africa* (Cambridge, 1969).

Fanso, Verkijika G., *Trans-Frontier Relations and Resistance to Cameroun – Nigeria Colonial Boundaries 1916 – 1945* (Doctorat d'Etat Thesis, Yaounde, 1982).

Ferrandi, Jean, *La Conquête du Cameroun-nord 1914 – 1915* (Paris, 1928).

Fitzgerald, Walter, *Africa* (London, 1955).

Forkusam, Austin Langmia, *The Evolution of Health Services in the Southern Cameroons Under British Administration* (DES Dissertation, Yaounde, 1978).

Franceschi, Roger, *Le Mandat Français au Cameroun* (Paris, 1929).

Gann, L.H. and Duignan, Peter, *The History and Politics of Colonialism 1914 – 1960* (Cambridge, 1970).

Gann, L.H. and Duignan, Peter, *The Rulers of German Africa 1884 – 1914* (Stanford, 1977).

Gardinier, David E., *Cameroon: United Nations Challenge to French Policy* (London, 1963).

Gifford, Prosser and Louis, William R. (eds), *Britain and Germany in Africa: Imperial Rivalry and Colonial Rule* (New Haven and London, 1967).

Gifford, Prosser and Louis, William R. (eds), *France and Britain in Africa: Imperial Rivalry and Colonial Rule* (New Haven and London, 1971).

Gonidec, P.F., *La République Fédérale du Cameroun* (Paris, 1969).

Gorges, E.H., *The Great War in West Africa* (London, 1927).

Gray, Richard (ed.), *Cambridge History of Africa: c.1600 – c.1970* (Cambridge, 1975).

Groves, C.P., *The Planting of Christianity in Africa,* 4 vols (London, 1958).

Hailey, Lord, *An African Survey* (Revised Edition, New York, 1957).

Hall, Hessel Duncan, *Mandates, Dependencies and Trusteeship* (Washington, DC, 1948).

Hazlewood, Arthur (ed.), *African Integration and Disintegration* (Oxford, 1967).

Hertslet, Sir Edward, *The Map of Africa by Treaty,* Vol. 1 (London, 1894).

Hopkins, A.G., *An Economic History of West Africa* (London, 1973).

Joelson, F.S., *Germany's Claim to Colonies* (London, 1939).

Johannsen, G. Kurt and Kraft, H.H. *Germany's Colonial Problem* (London, 1937).

Johnson, Willard, R., *The Cameroon Federation: Political Integration in a Fragmentary Society* (Princeton, 1970).

Joseph, Richard, *Radical Nationalism in Cameroun: Social Origins of the UPC Rebellion* (Oxford, 1977).

Kale, P.M., *Political Evolution in the Cameroons* (Buea, 1967).

Kirk-Greene, A.H.M., *Adamawa Past and Present* (London, 1969).

Kofale-Kale, Ndiva (ed.), *An African Experiment in Nation Building: The Bilingual Cameroon Republic Since Reunification* (Boulder, 1980).

Labouret, Henri, *Colonisation, Colonialisme, Décolonisation* (Paris, 1952).

Lembezat, Bertrand, *Le Cameroun* (Paris, 1954).

LeVine, Victor T., *The Cameroon Federal Republic* (Ithaca, 1971).

LeVine, Victor T., *The Cameroons From Mandate to Independence* (Berkeley and Los Angeles, 1964).

LeVine, Victor T. and Nye, Roger, *Historical Dictionary of Cameroon* (Metuchen, 1974).

Lewin, Evans, *The Germans in Africa* (New York, 1915).

Lewis, Thomas, *These Seventy Years* (London, 1929).

Logan, Rayford W., *The African Mandates*

in World Politics (Washington, DC, 1948).

Louis, William Roger, *Great Britain and Germany's Lost Colonies 1914 – 1919* (Oxford, 1967).

Lugard, Sir F.D., *The Dual Mandate in British Tropical Africa* (London, 1923).

Mair, Lucy, P., *Native Policies in Africa* (London, 1936).

Manue, Georges R., *Cameroun, Création Française* (Paris, 1938).

Marshall, D. Bruce, *The French Colonial Myth and Constitution-Making in the Fourth Republic* (New Haven, 1973).

Mazrui, Ali A., *The Africans: A Triple Heritage* (London, 1986).

McCulloch, Merran, et al., *Peoples of Central Cameroons* (London, 1954).

Middleton, John and Tait, David (eds), *Tribes Without Rulers* (London, 1970).

Moberley, F.J., *History of the Great War, Military Operations: Togoland and the Cameroons 1914 – 1916* (London, 1931).

Mortimer, Edward, *France and the Africans 1944 – 1960: A Political History* (London, 1969).

Murray, James N., *The United Nations Trusteeship System* (Urbana, Illinois, 1958).

Mveng, Engelbert, *Histoire du Cameroun,* Tome II (Yaounde, 1985).

Njeuma, M.Z., *Fulani Hegemony in Yola (Old Adamawa) 1809 – 1902* (Yaounde, 1982).

Nkwi, P.N., *Traditional Government and Social Change* (Friburg, 1976).

Nkwi, P.N. and Warnier, J.-P., *Elements for a History of the Western Grassfields* (Yaounde, 1982).

Oehler, Anna, *L'Oeuvre de la France au Cameroun* (Yaounde, 1936).

Oliver, Roland (ed.), *Cambridge History of Africa: c.1050 – c.1600* (Cambridge, 1977).

Osuntokun, Akinjide, *Nigeria in the First World War* (London, 1976).

Perham, Mergery and Simmons, Jack (eds), *African Discovery: An Anthology of Explorations* (London, 1942).

Prouzet, Marcel, *Le Cameroun* (Paris, 1974).

Roberts, Stephen H., *History of French Colonial Policy* (London, 1929).

Robinson, Kenneth and Madden, Frederick (eds), *Essays in Imperial Government: Presented to Margery Perham* (Oxford, 1963).

Robinson, Ronald and Gallagher, John, *Africa and the Victorians: The Official Mind of Imperialism* (New York, 1961).

Rotberg, Robert I. (ed.), *Africa and its Explorers* (Harvard, Massachussetts, 1970).

Rotberg, R. and Mazrui, Ali A., *Protest and Power in Black Africa* (New York, 1970).

Royal Empire Society, *Notes on Conditions in the British Cameroons* (London, 1956).

Royal Institute of International Affairs, *Germany's Claim to Colonies* (London, 1939).

Rubin, Neville, *Cameroon: An African Federation* (New York, 1971).

Rudin, Harry H., *Germans in the Cameroons 1884 – 1914* (New York, 1969).

Sady, Emil J., *The United Nations and Dependent Peoples* (Washington, DC, 1956).

Shram, Ralph, *A History of Nigerian Health Services* (Ibadan, 1971).

Stanford Research Institute, *The Economic Potential of West Cameroon* (Menlo Park, 1965).

Stearns, Raymond Phineas, *Pageant of Europe* (Revised Edition, New York and Burlingame, 1961).

Steer, George L., *Judgement on German Africa* (London, 1939).

Stoeker, Helmuth, *German Imperialism in Africa* (Berlin, 1986).

Suret-Canale, Jean, *French Colonialism in Tropical Africa 1900 – 1945* (London, 1971).

Tardits, Claude, *Le Royaume Bamoum* (Paris, 1980).

Tardits, Claude (ed.), *Ethnography and History in Cameroon,* 2 vols (CNRS, Yaounde, 1981).

Townsend, Mary Evelyn, *The Rise and Fall of Germany's Colonial Empire* (New York, 1930).

Vansina, J. et al., *The Historian in Tropical Africa* (London, 1964).

Verdzekov, Paul (ed.), *The Pope in Cameroon: Homilies and Addresses* (Yaounde, 1986).

Vernon-Jackson, H.O.H., *Language, Schools and Government in Cameroon* (New York, 1967).

Victoria Centenary Committee, *Victoria Southern Cameroons 1858 – 1958,* Victoria, 1958.

Webster, J.B. and Boahen, J.B., *The Growth of African Civilisation: The Revolutionary Years of West Africa Since 1800* (London, 1967).

Welch, Jr, Claude E., *Dream of Unity: Pan-Africanism and Political Unification in West Africa* (Ithaca, 1966).

Wright, Quincy, *Mandates Under the League of Nations* (Chicago, 1930).

Articles, pamphlets and manuscripts

Ardener, Edwin, 'Crisis of Confidence in Cameroon', *West Africa,* 12 August 1961.

Ardener, Edwin, 'The Political History of Cameroon', *The World Today,* XVIII, 1962, pp.341 – 50.

Austen, Ralph A., 'Duala vs Germans in Cameroon', *Revue Française d'Histoire d'Outre-Mer,* LXIV, 4, 1977, pp.477 – 97.

Bah, Thierno Mouctar, 'Contribution a l'Etude de la Résistance des Peuples Africains à la Colonisation: Karnou et l'Insurrection des Gbaya', *Afrika Zamini,* III, 1974, pp.105 – 61.

Bayart, J.F., 'One-Party Government and Political Development in Cameroon', *African Affairs,* Vol. 73, No. 287 (April 1973), pp.125 – 44.

Bederman, Sanford H., 'The Cameroons Development Corporation: A Unique Example of Government's Role in Commercial Tropical Agriculture', *Essays in International Relations,* Spring, Atlanta, Georgia, 1967, pp.8 – 19.

Bongfen, Emmanuel Ngwar, 'Western Education in Southern Cameroons Between the World Wars 1922 – 1939', MS, Yaounde, 1982.

Burnham, Philip, ' "Regroupement" and Mobile Societies: Two Cameroon Cases', *Journal of African History,* XVI, 4 (1975), pp.577 – 94.

Cameroons Peoples National Convention, *Plebiscite Message to all Workers of the Cameroons,* Times Press, Lagos, February 1961.

Chilver, E.M. and Kaverry, P.M., 'From Tribute to Tax in a Tikar Chiefdom', *Africa,* XXX, 1 (January 1960), pp.1 – 19.

Delancey, Mark W., 'Health and Disease on the Plantations of Cameroon 1884 – 1939', in Gerald W. Heartwig and K. David Patterson (eds), *Disease in African History,* (Durham, 1978).

Fanso, Verkijika G., 'Background to the Annexation of Cameroon 1875 – 1885', *Abbia,* Nos 29 – 30, 1975, pp. 231 – 80.

Fanso, Verkijika G., 'Party Politics in Post-Independence Black Africa, *Abbia,* Nos. 31 – 3, February 1978, pp. 196 – 204.

Fonlon, Bernard N., 'The Language Problem in Cameroon: An Historical Perspective', *Comparative Education,* Oxford, February 1969, pp.25 – 49.

Kamerun National Democratic Party (KNDP), *Newsletter,* July 1958, and sporadic.

LeVine, Victor T., 'A Contribution to the Political History of Cameroon: The United Nations and the Politics of Decolonization – The Termination of the British Cameroons Trusteeship', *Abbia,* No. 24, January – April 1970, pp.65 – 90.

Mohamadou, Eldridge, 'L'Histoire des Lamidats Foulbe de Tchamba et Tibati', *Abbia,* No. 6, August 1964, pp.15 – 158.

Pare, I., 'Les Allemands à Foumban', *Abbia,* Nos. 12 – 13, Mars – Juin 1966, pp.211 – 31.

Quinn, Frederick, 'Charles Atangana and Ewondo Chiefs, a Document', *Abbia,* No.23, Septembre – Décembre 1969, pp.83 – 126.

Seino, Matthew A., 'The History of Cameroon for the GCE Examinations', MS, Kumbo, February 1980.

Index

epidemics: and population, 6
Essono Ela, 30
ethnic communities, 1, 153; and
  British, 86; and chiefs, 69;
  organisation of, 1–4; relations between, 4; and religion,
  6–7
explorers: German, 21, 22–5,
  36
Europeans: access by, to
  interior, 21; on Cameroon
  coast, 9–10; officials, shortage of, 85; teachers, 71;
  traders, 4, 74
evil: and witchcraft, 7
Ewondo, 24, 29, 51, 144; chief,
  69; and Germans, 30

famine: and population, 6
Federal: Economic and Social
  Council, 161; States, 163
Federal Republic of Cameroon,
  158–74; constitution of,
  158–63; end of, 173
Fernando Po, 11, 15, 69, 90,
  100; blockade of, 52; British
  Consul at, 12
First World War: in Cameroon,
  50–59, 142
fon, 2, 3, 22, 84, 86; of Nso,
  2–3, 27, 85
Foncha, J.N., 127–8, 130–31,
  133, 137–9, 145–6, 148,
  150–51, 153, 156–9,
  160–61, 163–5
Fonka, Hon. L.S., 175
Fouda, André, 111, 114
Foumban Constitutional
  Conference, 158–9
Fournea, Lucien, 59
France: fall of, and Cameroon,
  97–100
Free French, 97, 98, 100
French, in Cameroon, 12, 62, 80,
  107–24; and boundaries, 31, 33;
  colonial policies, 64–5, 101–2;
  Constituent Assembly, 108;
  constitution, 1946, 107–9; dislike of, 99–100; forces, 51; and
  independence, 151; language,
  123; mandate, 59–61, 62–81;
  and nationalism, 143–5;
  rebellion against, 77–80;
  traders, 12; treaties, 24; and
  trusteeship, 105; withdrawal,
  18; and war, 51, 52–3, 98–9
French Equatorial Africa,
  53–5, 64, 107
Fulbe, 1; administration, 36–7;
  domination by, 4, 78, 94;
  lamibe, 25, 28, 37; raids by,
  6; and war, 51

Gabon, 12, 33
Galega I, 22–3, 29–30; Fon
  of Bali, 125, 127
gallicised elite, 65, 66
Garoua, 28, 52, 60; schools in,
  43, 44, 47
Gbaya: revolt by, 78–80
German property: disposal of, 74
Germans: annexation of
  Cameroon, 9–20; arrival of,
  11–12; in Cameroon, 35–49,
  142; claims to Cameroon,
  95–7; expansion by, 21–34;
  expulsion of, 33, 50; forces,
  51; language of, 43, 100; at
  Nso, 2; planters, 86–7, 95;
  pro-German sympathy, 100;
  reactions to, 16–18; resistance to, 25–8; traders, 12,
  14–15; uprising against, 40
Gesellschaft Norwest-Kamerun,
  37
Gesellschaft Sudkamerun, 37
Gleim, Otto, 39
gods: minor, belief in, 7
governors: German, 37–40
grants: British, 135; French,
  74–5; German, 42
grasslands, 39, 46, 48, 69, 91;
  neglect of, 47; resistance in,
  25, 26
Guidder: revolt by, 80

headquarters: of administrative
  districts, 58, 59
head-tax, 41–2, 78
health: and British, 85, 86,
  91–3; centres, 48; and
  French, 71–3, 101, 122;
  services, 53; of workers, 48,
  75
Hewett, Consul Edward (Too
  Late), 16
High Commissioner: authority
  of, 62–3; *arrêté*, 68, 187;
  French, 62–4, 67, 116, 118,
  119; of S. Cameroon, 127, 129
hinterland: of Cameroon, 37;
  schools in, 42–3; 'theory', 21
Hitler, Adolf, 95–6
hospitals, 48, 73, 91–3
household: as unit, 6

income: *see* revenue
independence, 107, 108, 112,
  116, 117, 119–20, 121, 133,
  139, 142–8, 149–51; of
  French Cameroon, 151; and
  UN trusteeship, 104–5
Indian (British), Army, 51
indigénat, French, 68, 101, 102,
  111, 187

indirect rule: British, 82, 84–6;
  in N. Cameroons, 93–4
indirect taxes: *see under* taxes
industries: in Cameroon, 75,
  111, 171
infrastructure, 170; and French,
  74–5, 101, 121
investment: areas of, 123; by
  British, 88, 94; by French,
  74–5, 121–2; by Germans,
  47, 87
Islam: pre-colonial, 6, 7
ivory: cost of, 21; as gift, 30; as
  ransom, 27; source of, 25;
  trade, 37

Jamot, Dr Eugène, 71–3
Janikowski: and annexation, 18
Jantzen and Thormahlen:
  traders, 12, 16, 35, 37
Jehovah's Witnesses, 76–7
Jeucafra, *Jeunesse Camerounaise
  Francaise*, 96, 111, 143;
  demands of, 111
John Holt & Co., traders, 11
Jua, A.N., 163–5, 166
judicial system: in Adamawa, 2;
  Federal, 167–8; French, 67;
  German, in S. Cameroons, 129

Kamptz, Herr, explorer, 25, 27
Karnou: leader of Gbaya, 78, 80
KNC, Kamerun National
  Congress, 126–8, 131, 133,
  146, 148, 152
KNDP, Kamerun National
  Democratic Party, 127, 131,
  133, 137, 139, 144, 146, 148,
  152, 153, 154, 163–5
Kotoko chiefdoms, 1
KPP, Kamerun People's Party,
  127, 128, 131, 133, 146, 148,
  152
Kribi, 22, 47, 48, 55, 95
KUNC, Kamerun United
  National Congress, 130–31,
  145
Kund, Lt R., explorer, 23, 30

labour, 185; and CDC, 134;
  codes, 114–15; communal, 6;
  compulsory, 86; conditions,
  113–15; forced, 75, 78, 111,
  113; freedom of, 101, 102; as
  ransom, 27; recruitment of,
  36, 41, 48, 75, 84, 86;
  reforms, 114; shortage, and
  plantations, 22, 47–8, 86;
  source of, 25
Lamdo (Ardo), 2
Lamibe, 70
Lamido (Emir): of Adamawa, 2

Royal Navy, British: and slave trade, 11; supremacy, 50
rubber, 74, 87, 122; German monopoly, 37; as ransom, 27; source of, 25
rulers, traditional: and administration, 36, 37, 41

Sacred Heart, Society of, 45 – 6
sacrifices: religious, 6 – 7
Same, Pastor A.L., 142
sea communication, 87
schools: and British, 88 – 9; district, 71; French, 59, 70 – 71, 122; government, 43 – 4, 88, 122; higher primary, 71; private, 71; village, 71; *see also* mission schools
Second World War, 68, 95 – 102
Seitz, Theodore, governor, 39
self-government, 143; and UN trusteeship, 104 – 5, 149
settlement: choice of, 6
services: after First World War, 53
slave trade: abolition of, 11, 13, 21
slaves: demands for, 4; -mongers, 6
sleeping sickness: control of, 72 – 3; permanent mission, 73
smuggling: *see* trade, contraband
social: organisation, 1 – 4; reforms, French, 101, 121 – 3
society: pre-colonial, 6 – 7
SONARA, National Refining Company Ltd, 184
Southern Cameroons, British: constitution, 137; constitutional developments in, 125 – 8; economy, 133 – 6; Executive Council, 129, 131, 136; House of Assembly, 127, 129, 131, 137, 146; House of Chiefs, 129, 137, 139, 163; nationalism in, 145 – 8; plebiscite in, 139, 150, 151, 152 – 4; status of, 128; viability of, 135 – 6
sports: and Cameroon, 186
Stanley, H.M., 19
stations: German military, 36, 37; heads of, 36
strikes: labour, 114, 115, 116 – 17, 143
subsistence economy, early, 4 – 5
Sudanic people, 5
Sultans, 70
supercargoes, 11

Tappenbeck, Lt, explorer, 23, 30
tariffs, 41, 62; French trade, 12; German, 36
taxes, 186; and British, 84,

85 – 6, 94, 127; direct, 41; dog, 41; and French, 102; German, 29, 37, 41 – 2; head-tax, 41 – 2, 78; indirect, 41 – 2
teachers: lack of, 88; and Normal Class, 89; training of, 88, 89
terrorism: by UPC, 117, 118, 119, 144 – 5, 169
Tibati: resistance by, 28
Tikar, 25; fondoms, 1, 4
Tiko: port at, 87
timber production, 74, 122
Tombel (Bakossi) massacre, 168 – 9
tonte (aid association), 5
trade: competition in, 13 – 14; concessions, 38; contraband, 87 – 8; decline in British, 14; increase in German, 14, 22; traditional, 87 – 8; treaties, 15; trust system, 14
trade routes: coastal, 10; and markets, 5; network of, 5, 74
trade unions, 113 – 15, 123
traders, 111; British, 10 – 11; Duala as, 10; French, 12; German, 12; and German treaty, 17
transport, 47 – 8
treaties: British, 10, 11; French, 12; German, 15, 29, 35, 36
tribute, 70
trusteeship: in Cameroon, 102 – 5, 128, 134; Council, 103, 104, 148, 150; end of, 121; UN system, 102 – 5, 148
Tumi, Cardinal Wiyghan, 182 – 4

Ubangi-Shari (Central African Republic), 33, 72
UC, *Union Camerounaise*, 96, 110 – 11, 113, 119, 165 – 6
Uechtritz, Lt Edgar von, 27 – 8
Um Nyobe, Reuben, 112 – 13, 114, 116, 120, 144, 145; at UN, 150
Unicafra, *Union Camerounaise Française*, 111 – 12, 143
UNO, United Nations Organisation, 148 – 51; Charter, 103, 148; and trust territories, 102 – 5; Visiting Missions, 144, 145, 146, 148, 149 – 50, 151, 154
UPC, *Union des Populations du Cameroun*, 112, 115 – 17, 119 – 20, 131, 143 – 4, 149, 150, 151, 169
Upper Cross River valley: revolt in, 28
USCC, *Union des Syndicats Confédérés du Cameroun*,

114, 115, 143
University: centres, 184; of Yaounde, 172, 184

vaccinations, 92
Versailles Treaty, 95, 96, 97
Vichy regime, 98, 99
Victor Kanga affair, 169
Victoria Botanical Garden, 47
Victoria Plantations Company, 46, 47
Victoria, 11, 13, 16, 22, 53; and annexation, 17, 18; and Christianity, 7, 10; Court of Justice in, 11, 48; and education, 10, 42, 43, 44; and Germans, 35; hospital in, 92; port at, 87; traders at, 11, 12
von Pavel, 25
von Puttkamer, Jesko, governor, 37, 39
von Soden, Julius Baron, governor, 35, 36, 37; and education, 42
von Stetten, explorer, 24
von Zimmerer, Eugen, governor, 37
voting, 108; for women, 42; *see also* elections

wars: inter-group, 6; *see also* First World War; Second World War
water transport, 47
Williams, Chief Manga, 125, 129, 145
Wilmot, Commodore A.P.E., 13
Wilson, Pastor Joseph, 42
witchcraft, 4, 7; doctors, 7
witches: punishment of, 7
Woerman Co., Carl, 35, 37; agents, 46
workforce: organisation of, 6; *see also* labour
Wouri river, 55
Wovea, 10

Yaounde: administrative capital, 63; Catholic church in, 77; and elections, 109; Federal University of, 172; higher primary school, 71, 73; importance of, 23; in Second World War, 99; schools in, 43, 44, 47; station, 23, 24, 36, 37; strikes in, 117; and unions, 114
Yola, 55; Emir of, 53

Zimmerman, Lt-Col, 51
Zintgraff, Dr Eugen, explorer, 22-3, 29-30
Zubeiru, Lamido, 28